PARTICIPATORY DEMOCRACY

Populism Revived

Joseph F. Zimmerman

PRAEGER

New York
Westport, Connecticut
London

Library of Congress Cataloging-in-Publication Data

Zimmerman, Joseph Francis, 1928–
  Participatory democracy.

  Bibliography: p.
  Includes index.
  1. Referendum – United States. 2. Recall – United
States. 3. Neighborhood government – United States.
4. Populism – United States. 5. Political participation
– United States. I. Title.
JF493.U6Z56 1986   323′.042′0973   86-8129
ISBN 0-275-92132-8 (alk. paper)

Library of Congress Catalog Card Number: 86-8129
ISBN: 0-275-92132-8

First published in 1986

Praeger Publishers, 521 Fifth Avenue, New York, NY 10175
A division of Greenwood Press, Inc.

Printed in the United States of America

The paper used in this book complies with the Permanent
Paper Standard issued by the National Information Standards
Organization (Z39.48-1984).

10 9 8 7 6 5 4 3 2 1

PREFACE

Democratic theory is premised upon citizens playing an active and informed role in the governance system. Nevertheless, widespread citizen involvement in public affairs on a continuing basis has been a rarity with the exceptions of the smaller New England municipalities with the open town meeting. In part, the relative lack of public participation can be attributed to the limited opportunities for playing a meaningful role in the governance process beyond voting in elections.

The sharp rise in the number and apparent influence of pressure groups in legislative halls in the twentieth century has tended to undermine citizen confidence in traditional representative governance institutions. And public diffidence toward law-making bodies has been increased by decisions of the United States Supreme Court effectively gutting important provisions of state corrupt-practices acts regulating campaign finance, thereby increasing the political power of organized groups at the expense of the average citizen.

Dissatisfaction with decision making by elected and appointed officials also is reflected in the demands for the establishment in large cities of a system of neighborhood units governed by town meetings. Dramatic developments in many of these cities in the 1960s demonstrated the inability of established institutions to be responsive in an effective manner to the needs and desires of minority groups.

This book examines the principal forms of direct citizen decision-making in the United States and two relatively new systems for enhancing the role of citizens in large city governance – topics that generally have been neglected in political science literature. Only two major studies of the 356-year-old open town meeting have been conducted, and few political scientists have examined the relatively new systems installed in New York City to increase the role of citizens in the governance process. To a degree, this book is a reference work containing descriptive and analytical information on the New England town meeting, the referendum, the initiative, the recall, and New York City community school boards and community boards.

The law of citizen participation is subjected to detailed analysis because opponents of direct citizen action frequently resort to the courts seeking to forestall or invalidate such action. Comprehension of interest group behavior is not possible without a full understanding of the constitutional and statutory bases of direct citizen action devices.

v

Heavy emphasis is placed upon citizen participation in practice rather than in abstract theory. Hypothesis testing unfortunately is not possible in a relatively short book presenting a general overview of the subject throughout the United States. The approach is a posteriori and not a priori. Hopefully, a number of prescriptions contained herein will be rephrased as propositions and empirically tested on a case basis by theory builders.

The concluding chapter focuses heavily upon four themes. A major theme is the impact of direct citizen action upon representative government. A number of legislators and legislative observers are convinced that the direct initiative, the petition referendum, and the recall are serious threats to representative government. The rhetoric of extreme proponents of these devices, who view elected officials as Janus-faced, reinforces the fear that the traditional law-making system by elected representatives will be undermined. We will examine the reality of this concern.

A second major theme is the importance of open government and the provision of accurate and full information on issues to assist citizens in resolving issues. In particular, the governmental ethos guiding public officers should emphasize citizen participation and public disclosure of information to assist citizens in decision making and forbid the officers to engage in cooptation.

A third and related theme is the need for ethical standards to guide and a mechanism to provide advice on ethical issues to elected and appointed public officers to ensure that citizens are not burdened by malfeasance, misfeasance, and nonfeasance.

The need for a broad grant of local discretionary authority by the state is a fourth theme. Without such a broad grant, the electorate will be unable to participate fully in the governance process in political subdivisions that are the closest to the people.

Academics and government officials too numerous to acknowledge individually cooperated with the author by supplying information and answering inquiries. Without their cooperation, this book would not have been possible. Their assistance is greatly appreciated as is the editorial assistance of Margaret B. Zimmerman. I owe a debt of gratitude to Lisa MacLeman for her excellence in copyediting this manuscript. The manuscript was typed by Maxine H. Morman and Addie Napolitano. Any errors of fact or misinterpretation, of course, are the responsibility of the author.

CONTENTS

Contents

Chapter 1

PARTICIPATORY DEMOCRACY

Citizen participation in government is enshrined deeply in the political culture of the United States and is epitomized by the open town meeting in many New England towns today. The value of an active citizenry in promoting the health of the polity, of course, was recognized in ancient times. Aristotle, for example, placed greater faith in the collective wisdom of citizens than in the sagacity of any individual.[1]

According to G. D. H. Cole, "the social contract theory is as old as the sophists of Greece and as elusive."[2] The theory, including the concept of the general will as popularized by Jean Jacques Rousseau, greatly influenced many of the leaders of the American Revolution. Rousseau wrote:

> The general will is always right and tends to the public advantage; but it does not follow that the deliberations of the people are always equally correct. Our will is always for our good, but we do not always see what that is: the people is never corrupted, but it is often deceived, and on such occasions only does it seem to will what is bad.[3]

Rousseau was enough of a realist to know that "a real democracy is only an ideal."[4]

While there is agreement that citizens should play an informed and active role in the governance system, there is wide disagreement as to the forms and the extent that citizen participation should take. At one extreme, the view prevails that citizens directly should make laws and hold all offices on a part-time basis. The early New England town accepted this concept of citizen participation and made voting and office-holding by freemen compulsory.

1

At the other extreme, the leadership-feedback theory limits the role of the citizen primarily to electing periodically government officers who provide leadership in public affairs by proposing policies. This model is reflected in the due process requirement for public hearings on many types of proposed or requested governmental actions.[5] Citizen feedback on proposals may induce the elected officers to modify the proposals prior to their implementation. Decision-making responsibility, however, remains with the officers.

The wide diversity of governmental projects and programs, in terms of their importance and impact upon the citizenry, makes it apparent that there is greater scope and need for citizen participation in certain projects and programs than in others. Active citizen participation generally is not needed in a smoothly operating program that is noncontroversial and routine. On the other hand, public projects and programs involving large sums of monies and impacting in a major way upon citizens, one can argue, should be planned and executed with citizen involvement. If a major program is highly controversial, citizens will become involved automatically without formal participation machinery, and the participation may take the form of protest actions, including court suits to block the program.

To provide a broad framework for the subsequent chapters, this chapter examines the benefits and costs of citizen participation, examines voting statistics, and describes the various types of passive and active citizen involvement in public affairs. The chapter concludes with an overview of the open town meeting, the referendum, the initiative, the recall, and New York City community school boards and community boards.

Benefits and Costs of Citizen Participation

Governmental programs can be developed without formal direct citizen involvement by placing reliance entirely upon elected representatives to ensure that the public's views and needs are reflected in plans and programs developed by legislative bodies, professional planners, and bureaucrats. We are convinced, however, that active and widespread citizen participation is essential for the best functioning of the various units of government in the United States and that intermediary bodies do not always represent accurately the views of the citizenry.

The participation should be permanent and commence at the planning stage of a new program or project and continue after implementation to ensure the effectiveness of the project or program. To the extent possible, all citizens should be provided with an equal opportunity to participate in terms of the accessibility of hearing sites, availability of full information, and opportunity to express views, subjects examined in greater detail in Chapter 7. There are four major benefits flowing from a well-functioning participatory governance system.

Benefits

A strong case can be made for citizen involvement in an active and meaningful way because governmental programs directly affect their lives, and traditional institutions and processes are not always able to identify and solve the problems perceived to be serious by groups of citizens.

A second potential benefit of citizen involvement flows from the valuable inputs citizens can make into the planning and implementation processes based upon their detailed knowledge of local conditions, needs, and desires.

From the governmental standpoint, citizens sharing with elected officers the responsibility for decision making may have the third advantage of facilitating the implementation of plans and programs as residents will be more willing to accept and work for the successful completion of projects if they helped to plan the projects since they will understand better the reasons for the projects.

Fourth, involvement by citizens has democratic value by making it easier for them to hold elected and appointed officers accountable for their actions. Knowledge is power and informed citizens are better able to judge the quality of governmental performance of functions. Thomas Jefferson in 1782 wrote:

> In every government on earth is some trace of human weakness, some germ of corruption and degeneracy, which cunning will discover, wickedness insensibly open, cultivate, and improve. Every government degenerates when trusted to the rulers of the people alone. The people themselves therefore are its only safe depositories. And to render even them safe, their minds must be improved to a certain extent.[6]

In consequence, Jefferson strongly advocated an amendment to the Virginia Constitution providing for a system of public education. Jefferson in essence was placing his trust in Rousseau's belief in the virtue of enlightened citizen opinion.

Costs

Citizen participation is not without costs for seven principal reasons. First, governmental expenses may be increased by the added costs of keeping the public fully informed and in some instances holding referenda. Second, citizens' demands on occasion for additional studies may delay the preparation and implementation of plans, thereby resulting in significantly higher costs in a period of inflation.

Third, lay citizens may not possess the competence required to judge adequately the technical aspects of plans and programs, and major delays may result from attempts by governmental officials to explain subtle nuances. Fourth, the danger exists that citizens participating in the planning and/or implementing process may be parochial in outlook and concerned only with the impact of plans and programs on their neighborhoods, thereby generating a conflict between what is best for a given neighborhood and what is best for a wider geographical area. Fifth, individuals participating in programs and decision making may not be representative of citizens at large. Sixth, a value conflict may occur if participants hold values differing substantially from the values held by a majority of elected officers and bureaucrats. Such a conflict, however, may be viewed as healthy if elected officers and bureaucrats are forced to rethink their values. And they obviously will become more responsive to the citizenry if they change their values to conform to those held by citizen participants. Seventh, citizen-initiated measures on referenda ballots may be poorly drafted and create implementation problems as explained in Chapter 4.

While the above costs may be encountered in various citizen participation programs, the costs are a small price to pay for the benefits of a healthy political system.

A Reluctant Democracy

An examination of the percentage of eligible citizens registered to vote and the percentage of registered voters exercising the electoral franchise suggests the health of the polity is poor. Charles Johnson reported in a 1980 United States Bureau of the Census publication that presidential elections always have had low voter participation and 50 percent of the voting age population did not vote until 1928.[7] In 1976, for example, 46 percent of the voting age population did not cast a ballot; failure to register was responsible for 82 percent of those who did not vote.[8]

Voter turnout at the polls is typically lower at state elections than at presidential elections, and the lowest voter participation rate tends to be in local elections, which theoretically involve governments closest to the people. In Oregon, the percentage of registered voters casting ballots fell from 84.8 in 1960 to 77.1 in 1980, a reflection of the continuing national decline in voter participation.[9] On the other hand, the percentage of registered voters casting ballots in Virginia increased from 20.8 percent in 1948 to 48.6 percent in 1976.[10]

Of the various types of substate governments, special districts have the lowest rate of electorate participation, in part because they tend to be the least visible governments. The number of special districts increased from 18,323 to 28,588 in 1982, a 56 percent rise.[11]

The Massachusetts Constitution authorizes the General Court (legislature) to provide for compulsory voting, but the General Court has not enacted implementing legislation.[12] Although voting is compulsory in some nations, many Americans believe that eligible citizens in a democracy should not be forced to vote. Furthermore, compulsory voting by itself does not guarantee intelligent voting or ensure that voters have studied the qualifications of candidates or the merits of referred issues.

Citizens, however, can be encouraged by other citizens to register and vote. In August 1982, for example, Father George Clements of the Holy Angels School in Chicago announced that while students do not have to be Catholic, parents desiring to enroll their children in the school must be registered voters.[13]

An examination of voting and nonvoting data reveals significant differences in terms of various racial and ethnic groups.[14] In 1976, 39 percent of whites were nonvoters compared to 51 percent of blacks and 68 percent of Hispanics. The differences can be explained by several factors, including degree of formal education, income level, and facility with the English language. Although most legal impediments to voting no longer exist, the heritage of discrimination against blacks and Hispanics in some areas undoubtedly discourages registration and voting by members of these groups.

To obtain data on voting, the assessor and collector of taxes of Travis County, Texas mailed a questionnaire to 5,000 voters registered at the times of the 1980 party primaries, 1980 general election, and 1982 party primaries.[15] The recipients represented approximately 2 percent of the registered voters and were divided between the 2,000 individuals who voted in the three elections and the 3,000 who did not vote in any election.

Responses were received from 60 percent of the questionnaire recipients who had voted compared to less than 32 percent of the nonvoters who received a second mailing. Approximately 6 percent of the respondent nonvoters were unaware they were registered to vote. In addition, more than 30 percent indicated they did not know their precinct number, and an additional 40 percent indicated they knew their number but did not write it on the questionnaire as requested. Interestingly, 46.3 percent of the nonvoters reported they had voted in the party primaries in 1982.

Only 1.6 percent of the voter group reported voting in either few or none of the elections; more than 47.0 percent of the nonvoters described themselves in this manner. Nonvoters reported voting is essential if public policies are to be changed. In addition, they indicated they lacked adequate information on candidates and issues, and nearly one-half reported their interest in elections would be increased if additional televised debates were held.

Distrust of elected officers, dating at least as far back as the period of Jacksonian democracy, is reflected in the facts that a quarter of the nonvoters were convinced "politicians never keep their promises," and nearly one-half of the nonvoters and two-fifths of the voters felt they are faced with the choice of the "lesser of the evils" in most elections. Nevertheless, more than three-fifths of the voters and more than two-fifths of the nonvoters perceived public officers to be hard working and honest.

With respect to obstacles to voting, 7 percent of the nonvoters reported they did not know how to vote, over 10 percent indicated they did not know how to locate their polling places, and 12 percent were unaware they could vote by absentee ballot if they were out of town on election day.

More than 29 percent of the nonvoters reported they had not voted because they had moved from their place of registration and had not reregistered. Nine percent of the nonvoters indicated they had failed to vote because they had lost their voter certificate, although they would have been allowed to vote had they produced other identification such as a driver's license.

A demographic examination of office holders also reveals that certain groups, particularly blacks and Hispanics, are underrepresented. The explanation in part is lower voter participation by members of these two groups. Other reasons for underrepresentation include relative lack of funds for election campaigns and gerrymandering.[16]

Low voter participation is only one sign of a reluctant democracy. Robert A. Dahl in 1956 maintained "that only a quite tiny proportion of the electorate is actively bringing its influence to bear upon politicians" when policy decisions are being made.[17] In Dahl's view, a polyarchy exists in which "minorities rule" rather than a democracy in which the majority rules.[18]

Types of Citizen Participation

Voting in elections and referenda is only one form of citizen participation. Other forms are of equal or greater importance in certain situations. We classify the forms as passive and active.

Passive Forms

Passive forms of citizen participation involve efforts by public officers to inform citizens of problems and plans for their solution, and determine citizen perceptions of problems and opinions relative to alternative plans and options. Citizens play an active role in providing inputs into the planning system.

Public officers often use passive forms of citizen participation to mobilize public support for projects they wish to implement. The question obviously can be raised whether it is legitimate for public officers to engage in citizen support mobilization programs, a subject examined in the concluding chapter.

Relative to the informational aspects of passive participation, government officers prepare and distribute information publications to arouse interest and explain concepts, issues, and procedures. In addition, officers may encourage radio and television stations to broadcast programs dealing with public problems and proposed solutions. Of course, the stations may decide on their own initiative to broadcast such programs.

Officers also encourage newspapers to prepare and publish editorials, feature articles, and special supplements on governmental problems and projects.

Survey research is a valuable source of information needed by government planners and officers, provided the questions are worded properly and the results are analyzed carefully. A key question involves the design and analysis of surveys. An argument can be advanced that the survey should be conducted by a neutral organization, possibly a university or a private survey firm, which is not responsible for the preparation of plans or their implementation. Webb and Hatry cautioned that survey data and findings "should contribute to, but not substitute for, political and managerial judgment."[19]

Active Forms

Active forms of citizen participation range from the open town meeting in the New England states to the district initiative to the protest meeting.

The New England Town Meeting

The oldest and most direct form of citizen participation occurs in many New England towns where the voters attend town meetings and directly make decisions on all local issues. The voters, of course, are guided in the decision-making process by the town finance committee, town planning board, and other town officers. Chapter 2 examines the origin and evaluates operation of the open town meeting and its use in modified form – the limited or representative town meeting – in a number of larger towns.

Public Hearings

In local governments with elected councils, the oldest form of active citizen participation in public decision making involves the formal public hearing at which citizens are afforded the opportunity to express their views and in some hearings to question officers. State administrative procedures acts mandate that administrative agencies must hold public hearings prior to issuing rules and regulations or undertaking specified projects.

Public hearings do not change the locus of decision-making authority, but may induce public officers to modify their original proposals and views. Officers must give serious consideration to the expressed views of citizens, or the public hearing will be little more than a pro forma consultation ritual. Timing of public hearings is crucial. If held during business hours on a weekday, working citizens may be excluded and only the higher economic groups will be able to participate.

The requirement in the 1969 National Environmental Policy Act of the preparation of an environmental impact statement for federally-aided capital projects has widened the opportunity for the individual citizen and citizen groups to influence the planning and programming process since numerous state and local government capital projects – especially sewer, transportation, and water – are funded in part by federal funds and public hearings must be held on the environmental impact statements in addition to the traditional public hearings required by state law.[20]

An interesting and innovative approach was initiated by the Kentucky Department of Community and Regional Development, which in 1981 conducted a phone-in program on radio station KET, as an alternative to public hearings throughout the state, to obtain the views of citizens on the use of funds received by the state under the federal Small Cities Community Development Block Grant Program.[21]

Cynics maintain that the typical public hearing is an ineffective form of citizen participation, in part because citizens lack the information and staff support possessed by public officers. Research on the effectiveness of such participation in regulatory public hearings is limited. Judy B. Rosener studied the hearings held under the California Coastal Act of 1972 and concluded "that most of the time citizens did not participate in public hearings held by the Coastal Commission, although when they did, they were effective in increasing the denial rate."[22] The charge frequently is made that staff dominates decision making, yet Rosener reported that staff recommendations for denial of permits were rejected in 45 percent of the cases.[23]

Citizen inputs at public hearings are unlikely to serve as catalysts and result in major changes in plans unless the hearings commence in the early stages of and continue throughout the planning process. If citizens are kept in an information vacuum and involved only after detailed engineering plans for a construction project have been prepared, citizens will be afforded little opportunity to influence significantly the nature of the plans. The best approach is illustrated by a British Department of Environment report – *Participation in Road Planning: A Consultation Paper* – which announced a new departmental policy "to inform people at an earlier stage in the preparation of plans for building or substantially improving roads (including motorways) of practical alternative routes, or methods of improvement, that are available, and to obtain a full expression of people's views at that stage."[24]

Citizen Advisory Committees

The legitimate purposes of these two types of committees – permanent and ad hoc – are similar: (1) afford citizens an opportunity to participate in the decision-making process, (2) improve two-way communications between citizens and public officers, and (3) draw upon the expertise of citizens in various functional areas.

The process of selecting committee members is crucial in terms of giving them legitimacy and making them effective in achieving their assigned goals. Most committees are composed of only appointed members. The principal advantages of this selection method are the selection of persons for their expertise and interest, and the achievement of membership balance in terms of geographical, ethnic, racial, socio-economic status, and other characteristics.

Provision has been made in some cities for neighborhood organizations to make nominations for committee appointments and in other cities for neighborhood committee members to be elected. While election of members may appear to be more democratic, the use of this selection method has resulted in overrepresentation of certain groups and underrepresentation of other groups. A combined elected-appointed system sometimes is employed to achieve the advantages of each type with the election being held first and appointments being made to achieve more balance on the committee.

A survey by the United States Advisory Commission on Intergovernmental Relations and the International City Management Association revealed that approximately 95 percent of the cities and 91 percent of the counties reported they had one or more citizen advisory committees.[25] The survey also revealed that local government budgets frequently are reviewed by citizen advisory committees and in a number of political subdivisions the preliminary proposed budget is prepared by such a committee. As described in Chapter 2, the finance committee in New England towns lacking a town manager prepares the budget for action by the town meeting.

Officers, of course, can employ citizen committees to delay taking action on a critical issue or to give the appearance of initiating remedial action. In addition, citizen committees can be subject to cooptation — a process to secure the commitment and support of citizens for programs developed by elected officers and/or the bureaucracy.[26] Power is not shared if cooptation is successful as citizen participation is designed merely to give legitimacy and public support to a program.

If a citizen advisory committee lacks staff, the committee as a general rule can do little more than react to plans prepared by the professional staff who may attempt to coopt the citizens. Where cooptation occurs, a legal requirement for citizen participation becomes a device for manipulating citizens and the purposes of citizen involvement are perverted since the participation program is utilized as a mechanism to achieve consensus in support of a given project or program developed by the planners.

To prevent citizen disillusionment, public officers establishing advisory committees must ensure their recommendations receive serious consideration, and are acted upon by the appropriate officers and bodies within a reasonable period of time. If committee reports gather dust, public officers will encounter great difficulty in persuading citizens to serve on similar committees in the future and may discover a lack of citizen cooperation in implementing new proposals should the officers adopt policies in conflict with the ones recommended by the committees.

What appears to have been an abuse of citizen advisory committees occurred in New York City under the mayorship of Robert Wagner. A report in *The New York Herald Tribune* in 1965 indicated that there were "multitudinous committees" appointed by the mayor, but no one, including the mayor, knew how many committees there were or the amount of funds being spent by the committees.[27] The report added:

> Yet what frustrates many people — including those who seem so willing to serve — is not so much the waste of taxpayer's money as it is the waste of the efforts and studies that this money buys. While the Mayor is always eager that they serve, he seems far less eager to act on the conclusions they present. . . .
>
> A former member of the now disbanded Mayor's Committee

on Professional, Technical, and Managerial Manpower complains
that recommendations from a report which cost the City $120,000
and was received by the Mayor several years ago still has not been
acted upon.[28]

The Twin Cities Metropolitan Council

An interesting approach to planning and development has been taken
by Minnesota. The 1967 state legislature created a Metropolitan Council
for the seven-county Twin Cities area and authorized the governor to
appoint the chairman and sixteen citizens as members with Senate
approval.[29] The council was directed by the legislature to prepare a development guide which must be followed by all public agencies, including the state-controlled public authorities. The council also is required
to prepare and adopt policy plans for each metropolitan operating commission, and each commission must prepare a development program to
implement the policy plans subject to the council's approval.

Charter Drafting and Amendment

Citizens often play major roles in drafting and amending charters of
local governments. A charter is the fundamental law of a local government and in this respect is similar to the state or national constitution.
Only Alabama, Kentucky, and Virginia do not permit local governments
to draft charters, but in certain other states the authority to draft a
charter is restricted to specified types of units such as cities and towns
in Massachusetts or to population classes such as cities over 5,000
population in Texas.[30] In a number of states, citizens can use the initiative, described in Chapter 4, to create a charter commission. Typically, a citizens' charter committee is elected or appointed to draft a new
charter or review the existing charter and to determine the need for
amendments.

The Referendum

Citizens, by means of popular referenda, often are afforded the opportunity to inform elected decision-makers of popular views on a controversial issue or make the decision on an issue, a subject discussed in
greater detail in Chapter 3.

A governing body may decide to employ the advisory referendum,
a nonbinding one, to determine popular views on an issue. In other instances, the governing body may choose to allow the voters to make
the decision because of the great importance of the issue or a desire to
avoid taking a stand on an emotional issue that will antagonize a significant number of voters.

In several states, the protest or petition referendum can be employed by citizens to delay and possibly prevent a law enacted by a state or local legislative body from going into effect. A waiting period, usually of 90 days, is provided before a legislative act becomes effective in order to provide citizens with notice of the law. Within this period, objectors to the law may circulate petitions for a popular referendum on the law. If the required number of voters—2 to 10 percent of the votes cast for governor in different states—sign the petitions, the measure must be submitted to the voters at a special or general election, and by majority vote the law can be repealed.

The Initiative

Currently, 23 states permit the use of the initiative, a type of direct legislation that is positive in character, allowing voters to enact laws without action by the legislative body. Under the direct initiative, explained more fully in Chapter 4, a measure proposed by a petition signed by a specified number or percentage of voters is placed directly upon the ballot at the ensuing general or special election for approval or rejection by the electorate. Under the indirect initiative, the measure proposed by petition is transmitted to the legislative body, which has a stated number of days to act on the petition. If the legislative body fails to act or amends the petition, the original petition is placed upon the referendum ballot for voter determination.

Citizens also may circulate petitions to hold a nonbinding referendum on an issue. Voters in Anchorage, Juneau, and Fairbanks, Alaska, on October 5, 1982, in an advisory referendum approved a resolution calling for a freeze in nuclear weapons.[31]

The Recall

Examined in detail in Chapter 5, the recall is designed to make public officers continuously responsible to the voters by authorizing them to circulate petitions to hold a special election for the purpose of determining whether one or more public officers should remain in office. The constitutions of 14 states sanction the use of the recall, and numerous locally drafted and adopted charters also provide for the recall.

Volunteerism

The founding fathers placed great emphasis upon a self-reliant citizenry who voluntarily would work to solve common problems, thereby reducing the need for governmental action. Volunteerism is based on the old tradition of neighborly assistance and assumes many forms in the United States today.

Since his inauguration in 1981, President Ronald Reagan has been promoting volunteerism to solve public problems and appointed a Task Force on Private Sector Initiatives, which issued a final report in 1982.[32]

In the past, voluntary programs generally were organized by individuals and organizations. Special districts, which are units of government, providing fire fighting and emergency medical services historically have relied upon volunteers. More recently, general-purpose local governments have been calling upon volunteers for assistance. Yukon, Oklahoma, in 1981 discovered it would be very expensive to hire a professional firm to move books from the old library to the new city library, and decided to request citizens to assist in moving the books. As a consequence, a human chain of approximately 1,000 citizens formed two lines over a one and one-half block area and passed books in shelf order from the old to the new library.

The New York City Retired Senior Volunteer Program, organized in 1964 by the Community Services Society, has involved approximately 9,000 retired persons with city departments and nonprofit organizations.[33] The time devoted to voluntary work varies from four to forty hours per week. Also in New York City, the Mayor's Volunteer Action Center has placed over 72,000 volunteers with city agencies.[34]

Similarly, citizens in North Tonawanda, New York, have been called upon to play major roles in the Rape Task Force, create a centralized purchasing system, adopt playgrounds to prevent their closing, and sponsor the traditional Fourth of July fireworks celebration.[35]

In Kettering, Ohio, Area Citizens Together in Volunteer Endeavors (ACTIVE) has developed a citizens' skills and interest bank to match potential volunteers with city departments. Approximately four-fifths of the volunteers work on short-term assignments and the other 20 percent work on a full-time basis.

According to Volunteer, the National Center for Citizen Involvement, 19 percent of adult volunteers work "in religious settings, 12 percent in health-related areas, 12 percent in education, 7 percent in recreation, 6 percent in a political setting, 3 percent in areas related to the arts and cultural affairs, and 1 percent in justice."[36] Maintaining the interest of volunteers over extended periods of time can be a serious problem.

An Overview

A substantial body of literature exists on certain types of citizen participation in the governance process. Public administrators and urban planners have written extensively on the participatory processes in planning and implementing programs. Political scientists have been con-

cerned about voter behavior and turnout at elections, the public hearing
process, citizen advisory committees, danger of cooptation, the neighborhood government movement, open government, and citizen involvement in political parties and pressure groups, including public interest
and single interest groups.

Voter approval of Proposition 13 in California, imposing limits on
the general property tax, has been labeled the start of a "tax revolt" and
has attracted the attention of a number of economists, political scientists, and public administrators. Nevertheless, there has been relatively
few published studies based upon a systematic investigation of the initiative. Even fewer studies have been conducted relative to the petition
referendum and the recall, and there are only two major studies of the
New England town meeting. The neighborhood government movement
in large cities, originating at approximately the same time as the civil
disorders in the tumultuous 1960s, spurred studies of the underlying
causes of the movement and led to predictions of the impact of the establishment of neighborhood governments upon the system of urban
governance. However, few scholars have analyzed two important in-
stutional changes in New York City that flowed in large measures from
the movement; that is, the system of community school boards and the
system of community boards combined with administrative decentralization.

Chapter 2 examines the origin and development of the open town
meeting and an associated modification – the limited or representative
town meeting – in New England and addresses the question of whether
law making by an assemblage of voters represents pure democracy in
action.

The subject of Chapter 3 is the various types of referenda – advisory, mandatory, voluntary or indirect, petition or protest, and mail.
The arguments for and against referenda are assessed and conclusions
are drawn relative to the various types of referenda.

Chapter 4 focuses upon the indirect and the direct initiative, and
analyzes the pro and con arguments associated with each type.

The recall, which seldom has been employed on the state level, is
examined in Chapter 5 and conclusions are drawn with respect to its
desirability in a representative system of government.

The neighborhood government movement, community school boards,
and community boards in New York City and administrative reforms
are assessed in Chapter 6.

In Chapter 7, conclusions are drawn and prescriptions are offered
relative to the New England open town meeting, referendum, initiative,
recall, and community school boards and community boards in New
York City. To maximize the effectiveness of citizen involvement in the

decision-making process, recommendations are advanced to promote open government, high ethical standards for public officers, and a broad state grant of discretionary authority to political subdivisions. Without full information, citizens will be unable to make rational decisions. Without mandated ethical standards, public officers may attempt to manipulate the citizenry as well as engage in corrupt activities. Similarly, public participation at the local government level will be discouraged if the state constitution and/or legislature do not provide political subdivisions with a broad grant of discretionary authority.

The question whether direct legislation and the recall undermine government by elected representative is addressed specifically in Chapter 7. There is, of course, no need to examine this question in Chapter 2, which focuses upon the open town meeting.

Notes

1. Benjamin Jowett, trans., *Aristotle' Politics* (New York: Carlton House, n.d.), pp. 145–46.

2. G. D. H. Cole, "Introduction" in Jean Jacques Rousseau, *The Social Contract and Discourses* (New York: E. P. Dutton, 1913), p. xviii.

3. Rousseau, *The Social Contract and Discourses*, p. 25.

4. Ibid.

5. For an interesting analysis of administrative due process, see Barbara R. Grumet, "Who is 'Due' Process?" *Public Administration Review* 42 (July/August 1982): 321–26.

6. Paul L. Ford, ed., *The Works of Thomas Jefferson*, vol. 4 (New York: G. P. Putnam's Sons, 1894), p. 64.

7. Charles Johnson, *Nonvoting Americans* (Washington, D.C.: United States Bureau of the Census, 1980), p. 8.

8. Ibid., p. 9.

9. Data supplied to author by Oregon secretary of state, Norma Paulus, 1983.

10. Larry Sabato, *Virginia Votes 1975–1978* (Charlottesville: Institute of Government, University of Virginia, 1979), p. 11.

11. U.S. Bureau of the Census, *1982 Census of Governments: Governmental Organization*, vol. 1 (Washington, D.C.: United States Government Printing Office, 1983), p. vi.

12. *Constitution of Massachusetts*, articles of amendment, Art. 61.

13. "Pastor Requires Voter Registration as Condition of School Enrollment," *Election Administration Reports* 12 (September 27, 1982): 6.

14. The following data are taken from Johnson, *Nonvoting Americans*.

15. Bill Alshire, *A Study of Voters and Non-Voters in Travis County* (Austin, Texas: Travis County Assessor and Collector of Taxes, 1983).

16. Gerrymandering is the deliberate drawing of district election boundaries to favor a political party or candidate.

17. Robert A. Dahl, *A Preface to Democratic Theory* (Chicago: University of Chicago Press, 1956), p. 130.

18. Ibid., pp. 131–33.

19. Kenneth Webb and Harry P. Hatry, *Obtaining Citizen Feedback* (Washington, D.C.: The Urban Institute, 1973), p. 65.

20. *National Environmental Policy Act of 1969*, 83 Stat. 852, 42 U.S.C. 4321 and 4331–332 (1977 and 1980 supp.).

21. *Sunday Herald-Leader* (Lexington, Kentucky), November 29, 1981, p. E6.

22. Judy B. Rosener, "Making Bureaucrats Responsive: A Study of the Impact of Citizen Participation and Staff Recommendations on Regulatory Decision Making," *Public Administration Review* 42 (July/August 1982): 343.

23. Ibid.

24. Department of the Environment, *Participation in Road Planning: A Consultation Paper* (London: Her Majesty's Stationery Office, 1973).

25. *Citizen Participation in the American Federal System* (Washington, D.C.: United States Advisory Commission on Intergovernmental Relations, 1980), p. 275.

26. The classic study of cooptation is Philip Selznick's *TVA and the Grass Roots* (Berkeley: University of California Press, 1949).

27. Barry Gottehrer and Tim Hutchens, "New York City in Crisis: Mayor's Multitudinous Committees," *The New York Herald Tribune*, February 22, 1965, p. 7.

28. Ibid.

29. *Minnesota Statutes*, chap. 473B.

30. See Joseph F. Zimmerman, *Measuring Local Discretionary Authority* (Washington, D.C.: United States Advisory Commission on Intergovernmental Relations, 1981).

31. "Alaska, Colorado Voters for Freeze," *Times Union* (Albany, New York), October 7, 1982, p. D9.

32. *Building Partnerships* (Washington, D.C.: The President's Task Force on Private Sector Initiatives, 1982).

33. Laurie Johnston, "Retirees Volunteer Wealth of Expertise," *The New York Times*, July 7, 1984, pp. 25–26.

34. "Volunteers: Our Greatest Natural Resource," *Community News*, April 1983, p. 1.

35. Patrick J. Brady, "Citizens Become Involved in North Tonawanda," *New York State Municipal Bulletin* (July-August 1982): 6–7.

36. *The Status of Volunteering* (Boulder, Colo.: Volunteer, 1982, Mimeographed), p. 2.

Chapter **2**

CITIZEN LAW MAKING:
The Town Meeting

The only example of direct democracy – law making by an assemblage of voters – in the United States is the open town meeting in the New England states. Originating in the Massachusetts Bay Colony in the latter part of the second decade of the seventeenth century, the open town meeting spread to New Hampshire, Connecticut, Rhode Island, Vermont, and Maine. Direct democracy also is used by a number of city school districts in New Hampshire and Vermont, and other special districts in all New England states.

The town meeting has been praised by Thomas Jefferson, Alexis de Tocqueville, and Lord Bryce among others. Jefferson wrote in 1782 "every government degenerates when trusted to the rulers of the people alone. The people themselves therefore are its only safe depositories."[1] Alexis de Tocqueville reported that direct democracy in the New England towns avoids "the commotion of municipal discord," and Lord James Bryce observed "the primary assembly is admittedly the best. It is the cheapest and the most efficient; it is the most educative of the citizens who bear a part in it."[2] In effect, these observers were agreeing with Aristotle who pointed out:

> For the many, of whom each individual is but an ordinary person, when they meet together may very likely be better than the few good, if regarded not individually but collectively, just as a feast to which many contribute is better than a dinner provided out of a single purse.[3]

In the twentieth century, criticism of the open town meeting has become relatively common. John W. Alexander and Morroe Berger in

1949 suggested that the town meeting is "a sacred cow that deserves to be laid to rest."[4] A 1965 editorial in a national publication maintained the open town meeting "still lingers on as an instrument of control by small groups of self-seekers and without participation by 90 per cent of the eligible voters."[5] And the Committee for Economic Development in 1966 argued the town meeting "met the needs of simpler earlier times, but was not designed to handle the complex modern problems confronting rapidly growing areas."[6]

An evaluation of the open town meeting is facilitated by an understanding of its origins and operational procedures. Special attention must be paid to Massachusetts initiative Proposition 2½ as it restricts the revenue-raising competence of the town meeting.

Genesis of the Town Meeting

The Pilgrims

Although an English colony was established in New England as early as 1607,[7] the first permanent settlement dates to the Plymouth Colony established in Massachusetts in 1620 by the Pilgrims. Originally known as "Separatists" because they had left the Church of England and in 1606 formed their own church, the Pilgrims were a small group of artisans and farmers living in Scrooby, England.[8] Concluding that England represented a hazard to their spiritual welfare, the Pilgrims emigrated to the Netherlands in 1607.

The Pilgrims were shocked by the light-hearted behavior of their Dutch neighbors on Sundays and feared church members would be absorbed by the Dutch since many Pilgrim children were speaking Dutch by 1620 and a number of church members had become Dutch citizens. In consequence, a decision was made to emigrate to Virginia with the permission of the Virginia Company of London. Whether by mistake, adverse weather, or a deliberate decision, the Pilgrims landed in Massachusetts.

Lacking a royal charter, on November 11, 1620, the Pilgrims signed the Mayflower Compact, which served as their government document. The Plymouth Colony, according to fragmentary available evidence, possessed complete power over its residents and would refuse permission to newcomers to locate in the colony unless they were considered to be prospective members of the church. The apparent disinterest of the Pilgrims in governmental institutions and political philosophy was a product of the great importance they attached to church doctrines designed to promote their spiritual welfare.[9]

The early government of the colony is an enigma, but it is evident that the contribution of the colony to the development of the town meeting was minor as the colony was ruled directly by the governor and council. With the exception of Scituate residents who were empowered in 1636 "to make such orders . . . for their convenient and comfortable living as they shall find necessary,"[10] the colony performed all governmental functions until Sandwich was allowed in 1651 to elect a board of selectmen authorized to call town meetings.[11]

The Puritans

The Puritans were men of station and wealth who wished to "purify" the liturgy of the Church of England and were upset by the political struggles between the Crown and Parliament. While not persecuted, the Puritans decided the task of reforming the church was hopeless and concluded they should emigrate to Massachusetts Bay. The Massachusetts Bay Company, a joint stock company, received a royal charter from Charles I on March 4, 1628–9 which provided for a governor, deputy governor, and 18 assistants who were empowered to hold a General Court, admit freemen, elect officers, and enact laws.[12]

In England, the Puritans had developed a concept of an ideal society and a plan for its future development, including political and economic institutions borrowed from England and adapted to the exigencies of colonial life.[13] Company records are not as complete as desired by scholars, but it is clear that the charter did not provide for town government.

A folkmoot, an extra-legal and informal assemblage of the freemen, governed the early towns. Attendance was compulsory and decisions were made on all matters affecting the welfare of the town, including the building of a church, hiring a minister, and division of land. Town government was completely informal and no town officials were elected.

The weekly primary assembly soon gave way to a monthly meeting.[14] Watertown in 1663 decided to hold an annual town meeting on the first Monday in September.[15] Although practices at the early town meeting were not documented adequately, evidence suggests that all male town residents were permitted to attend and speak, but only freemen typically were authorized to vote. The latter originally were the shareholders of the Massachusetts Bay Company and later included men granted political freedom.[16] Available evidence indicates freemen constituted a very small percentage of the adult male population in the colony.[17]

The town meeting alone soon proved inadequate for the governing of towns, and officials began to appear. With their appearance, town meetings were held with less frequency and often only once a year to elect officers and conduct business; special meetings were held if needed. The constable was the first appointed town official to appear in the records of the Massachusetts Bay Company.[18] Selectmen – a plural executive – were the first locally elected town officials to appear in early town records; the *Dorchester Records* referred to them on October 8, 1633.[19]

The Open Town Meeting

The open town meeting is held in response to the issuance of a warrant – a fixed agenda – by the selectmen. More than one meeting may be called by a single warrant, and routine articles may be listed first in the warrant as they will be considered early in the evening when attendance is smaller. The warrant contains articles the selectmen want the town meeting to consider, including articles requested by various town officers and boards, and citizens. By initiative petition, citizens can force the inclusion of an article in the warrant, but such petitions rarely are necessary.

Whereas officials were elected and business was conducted on the same day when all towns were small, the larger towns typically hold a two-part meeting with officials elected on a given day and business conducted at an adjourned session on a different day(s). Since the town meeting is not a continuing body, it is dissolved automatically upon completion of action on all articles in the warrant. The town meeting in certain Connecticut and Rhode Island towns is a budget town meeting only.

All mundane matters, major or trivial, affecting the town may be brought before the meeting to be debated and decided. Each warrant article is taken up and considered; the consideration may be no more than a motion and a vote to "pass over" the article. Debate tends to be practical rather than philosophical in nature. The quality of the debate varies from the dull, shallow, specious, and the superfluous to the didactic and the profound, but generally is sensible.

Voting most commonly is *viva voce,* but a show of hands, standing votes, a division of the meeting, a roll call, and written ballots may be employed. A roll call seldom is demanded because it is too time consuming in most towns. Secret ballots are used in voting on highly emotional issues to protect voters fearing recriminations if their votes were public. Such voting may require 30 or more minutes to cast the ballots and another 15 minutes to count them.

Table 2–1 reveals that attendance at the annual town meeting generally is related inversely to the size of the town, ranging in 1982

Table 2-1. Annual Town Meeting Attendance by Population Groups and States, 1982 (%)

| | Population Group | | | | | | |
	Under 2,500	2,500– 4,999	5,000– 9,999	10,000– 14,999	15,000– 19,999	20,000– 24,999	Over 25,000
Connecticut	NA	5.8 (10)	7.0 (7)	6.1 (6)	3.9 (4)	1.0 (1)	2.5 (2)
Maine	24.6 (22)	16.4 (20)	5.6 (5)	20.0 (1)	NA	NA	NA
Massachusetts	NA	14.8 (28)	9.5 (33)	6.4 (13)	4.6 (8)	3.1 (2)	NA
New Hampshire	NA	22.6 (5)	15.0 (5)	11.8 (3)	NA	5.0 (1)	NA
Vermont	21.5 (8)	14.6 (3)	NA	NA	NA	NA	NA

NA: Data not available.

Source: Compiled by author.

from an average in Massachusetts of 14.8 percent in towns under 5,000 population downward to 9.5 percent in towns of 5,000 to 9,999 population, to 6.4 percent in towns of 10,000–14,999 population, to 4.6 percent in towns of 15,000 to 19,999 population, to 3.1 percent in towns over 20,000, an average attendance of 10.0 percent of the voters. A similar pattern exists in the four other states listed in Table 2-1. The aggregate figures for the various population groups, of course, hide the range of attendance figures. Connecticut towns in the 5,000 to 9,999 population group had attendance ranging from 0.3 percent to 25.0 percent. Similarly, Massachusetts towns in the 2,500 to 4,999 population group had attendance ranging from .05 percent to 57.0 percent.

A similar relationship exists between voter attendance and town size relative to special town meetings (see Table 2-2). However, there are exceptions to the inverse relationship. Only 0.9 percent of the voters in Massachusetts towns in the 15,000 to 19,999 population category attended special town meetings in 1982, but the attendance percentage was 4.0 in towns in the 20,000 to 24,999 population group. While the presence of controversial articles in the warrant boosts attendance, the presence of such articles is particularly noticeable at special town meetings. If the warrant for such a meeting contains only articles proposing

Table 2-2. Special Town Meeting Attendance by Population Groups and States, 1982 (%)

| | Population Group | | | | | | |
	Under 2,500	2,500– 4,999	5,000– 9,999	10,000– 14,999	15,000– 19,999	20,000– 24,999	Over 25,000
Connecticut	NA	3.8 (8)	3.5 (14)	1.7 (7)	1.1 (4)	0.1 (1)	1.0 (1)
Maine	10.9 (22)	4.5 (20)	1.8 (5)	2.0 (1)	NA	NA	NA
Massachusetts	NA	10.0 (28)	6.0 (33)	2.5 (13)	0.9 (8)	4.0 (2)	NA
New Hampshire	NA	13.1 (5)	4.5 (4)	8.6 (3)	NA	2.5 (1)	NA
Vermont	15.5 (5)	15.0 (2)	NA	NA	NA	NA	NA

NA: Data not available.

Source: Compiled by author.

the routine transfer of funds between accounts, attendance of voters will be minuscule. On the other hand, the town hall will overflow with voters if a controversial zoning change is in the warrant.

Surveyed New England town clerks overwhelmingly report town meeting debate is of good quality, and a few clerks felt debate was of exceptional quality. On the other hand, a very small number of clerks rated town meeting debate as fair or poor, and a handful described the quality of debate as terrible. One clerk reported debates "sometimes are good and sometimes are terrible."

A relatively recent development is the use of town meetings by the national and regional interest groups as "straw polls" attracting widespread media coverage. Warrant articles relating to the proposed Panama Canal treaties appeared in many town meeting warrants in New Hampshire in 1978, and similar articles dealing with El Salvador and nuclear disarmament appeared in warrants in New Hampshire and Vermont in 1983. Acid rain was a prominent warrant issue in these states in 1984 and 1985.

Writing in 1983, Jeffrey Good, who had lived in Vermont for four of the previous six years, maintained Vermonters "don't want to New Hampshireize Vermont" by placing the El Salvador issue in warrants and added "local and outside activists and network executives must recognize the fragility of this most stubbornly Yankee of traditions and resist the urge to dilute it, to create still more illusion."[20] On the other hand, a number of native Vermonters argue the town meeting traditionally has been a revolutionary body dating to the colonial period and often is the only forum for the expression of views.

A common charge against the open town meeting is that it is controlled by special interests who pack the town hall. There is no denying the fact that town employees, members of the volunteer fire company, school teachers and parents of schoolchildren, and business association members tend to have excellent attendance records and undoubtedly exercise influence relative to the articles they are interested in. More recently, senior citizens have been attending meetings in sharply increased numbers in certain towns. Single issue groups also are formed and typically disappear within a relatively short period of time. A Connecticut town clerk wrote in 1983 that "special interests do have a major impact on the meeting; these groups are usually the pro-budget people present to prevent cuts to the education budget and the anti-budget group (presently a 'Homeowners Association') which wishes no tax increase at all, no matter the effect on the ability to function."

A related charge is that the town meeting is an unrepresentative body because of relatively low attendance by townspeople. In comparison with the early town meeting, the meeting today has a lower voter attendance with the exceptions of the very small towns. In effect, the town meeting typically is a de facto representative town meeting (RTM). Meetings held by the citizens' finance or advisory committee on all warrant articles or finance articles prior to the town meeting result in the resolution of many issues in advance of the de jure town meeting.

Most warrant articles are routine and do not generate debate. As a consequence, the town meeting often gives the appearance of being an unexciting assemblage of citizens for ratification purposes. Occasionally, a contentious issue is brought to the town meeting and debate is protracted as it was at the 1982 annual meeting in Chesterfield, New Hampshire, when citizens spent five hours debating, prior to defeating, an article creating a police commission to supervise the police department.

The general lack of controversy surrounding most warrant articles does not encourage attendance in an era when town populations generally have become more transient and the number of diversions, including cable television, is increasing. A Massachusetts town clerk in 1983 attributed the decline in attendance to selectmen performing functions the town meeting formerly performed, particularly work that had been conducted by special committees of the town meeting. According to data contained in Table 2–3, 82 percent of the reporting open town meetings in four of the New England states seldom or never established select committees.

Table 2-3.   Creation of Town Meeting Select
Committees by States, 1982

	Often	Seldom	Never
Connecticut	5	24	7
Maine	7	29	12
Massachusetts	19	61	10
New Hampshire	4	10	0
Vermont	0	8	2
Total	35	132	31

Source: Compiled by author.

Heavy reliance is placed by the electorate upon permanent citizen committees – particularly the finance committee and the planning board – for information and guidance on warrant articles, and the typical town meeting attendee is reluctant to challenge the recommendations of such committees, which have been studying the issues throughout the year. Relative to Massachusetts towns in the 5,000 to 9,999 population group, Table 2-4 reveals that three town meetings accepted all the recommendations of the finance committee in 1982, 24 town meetings accepted most recommendations, and four town meetings accepted some recommendations. Interestingly, the town clerks in two Maine towns and in one New Hampshire town reported that the open town meeting accepted none of the finance committee's recommendations in 1982.

Public understanding of town affairs is facilitated by the finance committee, which translates financial complexities into understandable terms and relieves the average townsperson of the inordinate burden of making a detailed investigation of each warrant article. Furthermore, the committee speeds up the decision-making process, thereby enabling the meeting to complete action on an ever-lengthening warrant without producing voter fatigue.

One of the committee's major functions is to serve as a counterpoise to pressure groups at town meetings; this function is particularly important in view of the amount of absenteeism at the annual town meeting and the sparse attendance at many special meetings. Without a finance committee, a meeting is apt to respond to the section of town or interest group exerting the most pressure. The committee may be able to convince the meeting that a careful study reveals the request of a stentorian minority deserves a low priority in view of other pressing town needs.

Table 2-4. Adoption of Finance Committee Recommendations, by Population Groups and States, 1982

		Population Group					
	Under 2,500	2,500– 4,999	5,000– 9,999	10,000– 14,999	15,000– 19,999	20,000– 24,999	Over 25,000
Connecticut	NA	0 All	0 All	1 All	1 All	0 All	1 All
	NA	7 Most	9 Most	7 Most	1 Most	1 Most	1 Most
	NA	2 Some	2 Some	1 Some	1 Some	0 Some	0 Some
Maine	4 All	1 All	1 All	0 All	NA	NA	NA
	15 Most	16 Most	2 Most	1 Most	NA	NA	NA
	4 Some	2 Some	2 Some	0 Some	NA	NA	NA
	1 None	1 None	0 None	0 None			
Massachusetts	NA	3 All	3 All	0 All	1 All	0 All	NA
	NA	13 Most	24 Most	14 Most	3 Most	3 Most	NA
	NA	8 Some	4 Some	0 Some	3 Some	1 Some	NA
New Hampshire	NA	3 All	0 All	0 All	NA	0 All	NA
	NA	2 Most	4 Most	1 Most	NA	1 Most	NA
	NA	0 None	0 None	1 None	NA	0 None	NA
Vermont	0 All	0 All	NA	NA	NA	NA	NA
	4 Most	2 Most	NA	NA	NA	NA	NA
	3 Some	0 Some	NA	NA	NA	NA	NA

NA: Data not available.

Source: Compiled by author.

The committee also serves as a training school for future town leaders. Citizens are afforded the opportunity to obtain an overview of town government, and creditable service on the committee facilitates appointment or election to other town offices.

Proposition 2½

That one form of direct citizen action may affect adversely another form of such action is illustrated by the impact of the voter-approved initiative Proposition 2½, limiting the general property tax, on Massachusetts town government.

The Massachusetts Constitution authorizes citizens to employ the indirect initiative under which petitions signed by voters equal to 3.0 percent of the votes cast for governor in the last state election are sent to the General Court (state legislature) for its action.[21] Should the General Court reject, amend, or take no action on the petitions by May 1, the petitions' sponsors must collect an additional number of signatures, equal to 0.5 percent of the votes cast for governor in the last state election, to place the proposition on the November referendum ballot. The General Court also may place its own proposition on the referendum ballot.

Because the general property tax rates were 70 percent higher than the national average in the late 1970s, citizen concern with the property tax had been increasing for many years. In 1978, voters approved, by a three to one margin, an advisory referendum proposition that the General Court should act to reduce property taxes, increase state aid to cities and towns, and limit increases in state and local taxes.

In 1980, Citizens for Limited Taxation secured the necessary signatures to place Proposition 2½ on the November ballot, and voters, by nearly a three to two margin, approved the proposition, which sought to reduce property taxes by an average of 40 percent for a total of approximately $385 million effective January 1, 1981. In contrast to the California state government when Proposition 13 was ratified by the voters, a subject discussed in Chapter 4, the Massachusetts state government did not have a budgetary surplus that could be drawn upon to assist local governments financially.

Provisions

The proposition is named after its major provision limiting the municipal general property tax levy to 2½ percent of the "full and fair" cash value of property located in a city or town. In 1980, approximately one-third of the cities and towns were assessing property at "full and fair" cash value even though a 1971 Supreme Judicial Court decision required assessment at 100 percent of "full and fair" cash value.[22]

If the property tax levy exceeds 2½ percent in a city or town, the levy must be decreased by 15 percent annually until the allowable maximum is reached. A total of 182 of the Commonwealth's 351 cities and towns exceeded the limit and generally were the larger municipalities. If the rate was below 2½ percent, the rate was lowered to the 1979 level and future increases were restricted to 2½ percent annually. The 2½ percent limit could be exceeded by a two-thirds vote of the local electorate provided the General Court placed the override question on a state election ballot in a city or town.

The Massachusetts General Court in December 1981 approved a bill, amending Proposition 2½.[23]

Effective July 1, 1982, the board of selectmen or council in a town and a city council by a two-thirds vote may place on the referendum ballot at any time the question whether the 2½ percent limit should be exceeded.

A two-thirds vote of the electorate is required for approval of the question only if the referendum proposal is to override the limit by more than 2½ percent or a total exceeding 5 percent. In other cases, only a majority vote is required. In addition, only a majority vote is required to reduce the 15 percent reduction in the general property tax rate in one year to 7½ percent in cities and towns exceeding the 2½ percent limit. Under no circumstances, however, may a city or town under the 2½ percent cap exceed the cap in any given year. To date, town voters have been reluctant to override the limit established by the initiative proposition.

Impact

Proposition 2½ rapidly achieved its major objective as the percentage of revenue raised by the general property tax was decreased from 43 to 32 between 1975 and 1982.[24] In the period July 1, 1981 to December 1, 1982, property tax revenues were reduced by $311 million or 9.3 percent.[25] In part, the reduction was due to increased state financial assistance which enabled cities and towns to reduce their spending cuts, as required by the proposition, by nearly 50 percent. The most major spending cuts were made in the area of capital improvements.

Cities and towns have become more dependent upon state financial assistance, which has increased by more than 50 percent, with a consequent loss of some local discretionary authority.

In towns with a general property tax rate exceeding or near the maximum allowable rate, the ability of the town meeting attendee to influence spending decisions has been curtailed greatly and the influence of the finance committee increased correspondingly. In order to win support for spending exceeding the finance committee's recommendation or to add an item to the committee's budget, a citizen or citizen group must convince the meeting to delete an item(s) from the committee's recommended budget. Some selectmen complain the finance committee has been attempting to act as a "super board of selectmen."

The Association of Town Finance Committees recognized the adverse impact of Proposition 2½ on the town meeting in many towns and offered the following "sage" advise to its members in 1983.

> To repeat sage counsel – try not to recommend a budget which presses all the way to the levy limit. This results in a budget so rigid that no item can be increased unless one or several inoffensive items are cut an equivalent amount. The voter who favors such an increase must either get in his licks before the budget is set in stone, find a soft spot in the budget or, more likely, give up and stay silent or even stay home. The town meeting will still have zoning and non-financial matters to consider but attendance will suffer badly unless there is *some* leeway for town meeting fiscal action. Perhaps 1 percent or 2 percent of the levy will be enough slack so that its appropriation will be worth the time and attention of a quorum.[26]

The Representative Town Meeting

Town records indicate the open town meeting functioned adequately albeit tumultuously on occasion for at least its first century and a half in all towns. It was not until the 1780s that there were rumblings of discontent with the plenary meeting as the local legislative body began to develop in Boston as its population increased. However, Boston did not abandon the open town meeting in favor of a city charter until 1822 when the town's population exceeded 43,000.

As town populations grew in the nineteenth and early twentieth centuries, the electorate in the larger towns decided to abandon the open town meeting for the only existing alternative – a city government. Alfred D. Chandler of Brookline, Massachusetts, is considered the father of the RTM as he first attempted to persuade his town to adopt the plan at the end of the nineteenth century. He was successful in 1915 when town voters adopted a RTM charter enacted by the General Court.[27] Whereas 45 Massachusetts towns operate a RTM, there are only 7 in Connecticut, 1 in Maine, 1 in Vermont, and none in New Hamp-

shire and Rhode Island. Greenfield, Massachusetts, in 1983 replaced its
243-member RTM with a 27-member town council.

The limited or representative town meeting is a hybrid political
institution which seeks to combine certain features of the open town
meeting with a representative body; the voters delegate legislative
powers to a relatively large number of elected representatives, yet reserve the right to attend and speak at town meetings and by referenda
reverse most actions of their elected representatives. State enabling
legislation or town charters often designate or authorize the town to
designate by bylaw specified town officers as members ex officio to participate in the meeting as members-at-large. Elected town meeting
members in Massachusetts towns range from 50 to 370 with an average
of 225.

The number of candidates for the office of town meeting member
is relatively small and frequently is equal to, or less than, the number
of town meeting members to be elected. Only on rare occasions are
there two candidates for each position. The number of candidates would
be even less except for the active recruitment of candidates by the town
clerk and other town officials.

In theory, town meeting members should be more conscientious
than townspeople in attending a town meeting as the former have accepted a civic responsibility by seeking public office. Nevertheless, the
RTM often has experienced attendance problems at adjourned sessions
of the annual meeting and at special meetings.

Surveyed town clerks described debate at a representative town
meeting as good, and only two clerks indicated special interests tended
to control the meeting. One town clerk noted that the referendum was
employed often to reverse the decisions of town meeting members. The
other clerks reported the referendum never or seldom was utilized.

The Changing Town Meeting

If a participant in a seventeenth-century New England town meeting
attended such a meeting in 1986, he would note certain similarities and
differences. The open town meeting in many towns is conducted in the
same manner as the seventeenth-century meeting with the most noticeable difference being the separation of the election of officers from the
conduct of town business. The seventeenth-century visitor undoubtedly
would be impressed by the overflow crowd of citizens in the town hall
in a number of towns, but would be dismayed to learn attendance was
not compulsory and only a minuscule percentage of the electorate was
in attendance. The visitor would be even more amazed by the represent-

ative town meeting when informed that only elected town meeting members can vote.

The visitor would feel most at home in the small towns in Maine and New Hampshire where relatively few changes have been made in the governance system. Although Vermont has many small towns, the meeting has less importance today because the town meeting no longer is the sole legislative body as the board of selection can adopt ordinances subject to a 30-day permissive referendum. In Massachusetts, the major changes have been the adoption of the RTM and the replacement of the meeting by a town council in six towns—Agawam, Franklin, Greenfield, Methuen, Southbridge, and Watertown.

Currently, 99 of Connecticut's municipalities are chartered and 73 are unchartered. A shared power arrangement exists in 32 of the chartered municipalities with legislative power shared by the council and the open town meeting. One RTM shares legislative authority with the town council while six other RTMs have full legislative authority. In 39 chartered municipalities, there no longer is a town meeting and only 16 of the chartered municipalities reserve full legislative authority to the open town meeting. In towns with legislative authority shared between the town meeting and the town council, the former is basically a budget town meeting. Although there has been a reduction in the legislative authority of the town meeting in many of these chartered towns, there has been a tendency to increase the potential for citizen participation by adding charter provisions for the initiative, referendum, and recall, which are examined in the following three chapters.

All Rhode Island towns have councils, and six councils possess full legislative authority. In the other towns, an annual financial town meeting is held. At present, there is no active movement to abolish the financial town meeting where it exists.

Pure Democracy in Action?

All venerable political institutions should be re-examined periodically to determine their viability and whether they deserve to survive. Are the eulogies of the open town meeting deserved or folklore? Is the New England town meeting a viable example of "pure" democracy or a degenerate descendant of a formerly great institution of local government? Do poor attendance and relative lack of debate constitute its syndrome? Have population growth and the increase in societal complexity undermined the raison d'être of the town meeting?

A question can be raised whether critics are evaluating the open town meeting against an idealized version conjured up in their minds which never has existed or are they evaluating the town meeting in terms of their subjective views of what it should be? The twin problems of poor attendance and relative lack of debate are the two major charges hurled against the open town meeting.

For sundry reasons, a large percentage of the registered voters voluntarily abdicate power that is rightfully theirs, and their non attendance at an open town meeting may be interpreted as a vote of confidence in a de facto representative town meeting. Fortunately, attendance appears to be a function of the importance of the unresolved issues; voter apathy tends to disappear when a major issue is brought to the meeting for resolution. And there is little evidence that the de facto RTM consistently thwarts the general will of the electorate. On the contrary, evidence reveals that town meeting attendees are well informed and typically represent a broad spectrum of viewpoints in the town.

A survey by the United States Advisory Commission on Intergovernmental Relations and the International City Management Association supports the conclusion that the town meeting affords the best opportunity for citizens to participate in decision making on fiscal matters.[28] The survey also reported that participation by citizens in town meetings is at a considerably higher rate than such participation in other forms of local governments, and "participation was judged to be quite meaningful."[29]

Most surveyed town clerks rated debate at open town meetings as of good quality, and a few clerks described the debate at their town meetings as exceptional in quality. Copious oratory generally is a thing of the past. In certain towns the population is relatively homogeneous, and a consensus on solutions to problems has been achieved; town meeting proceedings are decorous. Occasionally, the consensus breaks down and debate becomes acrimonious. In other towns where the population is more heterogeneous, battle lines on major issues are drawn sharply and considerable pungent debate takes place.

The amount of debate at town meetings in general, however, has declined. At the typical meeting, business is dispatched perfunctorily and swiftly, relatively few in the audience speak, and articles commonly are approved as recommended by the finance committee unanimously with little or no debate. The impression is given that complicated issues have not been debated fully. To an outsider, the meeting may appear to be a relatively dull ratification assembly, and the erroneous conclusion may be drawn that no serious debate has taken place.

The reduction in the amount of debate at town meetings is attributable in part to refinements in governmental procedures resulting in the resolution of most issues prior to the meeting. There is conflict in

varying degrees in every town, but the quantity of town meeting debate
is not always a reliable index of the degree of conflict. The veil of
decorum at the meeting may be hiding factional differences. The "pre-
town meeting meeting," held by the finance committee or the League
of Women Voters in many towns, and informal gatherings that discuss
town issues also contribute to the reduction of debate at town meetings
as many issues were debated thoroughly prior to the meeting. And the
minority may have concluded it was pointless to contest the issues again
and, consequently, may boycott the meeting.

Sentiment alone is not responsible for the tenacity of the open
town meeting. Townspeople generally are convinced they can make decisions as good as, or superior to, decisions made by elected representatives. Town meeting attendees generally have access to full information
on issues through the reports of the finance and advisory committees,
and the local law-making process appears to be functioning adequately in most towns. No evidence has been presented that an alternative
would exercise more sagacity in choosing solutions for town problems.

Interestingly, Montana voters in 1972 approved a new state constitution containing a provision requiring each local government to
review its form of government and submit an alternative form to the
voters for their action.[30] In implementing this provision, the 1975 Montana legislature authorized small towns to adopt town meeting government, but none has adopted such a form to date.[31]

Abandonment of town meeting government in favor of the city
form of government is not common. Lebanon, New Hampshire, in 1957
decided to make such change, primarily because of a post–World War
II influx of new residents. However, Lebanon voters are not entirely
pleased with city government. A former mayor of the city maintains
that there has been over-taxation and over-regulation under the city
form of government which would not have occurred under town meeting
government and asked: "An interesting question for the other side to
answer is why they are afraid of a town meeting. It's that elitist attitude:
'You're too frigging dumb. It's too complex.'"[32]

With continued population growth, a number of towns will be faced
with the problem of an inadequate facility for the town meeting. In the
larger Massachusetts towns, the open meeting has been conducted in
two or three auditoria connected by loudspeakers, but this arrangement
clearly is unsatisfactory. Towns of this size should select an alternative – the RTM, town council, or a city council.

In sum, the open town meeting is not an anachronism and may
be viewed as a safety valve allowing all voters to participate in town
governance and offering apathetic and lethargic citizens when sufficiently aroused to control town decision making. As we shall see in Chapter

6, the suggestion has been advanced that large cities should be broken up into neighborhood governments with town meetings.

As noted, voters dissatisfied with a representative town meeting vote may be able to employ the referendum to reverse the decision. The referendum assumes several forms as explained in Chapter 3.

Notes

1. Paul L. Ford, ed., *The Writings of Thomas Jefferson*, vol. 4 (New York: G. P. Putnam's Sons, 1894), p. 64.

2. Alexis de Tocqueville, *Democracy in America*, 3rd. American ed. (New York: George Adlard, 1839), pp. 62–63, and James Bryce, *The American Commonwealth*, 2nd ed. rev., vol. 1 (London: Macmillan, 1891), p. 591.

3. Benjamin Jowett, trans., *Aristotle's Politics* (New York: Carlton House, n.d.), pp. 145–46.

4. John W. Alexander and Morroe Berger, "Is The Town Meeting Finished?" *The American Mercury* (August 1959): 151.

5. "The Fading Town Meeting," *National Civil Review* 54 (October 1965): 522.

6. *Modernizing Local Government* (New York: Committee for Economic Development, July 1966), p. 30.

7. Nathaniel B. Shurtleff, ed., *Records of the Governor and Company of the Massachusetts Bay in New England*, vol. 1 (Boston: From the Press of William White, Printer to the Commonwealth, 1953), pp. 2–28.

8. Roland G. Usher, *The Pilgrims and Their History* (New York: Macmillan, 1918).

9. Francis Baylies, *Historical Memoir of the Colony of New Plymouth* (Boston: Wiggin & Lunt, 1866), pp. 256–57.

10. Nathaniel B. Shurtleff, ed., *Records of the Colony of New Plymouth in New England* (Boston: From the Press of William White, Printer to the Commonwealth, 1855), p. 44.

11. Henry C. Kittredge, *Barnstable: 1639–1939* (Barnstable, Mass.: Tercentenary Committee, 1939), p. 12.

12. Shurtleff, *Massachusetts Bay Records,* vol. 1, pp. 10–17. The Julian calendar was in use and the year legally commenced on March 25. The first date in a double date refers to the legal year and the second date to the historical year.

13. William Haller, Jr., *The Puritan Town-Planting in New England Colonial Development: 1630–1660* (New York: Columbia University Press, 1951), p. 13.

14. *The Records of the Town of Cambridge (Formerly Newtowne) Massachusetts: 1630–1703* (Cambridge: Printed by order of the City Council under direction of the City Clerk, 1901), p. 4; and *Second Report of the Record Commissioners of the City of Boston* (Boston: Rockwell and Churchill, 1877), pp. 2–9 and 222–40.

15. *Watertown Records* (Watertown: Press of Fred G. Barker, 1894), p. 78.

16. Shurtleff, *Massachusetts Bay Records*, vol. 1, pp. 78–80, 87, 168, and 367–70.

17. Haller, *Puritan Town-Planting*, p. 22.

18. Shurtleff, *Massachusetts Bay Record*, vol. 1, pp. 76 and 79.

19. *Dorchester Town Records: Fourth Report of the Record Commissioners of the City of Boston*, 2nd ed. (Boston: Rockwell and Churchill, 1883), p. 3.

20. Jeffrey Good, "Vermont Spoilers," *The New York Times*, March 26, 1983, p. 23.

21. *Constitution of the Commonwealth of Massachusetts*, articles of amendment, Art. 48, 74, and 81.

22. *First National Stores Incorporated v. Board of Assessors of Somerville*, 358 Mass. 554, 265 N.E. 2d 848 (1971).

23. *Massachusetts Laws of 1981*, chap. 782. *Massachusetts General Laws*, chap. 4, § 4B; chap. 59, § 21 (a–d); chap. 62, § 3 (B)(9); and chap. 71, § 34 (1982 supp.). Relative to sewer and water districts, see *Massachusetts Acts of 1982*, chap. 550.

24. Governor Edward J. King, *Testimony Before the Joint Economic Committee* (Boston: Massachusetts Executive Department, February 24, 1982), p. 4.

25. "Property Taxes Decline 9.3% with Massachusetts Measure," *The New York Times*, December 20, 1982, p. B16.

26. *Memorandum to All Finance Committee Chairmen & Secretaries* (Boston: Association of Town Finance Committees, April 1, 1983), p. 2.

27. *Massachusetts Act of 1915*, chap. 250.

28. *Citizen Participation in the American Federal System* (Washington, D.C.: United States Advisory Commission on Intergovernmental Relations, 1980), p. 238.

29. Ibid.

30. *Constitution of the State of Montana*, Art. 11, § 9.

31. *Revised Code of Montana*, § 47A–3–207 (1975 supp.).

32. "The Move to Go Back: The Hard Talk Around Dulac's Hardware," *Valley News* (White River Junction, Vermont), March 31, 1981, p. 5.

Chapter **3**

PLEBISCITARIAN DEMOCRACY:
The Referendum

The referendum, based upon the concept of shared decision making, is a natural extension of the New England town meeting and allows voters to determine whether referred matters are to become parts of the state constitution, state statutes, local charters, or local ordinances. Not surprisingly, the first referendum was held in the Massachusetts Bay Colony in 1640.[1]

This chapter traces the development of the referendum, describes the types of referenda and associated legal issues, and evaluates this variety of citizen law making. The question of the types of propositions that should be submitted to the voters is addressed, and a prescription for improving the petition or protest referendum is advanced.

Development of the Referendum

Following the issuance of the Declaration of Independence in 1776, constitutional conventions in Massachusetts and New Hampshire referred draft constitutions to the voters for their action. Although Massachusetts voters rejected the document submitted by the General Court (state legislature) in 1778, they approved in 1780 a new document drafted and submitted by a constitutional convention.[2] New Hampshire voters rejected a constitution drafted by a convention in 1778, but approved in 1784 a new document submitted by a second convention.[3] The practice of submitting proposed constitutions to the voters spread to Connecticut in 1818 and Maine in 1819. New York, in 1821, was the first state outside of New England to submit a proposed fundamental document to the electorate for ratification or rejection.

Legislative Power Delegation

While the practice of submitting the fundamental state document to the electorate became well established in the nineteenth century, courts generally held that a state legislature, acting under authority delegated by the people, could not redelegate its power. In a 1853 decision relative to the New York Free School Law of 1849 providing the voters were to determine whether the act would become effective, Chief Justice Ruggles of the New York Court of Appeals wrote:

> The exercise of this power by the people in other cases is not expressly and in terms prohibited by the Constitution; but it is forbidden by necessary and unavoidable implication. The Senate and Assembly are the only bodies of men clothed with the power of general legislation. They possess the entire power. . . . The people reserve no part of it to themselves excepting in regard to laws creating public debt, and can therefore exercise it in no other case.[4]

Similarly, the Iowa Supreme Court held in 1855 that "the people have no power in their primary or individual capacity to make laws."[5]

The rule *delegata postesta non potest delegari* was followed consistently relative to state laws with one exception. Thomas M. Cooley in his classic work on *Constitutional Limitations* referred to the people tying "their own hands" when they adopt a constitution and added:

> One of the settled maxims in constitutional law is, that the power conferred upon the legislature to make laws can not be delegated by that department to any other body or authority . . . and by the constitutional agency alone the laws must be made until the constitution itself is changed.[6]

The only nineteenth-century judicial exception to this maxim relative to a general law was the decision of the Vermont Supreme Court upholding as constitutional a liquor prohibition law enacted in 1852 by declaring that approval of the voters was a sufficient contingency for making a state law effective.[7]

Courts in the nineteenth century, however, sanctioned legislative power delegation to municipal corporations. Cooley wrote this exception "is to be understood in the light of the immemorial practice of this country and of England, which has always recognized the propriety and policy of vesting in the municipal organizations certain powers of local regulation, in respect to which the parties immediately interested may fairly be supposed more competent to judge of their needs than any central authority."[8] In 1822, for example, the Massachusetts General Court approved an act establishing the City of Boston that would be invalid "unless the inhabitants, shall, by written vote, determine to adopt the same within twelve days."[9] The Supreme Judicial Court ruled that there was "no impropriety, certainly no unconstitutionality, in giving the people the opportunity to accept or reject such provisions."[10]

Massachusetts thus became the first state to resurrect the popular referendum. Three years later, the Maryland legislature approved an act for a system of primary education subject to a veto by the voters in a referendum in any county.[11]

Conditional Laws

Growing distrust of the state legislature by the voters in the nineteenth century led to constitutional amendments or new constitutions providing for conditional laws; that is, ones that do not become effective without voter sanction. Most restrictions involve borrowing of funds and taxation, and are found in many constitutions today. The first such restriction was placed in the Rhode Island Constitution of 1842, drafted by a convention and ratified by the voters. The legislature was forbidden to incur debts exceeding $50,000 without the consent of the electorate except during a war, insurrection, or invasion.[12] In 1843, the Michigan Constitution was amended to prohibit the legislature from incurring any debt without the consent of the voters with the exceptions of raising funds "for defraying the actual expenses of the legislature, the judicial and state officers, for suppressing insurrection, repelling invasion, or defending the State in time of war."[13]

The 1876 Colorado constitutional convention drafted a constitution, ratified by the electorate, containing a maximum property tax limitation that could not be exceeded without the approval of the electorate.[14] Similar restrictions have been incorporated in other constitutions relative to state taxation and/or local taxation.

Direct Legislation

The referendum entered a new era in 1898 when South Dakota voters amended their constitution to provide for the statutory initiative and referendum by stipulating that they "expressly reserve to themselves the right to propose measures, which measures the legislature shall enact and submit to a vote of the electors of the State" and "to require that any laws which the legislature may have enacted shall be submitted to a vote of the electors of the State before going into effect. . . . "[15] The only exceptions to the referendum requirements were laws designed to preserve "the public peace, health or safety, support of the State government and its existing institutions."[16] The petition or protest referendum is examined in greater detail in a subsequent section.

The petition referendum, the initiative, and the recall were advocated strongly by the progressive and municipal reform movements at the turn of the century. These reformers were convinced that population growth and urbanization had made it difficult for citizens to keep officials as responsive as they had been when society was less complex. Interestingly, a number of the early municipal reformers, Richard S. Childs in particular, favored the short ballot to relieve the burden placed on the voter at the same time the reformers favored the initiative, referendum, and recall.[17]

Progressives in the Midwest and the West viewed the initiative and the referendum as weapons to be employed by citizens to break the power of the railroads in state legislatures. V. O. Key, Jr. and Winston W. Crouch described the movement for the initiative and the referendum in California as "a revolt against a monopoly-control situation."[18]

The Referendum Today

The Delaware Constitution is the only constitution that does not provide for a referendum on constitutional amendments enacted by the state legislature. An amendment to this constitution becomes effective upon approval by a two-thirds vote of each house of the state legislature in two consecutive sessions.[19]

In the other states, the size of the legislative and referendum votes required for approval of a constitutional amendment varies. An extra-majority vote of the state legislature and a simple popular majority vote are required in 33 states, and a simple legislative majority and a simple popular majority are required for approval in the remaining states. However, a simple legislative majority at two successive sessions and a simple popular majority are required in two states for approval of an amendment, and approval by two consecutive legislative sessions is required in 12 states.

As of 1982, voters had ratified 4,430 of the 7,021 amendments proposed by state legislatures.[20] Proposed constitutional amendments affecting local governments only are common in six states—Alabama, Georgia, Louisiana, Maryland, Missouri, and Texas—where voters in 1982 approved 99 of 114 proposed local amendments.[21]

Thirty-six state constitutions contain provisions for referenda on certain laws enacted by the state legislature. First, an act pledging the "full faith and credit" of the state as backing for a bond issue requires the affirmative majority vote of the electorate in 25 states.[22] Exceptions

to the referendum requirement for specified purposes have been made
by constitutional amendments. Three amendments to the New York
Constitution allow the state legislature to issue "full faith and credit"
bonds without voter approval.[23]

Second, registered voters in 25 states may petition for a referendum on a law enacted by the state legislature. The filing of the required
number of signatures on petitions suspends the law, except appropriations and emergency ones in several states, until the electorate determines whether the law should be approved.

Third, the initiative, which is examined in detail in Chapter 4, may
be employed in 23 states to place proposed constitutional amendments
or laws on the referendum ballot. If competing measures are on the
ballot, the measure receiving the highest number of votes and meeting
the minimum percentage of the electorate specified is ratified.

Ten states currently require that a named official prepare and post
to each registered voter a pamphlet describing the referred issues and
the arguments for and against the propositions. The length and complexity of voters' guides vary considerably. In 1979, New York State
issued a $4'' \times 9''$ card describing a proposed bond issue and three constitutional amendments. In 1964, the Massachusetts Secretary of the
Commonwealth distributed a 21-page pamphlet describing four proposed constitutional amendments, one initiated measure, and one protest referendum.[24]

In 1972, New Hampshire distributed a voter's guide to a proposed
constitutional amendment that was four pages in length: page one contained the title of the guide; page two contained a brief statement by
the two legislative leaders; page three contained the question plus "A
YES vote means you must be twenty-one to be elected to office other
than governor, state senator, or governor's councilor" and "A NO vote
means you can be elected to any office except governor, state senator,
or governor's councilor at eighteen"; and page four simply stated "IM-
PORTANT BE SURE TO READ THIS PAMPHLET."[25]

A proposed California state constitutional amendment making the
Communist party illegal was complex and lengthy, and could not be
described within the statutory 500-word maximum limit for the voter's
pamphlet, and permission was granted to the Chief Deputy Legislative
Counsel to employ 558 words to explain Proposition 24.[26]

The cost of publishing and distributing voter information hand-
books and pamphlets on referenda questions ranges from more than
$400,000 in Massachusetts to in excess of $1 million in California. Exit interviews at the polls on November 2, 1976 by staff of the Massachusetts Secretary of the Commonwealth revealed 58 percent of the
voters indicated "they depend heavily on the Secretary of State's In-

formation for Voters Guide for their information compared" to 39 percent who relied on newspapers and 32 percent who relied on television.[27]

Professor David B. Magleby of Brigham Young University, on the other hand, reported that California "voters rely almost entirely upon the mass media for information about propositions and not upon the handbook" and "voter pamphlets have readability levels beyond the ability of all but a few voters."[28]

An Oregon law, enacted in 1973 and amended in 1979, authorizes lawsuits for false publicity relating to any referendum measure, candidate, or political committee.[29]

Types of Referenda

In addition to distinguishing official referenda as state or local and constitutional or statutory, four other types of referenda may be identified.

Advisory Referendum

There are two varieties of advisory or nonbinding referenda expressing the opinion of the voters on issues. The first variety involves the legislative body seeking the advice of the electorate by placing a question on the ballot. The legislative body is only guided and is not bound by the outcome of the plebiscite.

The New York State Legislature in 1883 authorized an advisory referendum on contract labor in state prisons, and the Massachusetts General Court in 1895 held an advisory referendum on the question of granting suffrage in municipal elections to women. In 1974, the city commissioners of Cocoa Beach, Florida were unable to reach a decision whether topless bathing by women should be prohibited and referred the proposed anti-topless ordinance to the voters who rejected the proposal.[30]

The second variety involves the circulation of petitions by citizens to place a question on a nonbinding ballot. This variety has become common as national and regional interest groups discovered the advisory referendum is an effective means of publicizing their views. In Chapter 2, reference was made to the tendency in recent years for such groups to petition to have town meetings in New England vote on issues such as nuclear disarmament, El Salvador, and the proposed Panama Canal treaty.

On November 3, 1982, voters in many local governments and in eight states participated in the largest advisory referendum to date; that is, the issue of a freeze on nuclear armament. Proponents were in the majority in 8 states and in 27 of the 30 cities or counties where the

·question was on the ballot.[31] Sixty percent of the approximately 18 million voters who expressed an opinion on the issue approved the proposal.[32] Candidates for elective office favoring the freeze indicated their stand on the issue was not decisive in terms of their victories.

There is evidence that advisory referenda promote a larger voter turnout on election day. Exit interviews of voters at the polls in Worcester, Massachusetts, on November 3, 1982, revealed the attractive power of advisory referenda questions. One voter was quoted as stating "I wanted to have my say on the candidates, but primarily it's the referendum questions that made me come here today," and a second voter indicated she had voted for a proposal to assess residential property at a lower rate than commercial and industrial property because she was a homeowner.[33]

A development related to official advisory referenda is the unofficial plebiscite or straw poll organized by interest groups. In 1982, supporters of a nuclear freeze collected approximately 22,000 signatures to have the question of a freeze placed on the bond referendum ballot in Austin, Texas, but the city attorney ruled the freeze question was unrelated to a municipal issue and could not appear on the municipal ballot.[34] Proponents were not deterred and arranged for a private referendum with secret ballots being placed in locked boxes and counted under the supervision of the Travis County clerk.

Mandatory Referendum

Adoption of a new state constitution or constitutional amendment, except in Delaware, requires the affirmative majority vote of the electorate. In addition, a number of issues are determined by the state or local legislative body *ad referendum*, and a compulsory referendum typically is held on the question of adopting or amending local government charters and incorporating municipalities. The city charter of San Jose, California is an example of a local charter requiring a referendum on the proposed alienation of city parks.[35]

The constitution of Montana, adopted in 1972, contains an unusual provision for "Voter Review of Local Government"; the state legislature is directed to require "each local government or combination of units to review its structure and submit one alternative form of government to the qualified electors at the next general or special election."[36] In addition, the legislature is directed to "require a review procedure once every ten years after the first election."[37] Of the 182 units of local government voting on an alternative plan in 1976, voters in only 31 units approved the proposal.[38]

The Massachusetts Constitution of 1780 was the first one to require that a public referendum be held on the question of calling a constitutional convention.[39] The constitutions of 14 states currently require that the question of calling a convention be placed automatically on the referendum ballot periodically or the state legislature is directed to place the question on the ballot. In the period 1930–81, voters approved 35 proposals calling for the convening of a constitutional convention and rejected 27 proposals.[40] In recent years there has been a tendency for conventions to submit a proposed constitution as a series of proposition rather than risk the defeat of the entire proposed document.

A referendum, mandated by the state constitution, is held in a number of states and localities whenever the legislative body wishes to borrow funds and pledge the "full faith and credit" of the government as the enacted laws are "conditional" ones subject to referenda. Furthermore, bond referenda are held in many municipalities under state or local charter requirements (see Table 3–1). For example, California cities, counties, and school districts may issue general obligation bonds only if two-thirds of the voters give their consent.[41]

The constitutions of 13 states allow the state debt limit to be exceeded only upon the affirmative majority vote of the electorate.[42] To exceed state-imposed debt and tax limits, local voter approval often is a requirement.

The mandatory bond referendum requirement can be evaded as evidenced by the creation of public authorities authorized to issue "moral obligation" bonds and by entering into lease-purchase agreements. Public authorities are not subject to constitutional debt referendum requirements, and a number of such authorities have been created in various states with the power to issue bonds backed by a "moral obligation" or "indirect" guarantee that a future state legislature will appropriate funds to meet interest and principal payments should the issuing authorities be unable to meet their financial obligations.[43] These bonds carry a higher rate of interest than "full faith and obligation" bonds and, consequently, impose a heavier burden upon taxpayers.

Lease-purchase agreements involve a state or a local government entering into an agreement to purchase large capital equipment or facilities on the installment plan. In other words, a government signs a long-term contract providing that the government may use a facility constructed and financed by another government or a private firm with title to the project passing to the former government on a certain date.[44] In common with the "moral obligation" financing device, lease-purchase financing is more expensive than "full faith and credit" financing.

Although voters in each New York State school district, except

Table 3-1. Bond Elections Held from January 1976 to March 1982, by Population Group

Population group	No. of cities reporting (A)	No. of elections held per city										Total no. of elections held	Percent successful
		None		One		Two		Three		Four			
		No.	% of (A)	No.	% of (A)	No.	% of (A)	No.	% of (A)	No.	% of (A)		
500,000–1,000,000	14	7	50.0	1	7.1	0	0.0	2	14.3	4	28.6	23	100.0
250,000–499,999	20	8	40.0	2	10.0	3	15.0	4	20.0	3	15.0	32	75.0
100,000–249,999	70	36	51.4	10	14.3	10	14.3	6	8.6	8	11.4	77	75.3
50,000–99,999	68	51	75.0	8	11.8	5	7.4	1	1.5	3	4.4	33	84.8
25,000–49,999	56	46	82.1	5	8.9	4	7.1	0	0.0	1	1.8	17	58.8
10,000–24,999	105	75	71.4	17	16.2	8	7.6	2	1.9	3	2.9	51	74.5

Source: Kathryn E. Newcomer, Deborah L. Trent, and Natalie Flores-Kelly, "Municipal Debt and the Impact of Sound Fiscal Decision Making," The Municipal Year Book 1983 (Washington, D.C.: International City Management Association, 1983), p. 227.

dependent city districts, may reject a budget proposed by the school board, the latter may vote to adopt an "austerity" budget, as defined by the board, without voter sanction.[45] Typically upon the rejection of the first proposed budget, the board reduces items in the budget and resubmits it to the electorate. Proposed budgets have been defeated four or five times in a district before the board decides to implement an "austerity" budget, which typically is similar to the last proposal rejected by the voters.

A California constitutional provision limits state appropriations increases to changes in the state's population and cost of living, but excludes appropriations for debt service, federal court mandates, tax refunds, and insurance funds.[46] The restriction can be overridden with the approval of the electorate for a maximum period of four years.[47] New Jersey has a similar statutory provision limiting increases in state appropriations to increases in per capita income in the state between the second quarters of the preceding two years.[48] Voters in a statewide referendum may override this restriction.

To support public education, Minnesota statutes provide that a property tax of .024 mills is to be levied by each school district.[49] The school board or voters by petition may provide for a referendum on the question of authorizing an additional levy to finance school operations.[50] In Massachusetts cities and towns assessing property at "full and fair cash" value, a decision by the local legislative body to assess residential property at a lower rate than other types of property is subject to referendum.[51]

A number of mandatory referenda are the product of defensive incorporations; that is, a group of voters petition to hold a referendum on the question of incorporating a municipality in order to prevent the incorporation of part of the territory as a municipality by another group or annexation by another municipality. In 1974, a group of residents petitioned to incorporate the entire town of Harrison, New York, as a village to prevent residents of the Purchase Fire District, located in the town, from holding a referendum on incorporating a village which would remove a substantial portion of the tax base from the town as well as land use controls over the Purchase area.[52]

Annexation of land by a municipality typically requires approval of voters in the proposed annexation area to become effective. In several states, annexation requires an affirmative concurrent majority vote; that is, approval by the voters in the annexing central city and voters in the area sought to be annexed.[53] In Minnesota, a city may annex land without a referendum if the city borders 60 percent of the land to be annexed, but a town can object and demand a hearing before the Minnesota Municipal Commission, which possesses the authority to make the final decision.[54]

City–county consolidations without referenda occurred in Boston, Philadelphia, New Orleans, New York City, and San Francisco, and entire towns were consolidated by legislative edicts with the central city in the nineteenth century. Today, amalgamations of local governments typically require the consent of the concerned electorate. The consolidation of Indianapolis and Marion County by the Indiana legislature without a referendum, effective January 1, 1970, was exceptional.[55]

The fear of annexation with higher taxes and no guarantee that services would be provided in the proposed annexation area helped to persuade residents of such areas to vote in favor of proposed charters merging Nashville and Davidson Counties, Tennessee (1962), and Lexington and Fayette Counties, Kentucky (1972), since both proposed charters guaranteed provision of additional services.[56]

Laws relating to what may be labeled "moral" issues – such as the sale of alcoholic beverages and gambling – generally may be enacted only by means of a voter-approved referendum proposition. Many states have local option laws relative to the sale of various types of alcoholic beverages, and separate questions may appear on the ballot relative to whether a municipality should issue licenses for the sale of malt beverages, wines, and "hard" liquor, and whether restaurants should be allowed to serve wine with meals.[57] Statutes in several states also provide for a local option referendum on the issue of Sunday sales of alcoholic beverages.[58]

Voluntary Referendum

The voluntary or indirect referendum is initiated by a legislative body deciding to allow the voters to determine policy on an issue, often because of its controversial nature.

A number of issues – fluoridation of the water supply or the prohibition of the sale and consumption of alcoholic beverages – are emotionally charged issues that legislators know will result in the alienation of a significant number of citizens regardless of how the legislators vote on the issues. As a consequence, the state legislature frequently decides to authorize the electorate in each local government to hold a referendum to determine the policy on the issue within each community.

The Citizens' Veto

The petition referendum, also known as the protest or direct referendum, provides for a citizens' veto by allowing voters by petitions to stop the implementation of a law until a referendum determines whether the law is to be repealed. In 1970, the United States Court of Appeals for the Ninth Circuit defined a petition referendum as "an exercise by the voters of their traditional right through direct legislation to override the views of their elected representatives as to what serves the public interest. . . . "[59]

The petition referendum is similar to the initiative in that action to place a law on the referendum ballot originates with the voters. Successful collection of the requisite number of signatures results in a mandatory referendum.

This type of referendum may be employed in 24 states and first was authorized in South Dakota in 1898 when voters approved a constitutional amendment providing for the petition referendum and the initiative. In eight states – Alaska, Idaho, Massachusetts, Michigan, Missouri, Montana, South Dakota, and Wyoming – the petition referendum may be used only against an entire law, whereas in the other states the referendum may be employed against part or all of a law.

The constitutional provision for the petition referendum typically excludes certain topics – religion, appropriations, special legislation (a law affecting a single local government), and the judiciary – from the referendum. The longest list of excluded topics is contained in the Massachusetts Constitution.[60] The Massachusetts General Court on several occasions voted a salary increase for its members only to see the increase repealed by the electorate employing the protest referendum.

The Massachusetts Supreme Judicial Court in 1962 rejected the argument that a pay increase for legislators was equivalent to an appropriation of funds and, consequently, was included among the subjects exempted by the state constitution from the protest referendum.[61] The General Court in 1963 attached an emergency preamble to a bill providing a salary increase for legislators, thereby making the increase effective upon passage. The Supreme Judicial Court upheld the constitutionality of the law.[62]

Emergency and appropriation acts are excluded from the citizens' veto in ten states; appropriation and emergency acts are excluded in five additional states and four additional states, respectively.[63] All statutes are subject to the protest referendum in Arkansas, Idaho, Nevada, and North Dakota. Local government charters and state statutes often provide for a petition referendum on a local law or ordinance.[64]

In fourteen states, the petition referendum propositions appear only on the general election ballot. In nine additional states, issues may appear either on a general election ballot or a special election ballot. The governor in California, Maine, North Dakota, and Oklahoma may call a special referendum election, and the legislature in six states – Arkansas, Michigan, Missouri, Oklahoma, Oregon, and Washington – may schedule a special referendum election. Voters in Arkansas and Maine may call a special referendum election by petition.

To suspend a law and place it on the referendum ballot requires a number of signatures varying from 2 percent of the votes cast in the last gubernatorial election in Massachusetts to 15 percent of the number who voted in the previous general election and reside in at least two-thirds of the counties in Wyoming.[65] Typically, there is a requirement that a specified minimum number of signatures must be collected in each county or in a specified number of counties such as a majority in Utah and two-thirds in Wyoming in order to demonstrate there is interest in the issue in many sections of the state. The degree of difficulty encountered by dissatisfied voters in utilizing the protest referendum is affected directly by the signature threshold and distribution requirements.

The secretary of state or the local clerk or board is designated as the official who determines the sufficiency of the petitions, subject to appeal to the courts as described in a subsequent section. Prior to seeking signatures, proponents in 13 states are required to make a preliminary filing of the petition which is checked by a state official for compliance with legal requirements. Maine is the only state that does not specify the petition format.

Constitutional provisions require that petitions relative to a state law must be filed within a specified number of days – typically 90 days – subsequent to the adjournment of the state legislature. In Utah, the maximum time allowed is 60 days, whereas Montana allows 6 months. All but four states require simply a majority vote on the question to repeal a law. In the four states that are exceptions, the number of votes cast on the question must be equal to 30 to 50 percent of the votes cast in the previous general election. The state legislature in only six of the protest referenda states may not amend or repeal the decision of the voters.

States lacking the protest referendum at the state level authorize the use of this type of referendum at the local level. New Hampshire statutes, for example, authorize the owners of 20 percent either of the land area or lots to petition for a referendum on a change in land use regulations adopted by a town.[66] Residents of Connecticut towns with town meetings, a subject discussed in Chapter 2, are authorized by petition – 200 voters or 10 percent of the registered voters, whichever is less – to force a referendum on any item in the warrant calling a town meeting.[67]

The protest referendum can be employed by conservative or liberal groups, or by integrationists or segregationists. Relative to the latter, they employed the petition referendum in June 1963 to block the immediate implementation of a public accommodations law in Maryland.[68]

Whereas business groups typically do not employ the initiative to achieve their goals, such groups use the protest referendum to annul statutes. In 1982, for example, the Massachusetts Soft Drink Association filed petitions for the first referendum in the nation on the subject of repealing a mandatory bottle deposit law enacted by the General Court.[69] Although voters defeated a proposed bottle deposit law by a small margin in 1976, they rejected the repeal proposal in 1982.

The San Diego Mail Referendum

The first protest referendum conducted entirely by post occurred in San Diego on May 6, 1981, when voters turned down a proposal for a convention complex in downtown San Diego.[70] Voter participation in the referendum was 61.7 percent, which was approximately twice the participation in any previous special referendum in the city not held in conjunction with a general election.

Legal Issues

Opponents and proponents of measures on the referendum ballot typically seek judicial decisions to strengthen their respective positions and opponents of successful measures often seek to invalidate the referenda. The 1877 constitution of Georgia, for example, stipulated that only a constitutional convention may submit a completely revised constitution to the voters for their action.[71] The Georgia Supreme Court in 1946, however, upheld the right of the electorate to adopt a complete constitutional revision that was not submitted to them by a convention.[72]

Other issues referred to the courts include restrictions on the number of ballot questions, ballot language, extraordinary requirements for approval of measures, concurrent vote requirements, property voting requirements, zoning changes, rent control, and public housing.

Number of Ballot Questions

Illinois law restricts the number of questions that may appear on any local government referendum ballot to three.[73] A group of DuPage County voters petitioned for an advisory referendum on a nuclear arms freeze, but four binding referenda questions already had qualified for the ballot. Qualifying questions not specifying a date for a referendum in excess of three are placed on the next local election ballot.

Judge William T. Hart of the United States District Court for the Northern District of Illinois in 1982 upheld the Illinois law relative to the number of ballot questions, but invalidated the requirement that petitions for advisory referenda need the signatures of 25 percent of the registered voters.[74] The nuclear freeze group collected only one-eighth of the required signatures, and the judge ruled "we can not suppose the legislature intended that professional canvassers be employed in order to allow citizens to exercise their statutory right to place on the ballot advisory public questions."[75]

Ballot Language

Ballot language restricts voters to a "yes" or "no" choice. If several questions are on the referendum ballot, proponents of one proposal may discover that their campaign urging the electorate to vote "yes" inadvertently may encourage the electorate to vote "yes" on a second proposition the group opposes.

On the November 4, 1972, ballot in Yonkers, New York, there were two propositions one.[76] The League of Women Voters favored one proposition one, a state environmental bond issue, and opposed a second proposition one, a city charter amendment that would provide for a strong mayor as a replacement for the city manager. Since the environmental bond issue was the first state proposition on the ballot, the proposition was labeled number one. Similarly, the city charter amendment was the first local proposition and also was labeled number one. Citizens for Continued City Manager Government discovered the wording problem after distributing 50,000 flyers urging the defeat of proposition one.

In 1981, the Ohio Supreme Court directed the Ohio Ballot Board, a five-member bipartisan body charged with drafting the ballot language for proposed constitutional amendments, to rewrite the ballot wording drafted for an initiated constitutional amendment because the wording "is in the nature of an argument against adoption of the amendment."[77] Specifically, the court held the word "present," employed in conjunction with "at no cost to the Ohio taxpayers," created the impression taxpayers will have to bear some of the cost if the amendment is ratified.[78]

Similarly, the New Jersey Supreme Court in the same year upheld a ruling by the Appellate Division of the Superior Court that the wording on the November ballot explaining a proposed riparian land constitutional amendment, written by the attorney general's office, was not neutral and would discourage voter approval.[79] State officials agreed almost immediately to use the court's recommended explanatory statement although such use was not mandatory.

Petition Fraud

A major problem with the employment of the petition referendum (and the initiative and the recall) is fraudulent petition signatures. The cost of collecting signatures leads unscrupulous petition circulators to forge signatures on petitions. The secretary of state or State Ballot Law Commission is charged with examining and certifying signatures on state petitions, and local clerks or boards of registrars of voters typically are charged with a similar responsibility on the local government level. In 1972, six individuals were indicted on the basis of testimony by nine teenagers who had been promised five dollars each for signing names from street directories on petition forms to place a proposed $7.3 million Missouri transportation bond issue on the referendum ballot.[80]

In 1963, protest petitions were filed in Massachusetts seeking to invalidate a statute increasing the salary of members of the General Court.[81] The petitioners made a timely filing of 88,159 signatures from 12 counties; a total of 31,637 signatures were required.[82] The State Ballot Law Commission held public hearings relative to challenges to the validity of signatures, and all members agreed there were instances of fraud and perjury relative to the petitions. The majority of the commission members ruled that only 29,299 signatures were valid, and the minority member argued 39,040 signatures were valid. The difference involved the legal issue of whether a false jurat on a petition sheet invalidates the entire sheet and whether a forged signature on a sheet invalidates the entire sheet because the forgery affects the jurat of the circulator.

The Supreme Judicial Court rejected the contention that a provision in state law applicable to jurats on nomination papers applied to protest referendum petitions and ordered the printing of ballots containing the referendum question and an explanatory pamphlet for voters.[83]

Referendum Campaign Finance

State corrupt-practices acts regulate the financing of election and referendum campaigns. Historically, these acts required the reporting of campaign receipts and expenditures, and limited the amount that may be contributed to or spent in campaigns.

In 1976, the U.S. Supreme Court in *Buckley v. Valeo* examined the Federal Election Campaign Act of 1971 and its 1974 amendments.[84] The Court upheld the individual contribution limits, disclosure and reporting requirements, and public financing provisions, but held "the limitations on expenditures, on independent expenditures by individuals and groups, and on expenditures by a candidate from his personal funds are constitutionally infirm."[85] In particular, the Court ruled the limitation on personal expenditures by candidates "imposes a substantial restraint on the ability of persons to engage in protected First Amendment expression."[86]

The California Supreme Court in 1976 invalidated a provision of the state's Political Reform Act imposing limitations on contributions to referendum campaigns as violative of the freedom of speech guarantee contained in the First Amendment to the U.S. Constitution.[87]

Two years later, the U.S. Supreme Court invalidated a Massachusetts statute restricting corporate contributions to referendum campaigns by ruling that a corporation was protected by the First Amendment to the U.S. Constitution and could expend funds to publicize its views relative to a proposed state constitutional amendment authorizing the General Court to levy a graduated income tax.[88]

In 1981, the Court examined a City of Berkeley, California, initiated ordinance restricting campaign contributions by any one person to a maximum of $250.[89] The Court struck down the ordinance and noted:

> The Court has long viewed the First Amendment as protecting a market place for the clash of different views and conflicting ideas. That concept has been stated and restated almost since the Constitution was drafted. The voters of the City of Berkeley adopted the challenged ordinance which places restrictions on that market place. It is irrelevant that the voters rather than a legislative body enacted s 602, because the voters may no more violate the Constitution by enacting a ballot measure than a legislative body may do so by enacting legislation. . . . To place a spartan limit . . . on individuals wishing to band together, while placing none on individuals acting alone, is clearly a restraint on the right of association.[90]

Distinguishing between *Buckley v. Valeo* and the Berkeley case, Mr. Justice White dissented and pointed out the invalidated Massachusetts statute completely prohibited contributions and expenditures while the Berkeley ordinance allowed contributions up to a maximum of $250.[91] He added:

> The role of the initiative in California can not be separated from its purpose of preventing the dominance of special interest. That is the very history and purpose of the initiative in California and similarly it is the purpose of the ancillary regulations designed to protect it. Both serve to maximize the exchange of political discourse.[92]

Although decisions by the U.S. Supreme Court and the U.S. Court of Appeals have invalidated several state corrupt-practices acts' provisions restricting contributions by individuals to referendum campaigns, such provisions remain on the statute books in several states, including Massachusetts and Michigan.[93]

Extra-Majority Approval Requirements

Do charter provisions, state laws, and constitutional provisions requiring an extra-majority affirmative vote in referenda violate the "one person, one vote" doctrine of the U.S. Supreme Court? In 1969, the West Virginia Supreme Court concluded that an extra-majority requirement of the state constitution violated the federal Constitution's guarantee of equal protection of the laws.[94]

In 1971, however, the U.S. Supreme Court reversed the decision by holding that the requirement of an affirmative majority of 60 percent of the voters in a referendum before political subdivisions could incur bonded indebtedness or increase tax rates beyond the constitutional limits did not single out a "discrete and insular minority" for special treatment as the requirement applied to any bond issue for any purpose. The Court could not find a section of the population would be "fenced out" from the franchise by the vote they cast in such a referendum, and decided the extraordinary majority affirmative vote requirement was reasonable relative to bond issues since the credit of unborn generations, as well as children, would be affected.[95]

Concurrent Vote Requirements

The New York Constitution requires a popular referendum on the question of adopting a county charter and the transfer of functional responsibilities to a county from cities, towns, and villages; a proposal to become effective must be approved by city voters as one unit and town voters as a second unit.[96] If a proposed charter provides for the transfer of a village function to a county, separate approvals by city voters, town voters, and village voters are required for ratification. Village voters also vote as town voters since all villages are located within towns in the state of New York.

The U.S. District Court for the Western District of New York in 1974 invalidated the New York concurrent majority constitutional requirement as violating the U.S. Supreme Court's "one person, one vote" dictum.[97] The Supreme Court in 1977, however, upheld the constitutionality of the concurrent majority requirement by ruling it did not violate the "one person, one vote" dictum as cities and towns had interests that were distinct.[98]

Property Voting Requirements

Property ownership historically was a qualification for voting in many states in general elections. Although such a requirement in general has been abandoned, laws in several states restrict voting in special district elections and bond referenda to property owners.

In 1969, the U.S. Supreme Court struck down a property tax-paying requirement for voting in a revenue bond referendum.[99] Similarly the Appellate Division of the New York State Supreme Court affirmed the decision of the Supreme Court invalidating a town law provision restricting voting on propositions to raise, appropriate, or expend money, or dispose of town land and property to persons who own assessed property in the town.[100] Nevertheless, the town law provision remains on the New York statute books.[101]

Zoning Changes

Acting under the initiative and referendum provision of the Ohio Constitution,[102] voters amended the City of Eastlake Charter to require that a change in land use approved by the city council was subject to approval by 55 percent of the voters in a referendum. The amendment was approved while the application of a real estate developer for a zoning change was pending. The developer filed suit in state court seeking a judgment that the amendment was an unconstitutional delegation of legislative power to the voters who had rejected the proposed land use change while the court action was pending.

Although the charter amendment was upheld by the trial court and the Ohio Court of Appeals, the Ohio Supreme Court ruled the amendment to be a delegation of power violating federal constitutional due process guarantees as voters were not provided standards to guide their decision.[103] The U.S. Supreme Court reversed the Ohio Supreme Court's decision and concluded that

> a referendum cannot . . . be characterized as a delegation of power. Under our constitutional assumptions, all power derives from the people, who can delegate it to representative instruments which they create. . . . In establishing legislative bodies, the people can reserve to themselves power to deal directly with matters which might otherwise be assigned to the legislature.[104]

Mr. Justice Powell dissented on the ground the "normal protective procedures for resolving issues affecting individual rights" were bypassed, and Mr. Justice Stevens, joined by Mr. Justice Brennan, dissented on the ground "the popular vote is not an acceptable method of adjudicating the rights of individual litigants."[105]

Preemption by State Law

In 1983, a three-judge panel of the California State Court of Appeals invalidated as unconstitutional a rent control ordinance, adopted by Berkeley voters, on the ground that state law preempted the provisions of the ordinance allowing tenants to withhold rents if they believe land-lords are not complying with the ordinance.[106]

Civil Rights

The U.S. Supreme Court in 1969 invalidated a City of Akron, Ohio, charter amendment, ratified by the voters in a referendum, stipulating that an ordinance regulating real estate on the basis of color, national origin, race, or religion would not be effective unless approved by a ma-jority of citizens voting in a referendum.[107] The Court held that the referendum requirement denied equal protection of the laws by plac-ing "special burdens on racial minorities within the governmental pro-cess."[108]

Two years later, the Court upheld a California constitutional re-quirement that a public low-rent housing project could not be con-structed or acquired without majority voter approval in a local refer-endum.[109] Although the California Constitution provided for the initi-ative and the referendum, the California Supreme Court in 1950 ruled that the decision of a local housing authority to seek federal financial assistance for public housing projects was "executive" and "adminis-trative" rather than "legislative," and hence the decision was not sub-ject to the protest referendum.[110] Within one-half year of the court's ruling, voters adopted a new constitutional article bringing public hous-ing decisions under the protest referendum provision.[111]

A three-judge U.S. District Court for the Northern District of California in 1970 held that the new California constitutional referen-dum article denied the plaintiffs equal protection of the laws and en-joined enforcement of the referendum provision.[112] In overturning the district court's decision, the U.S. Supreme Court reported the law was not "aimed at a racial minority" and noted "California's entire history demonstrates the repeated use of referendums to give citizens a voice on questions of public policy . . . " and "an examination of California law reveals that persons advocating low-income housing have not been singled out for mandatory referendums while no other group must face that obstacle."[113]

FBI Involvement

Financing of expenses incurred by supporters of a referendum on the sale of alcoholic beverages in Bolton, North Carolina, by agents of the Federal Bureau of Investigation (FBI) led to the North Carolina Board of Elections in 1983 invalidating the referendum.[114] The FBI had been conducting an investigation of automobile theft, drug smuggling, and political corruption in Columbus County and decided a bar would pro-vide a good cover for their covert operations.

FBI agents provided funds to a political leader in Bolton, a town with less than 400 registered voters, to help finance the election of his supporters to the town council in 1981 with the understanding they would react favorably to a petition for a mixed beverage referendum. In December 1981, petitions containing in excess of 100 signatures were filed with the council, and a referendum was scheduled for April 30, 1982. Voters approved the proposal by 136 to 76.

An Evaluation

The arguments for and against the referendum, numerical democracy, analyzed in this section to a large extent apply as well to the initiative and the recall, subjects examined in detail in Chapters 4 and 5. In assessing the arguments, the reader should bear in mind that the goals of the governmental reformers in the late nineteenth and early twentieth centuries were to make governmental officials more responsive to the citizenry by reducing the power and influence of bosses and special interests, eliminate corruption in government, and increase economy and efficiency in the provision of public services. While the referendum adds to the length of the ballot and places a greater burden upon the voters, a number of advocates of the petition referendum also were members of the Short Ballot Organization seeking to reverse the influence of Jacksonian democracy, which was responsible in large measure for the long ballot.

Arguments in Favor

The early reformers based their arguments upon the model of the rational voter who faithfully followed public affairs and sought information on public issues. Survey evidence reveals that only a small percentage of the voters fit this model today. Seven major arguments have been advanced in support of the referendum.

1. *The citizen is sovereign and the referendum is a mechanism of "pure" democracy.* This *ipse dixit* argument is advanced by individuals who posit that political parties, political bosses, and special interest groups distort the views of the people and only the submittal of issues to popular ratification produces an accurate reflection of the public will. Furthermore, the petition referendum allows voters to repeal boss- or special-interest-sponsored laws. Walter E. Weyl argued in 1912 "the referendum is not perfect any more than the secret ballot or the policeman's club is perfect. It is merely the best expedient in the present circumstances. With the referendum we shall doubtless enact into law a vast deal of sublimated nonsense – as we do now with the referendum."[115]
Richard S. Childs, an early municipal reformer, wrote:

Although the people may be ready to vote overwhelmingly for a measure, their nominal agents and servants in the representative system will frequently maintain a successful indifference or resistance election after election. Our governments are less anxious to please the people than they are to please the politicians who thus become an irresponsible ruling class with a vast and marketable influence. Our representative system is misrepresentative. Many Americans, impatient with it, are demanding access to an additional and alternative system, namely, direct legislation by the Initiative and Referendum.[116]

2. *The petition referendum has the potential for making legislators more responsive to the citizenry since they are in a position to question the judgmental powers of the law-makers.* According to this line of reasoning, legislators will be reluctant to enact unpopular laws for fear the petition referendum will be employed to repeal them and in effect censure the legislature. A solution to the problem of unresponsive legislators is available that can obviate the need for the petition referendum; that is, the electorate can replace unresponsive legislators with responsive ones.

The Citizens League of the Twin Cities of Minnesota in a report on the initiative and the referendum noted:

In North Dakota the Legislature tends to construct its laws with an eye towards the possible submission of those laws to referendum. At times the legislature has been unwilling to pass what it thought was needed legislation because of the threat of referendum. At other times, what looks to the general observer to be good legislation has been repealed by referendum.[117]

3. *The referendum reduces citizen alienation and increases citizen interest in governmental affairs since the petition referendum provides for a veto without removing legislators from office.*

4. *The mandatory and the petition referenda foster a highly desirable movement for shorter state constitutions and local charters since there is less need for detailed restrictions upon the powers of the legislative body when its actions are subject to referenda.*

5. *Campaigns associated with the referendum produce discussion and debate on issues, thereby leading to the education of the public.* Misinformation, of course, can be disseminated during a referendum campaign. In 1982, Massachusetts Secretary of the Commonwealth Michael J. Connolly charged opponents of bottle deposit proposal with making a false claim that his office had indicated that a negative vote on the proposal would establish a clean-up and recycling project financed by the beverage and bottle industries.[118]

6. *The optional referendum can be employed to break a legislative deadlock.* Experience reveals the optional referendum seldom is employed for this purpose.

7. *The protest referendum is a natural extension of the principle of checks and balances inherent in the existing system of governance.*

Relative to the advisory referendum, proponents maintain it allows legislators to determine the general will on an issue instead of relying upon the views of an outspoken minority group.

Arguments in Opposition

Twelve major arguments have been advanced against the referendum, and the fear has been expressed that frequent employment of the referendum will undermine representative government.

1. *The referendum weakens representative government by discouraging energetic and innovative leaders from seeking election as legislators.* True leaders are innovators, and the acceptance by the public of new types of laws lags behind that of the innovators who may fear that their efforts have been wasted if the petition referendum is employed to repeal laws.

2. *The referendum encourages law-makers to pass the buck on emotional issues by referring them to the electorate.* In other words, representatives shirk their responsibilities. Walter E. Weyl concluded in 1912 the referendum "is likely to be used by weak-kneed legislators to throw the burden of an awkward decision back upon the electors."[119]

3. *The electorate is not sufficiently informed to deal rationally with complex and technical questions.* This argument, of course, is an aristocratic one.

4. *The protest referendum introduces unnecessary delays and uncertainty into the law-making process, which often is a lengthy one to begin with.* Although an act may be signed by the governor into law on April 1, petitions for a referendum may not be filed until July 1, and the referendum may not be held until November. Furthermore, opponents object to allowing a small percentage of the electorate to disrupt governmental operations pending a referendum in which the majority of the voters frequently approve the law in question.

5. *The referendum is based on the unrealistic assumption there is a simple "yes" or "no" answer to complex questions, and sets up a confrontation between supporters and opponents of a proposition.* In the legislative process, both sides on an issue can compromise and recognize points made by the other side that will improve the quality of a bill. There is no such opportunity for compromise with the referendum.

6. *The referendum fails to reveal the intensity of feeling behind each "yes" or "no" vote.* The majority of the electorate may be disturbed by only one provision of a law and would approve the law if the provision was repealed.

7. *Fewer voters typically mark referenda questions than vote for candidates, and measures may be approved or rejected by a small percentage of the registered voters.* Decisions, in other words, are made by a plurality rather than a majority of voters. While this argument cannot be denied, it must be pointed

out that many legislators are elected to office by a plurality and hence may not
represent the views of a majority of their constituents.

8. *Special interest groups are afforded the opportunity to employ the protest referendum to repeal laws whose enactment the groups were unable to prevent.* These groups typically have financial resources considerably larger than
the resources of public interest groups. Even if the protest referendum is not
used to repeal a law, well-financed special interest groups may be able to persuade voters to defeat a proposal that a legislative body approved *ad referendum.* In 1979, the Consolidated Edison Company spent approximately $700,000
and successfully defeated a Westchester County, New York, proposal authorizing the establishment of a county public utility agency to investigate the possible county assumption of the company's electric distributing facilities. The company channeled $612,540 through another organization – Westchester Citizens
Against Government Take Over.[120]

9. *The "tyranny of the majority" argument is advanced against the employment of the referendum.* Writing in *The New York Times* in 1977, Anthony Lewis
stressed:

> In voting to repeal a local law that protected homosexuals from
> discrimination in jobs and public accommodations, the people of
> Miami, Florida, sent an unintended message. They reminded us that
> the rights of minorities are too important to be trusted to the pas-
> sions of passing majorities.[121]

10. *The average voter is overburdened, and the statutory referendum increases unreasonably the burden placed upon the voter.* Proponents of a short
ballot point to the typically sharp fall-off in the vote on referenda questions compared to the vote for candidates as evidence that many members of the electorate cannot cope with referenda questions. This argument, while having some
validity, is not a major opposition argument as one generally would anticipate
that election campaigns will generate more votes for candidates than votes for
or against what are perceived to be, and often are, minor referenda proposals.
Chapter 4 examines voter turnout in referenda produced by initiative petitions,
and Chapter 7 draws conclusions relative to law making directly by a minority
of the voters.

11. *Inflexibility is produced by referenda in states where matters approved
by the voters cannot be amended or repealed by a legislative body.* Consequently, referenda represent an inflexible method of law making. Even in the absence
of a prohibition on legislative repeal or amendment, opponents of the referendum
argue that legislators are reluctant to tamper with a decision made directly by
the voters.

12. *Taxpayer costs are increased by the requirement that a voter information pamphlet be prepared and distributed.* Furthermore, costs may be increased substantially if referenda necessitate special elections.

A related problem involves the intervention of courts in the form of judicial
directives to local governments to take a certain course of corrective action dur-

ing the past three decades which has created dilemmas for local governments needing voter approval to borrow funds. President James R. Holland of the Association of County Commissioners of Georgia in December 1983 wrote:

> County governments are having a terrible struggle building new public facilities. On the one hand, we've got the courts and common sense telling us we ought to build new courthouses, jails, administration buildings, etc. . . . and on the other hand, we've got the citizens turning down bond issues. So often, they are only delaying the day of reckoning.[122]

Conclusions

Few question whether citizens are sovereign or the desirability of submitting proposed organic documents – state constitutions, constitutional amendments, local charters, and charter amendments – to the voters for a final determination. Optional and advisory referenda have not been initiated often by legislative bodies. Furthermore, there can be little objection to advisory referenda, initiated by voters, on issues such as acid rain and a nuclear freeze as these referenda assist elected representatives in divining the will of the electorate, by providing elected officials with an opinion spectrum supplementing their normal sources of information on public opinion.

Although the referendum on ordinary statutes is designed to be a complement to and not a replacement of law making by elected public representatives, the circulation of petitions and increased use of the referendum reflect a loss of voter confidence in elected representatives and an erosion of their position and importance. On the other hand, the availability of the protest referendum arms the citizens with a device for remedying what they perceive to be poor judgmental decisions by legislative bodies. If a late nineteenth-century populist or early twentieth-century progressive visited states today with the petition referendum, he probably would be pleased in general with its employment.

Petition fraud has not been a serious problem in most referenda campaigns, but evidence exists that the public can be misinformed by both proponents and opponents of a proposition. While official voters' information pamphlets apparently have been relatively ineffective in educating the electorate on the pros and cons of issues, there clearly is a need for an officially sponsored public information campaign to inform voters of the nature of the issues and what a "yes" or a "no" vote will mean. Heavier reliance should be placed by governments upon the mass media to inform the public of the nature of referenda issues.

Should elected officials be neutral on referred issues or should they actively campaign for or against propositions? Unfortunately, there is no clear-cut answer to this question. Certain state and local officials should be charged with ensuring that the public is provided with impartial factual information and the views of proponents and opponents on each issue. Other officials, such as the governor or the mayor, should be free to campaign for or against a referred proposition. Questions, however, may be raised as to whether public funds should be expended to promote voter approval of a referrred measure. In 1983, Governor Mario M. Cuomo of New York helped to organize a citizen's committee to promote a favorable vote on a transportation bond issue, and the state spent an estimated $75,000, not including staff time, to help ensure an affirmative vote on the proposal by the electorate.

There is no evidence that "conservative" groups make more use of the referendum than "liberal" groups, but there is evidence that voters take both a "conservative" and a "liberal" stance on different propositions on the same ballot. Massachusetts voters in 1982, for example, approved a death penalty proposition, generally considered to be a "conservative" issue, and a bottle deposit proposition and a nuclear freeze proposition, which are considered to be part of the "liberal" agenda.

Evidence is lacking that the mandatory referendum in general has resulted in poor quality decisions or that the protest referendum has been abused by special interest groups.

The danger of "moneyed" interests employing the petition referendum for their own benefit has been increased by the U.S. Supreme Court's decisions striking down state laws placing a limit on the amount of money that may be expended by individuals and corporations in referenda campaigns. This subject is examined in greater detail in Chapter 4 in connection with the employment of the initiative.

Voter intervention in the law-making process is not inherently bad as citizens have the right to reserve to themselves the power to participate in decision making on issues. Yet widespread use of the statutory referendum clearly is undesirable as compromises and amendments, a product of the representative decision-making process, improve the quality of laws.

In our judgment, extra-majority approval requirements for borrowing are highly undesirable as studies reveal that most rejected issues were approved by a majority of electors voting on the issues. Rejection of a proposed issue may increase the burden placed on the taxpayers in the future because of construction inflation and possibly higher interest rates, and also deprives citizens of needed facilities.

We conclude that the mandatory referendum on fundamental state and local government documents is desirable, but the mandatory referendum on "full faith and credit" borrowing is undesirable because the requirement has led to the employment of evasive devices – the "moral obligation" bond and lease-purchase agreements – which place an increased financial burden on the taxpayers. Furthermore, the requirement has led to the inability of local governments to modernize and construct needed facilities to improve service provisions, and to comply with court-ordered capital improvements, thereby setting up a confrontation with the courts.

One of the auxiliary advantages of the petition referendum, in conjunction with the initiative and the recall, is to encourage the electorate to revise state constitutions and local charters to make them short documents, confined to fundamentals and readable, since direct legislation and the recall provide the citizenry with mechanisms to ensure that legislators do not abuse the trust placed in them by the electorate. A state constitution confined to fundamentals and containing few restrictions on the powers of the state legislature and local governments would relieve voters of the need to make decisions on questions such as the following one, which appeared on the November 8, 1982, New York State ballot:

> Shall the proposed amendment of Paragraph E of Section Five of Article VII of the Constitution, permitting the exclusion of indebtedness contracted by a county, city, town, or village after January 1, 1982, and prior to January 1, 1984, for construction or reconstruction of sewage facilities in ascertaining the power of such county, city, town, or village to contract indebtedness within its constitutional debt limit, be approved?

The petition referendum is a form of citizens' veto designed to correct legislative sins of commission and should be available to voters as a safety valve to be employed to reverse unrepresentative legislative decisions. To date, there is little evidence that the protest referendum has weakened representative government by discouraging many able individuals from seeking or continuing in legislative office, or by encouraging legislative bodies to shirk their responsibilities by employing often the optional referendum.

While the typically lower voting rate on referenda issues compared to the voting rate on candidates is a matter of concern on the surface, one should not conclude that the failure to mark a referendum question means voters lack interest in the issue. It is possible that voters failing to mark referenda questions believe that persons with more concern with the issue should make the decision. A requirement that ratification must be by a majority of votes cast for candidates unfairly penalizes proponents of change.

Consideration should be given to a new type of petition referendum which, upon the filing of the requisite number of certified signatures, would suspend a law and require the legislative body to consider the repeal or amendment of the law within a stated number of days. Should the legislature fail to adopt the proposal contained in the petition within a specified number of days, regardless of whether the legislature is in session on the day the petitions are certified, a referendum automatically would be held on the proposal. At present, the filing of the requisite number of certified signatures results automatically in a referendum where voters are limited to a "yes" or "no" choice on the question of repealing the referred law. The proposed new type of petition referendum hopefully would encourage the legislative body to amend or repeal the law in question, thereby obviating the need for a referendum and its attendant expenses.

The initiative, a companion with the petition referendum in origin, allows registered voters directly to initiate the process of law making by means of petitions. Successful use of the direct initiative, the subject of Chapter 4, automatically results in a mandatory referendum.

Notes

1. Nathaniel B. Shurtleff, ed., *Records of the Governor and Company of the Massachusetts Bay in New England*, vol. 1 (Boston: From the Press of William White, Printer to the Commonwealth, 1853), p. 293.

2. *Journal of the Convention for Framing a Constitution of Government for the State of Massachusetts Bay from the commencement of their first session September 1, 1779 to the close of their last session, June 16, 1780* (Boston: Dutton and Wentworth, Printers to the State, 1832), p. 255. See also *The Acts and Resolves of Massachusetts Bay, 1779–80*, chap. 135.

3. *New Hampshire Constitution of 1784*. This document lacks article or section numbers in part 2. The constitution is the first one to provide for a referendum on the question of calling a constitutional convention. A referendum on this subject was to be held every seven years. See part 2.

4. *Barto v. Himrod*, 4 Seld. [N.Y.] 483 (1853).

5. *Santo v. State*, 2 Clarke [Iowa] 165 (1855).

6. Thomas M. Cooley, *A Treatise on the Constitutional Limitations Which Rest upon the Legislative Power of the States of the American Union*, 7th ed. (Boston: Little, Brown, 1903), pp. 56 and 163.

7. *State v. Parker*, 26 Vt. 357 (1854).

8. Cooley, *A Treatise on the Constitutional Limitations*, p. 165.

9. *Massachusetts General Laws*, chap. 110 (1822).

10. *Wales v. Belcher*, 3 Pick. [Mass.] 508 (1826).

11. *Maryland Laws of 1825*, chap. 162.

12. *Rhode Island Constitution of 1842*, Art. 4, § 13.

13. *Michigan Constitution of 1835*, amendment 2.

14. *Colorado Constitution of 1876*, Art. 10, § 11.

15. *Constitution of South Dakota*, Art. 3, § 1 (1898). The initiative is examined in detail in Chap. 4.

16. Ibid.

17. See Richard S. Childs, *The Short Ballot: A Movement to Simplify Politics* (New York: The National Short Ballot Organization, 1916).

18. V. O. Key, Jr. and Winston W. Crouch, *The Initiative and Referendum in California* (Berkeley: University of California Press, 1939), p. 424.

19. *Constitution of Delaware*, Art. 16, § 1.

20. *The Book of the States 1982-83* (Lexington, Ken.: The Council of State Governments, 1982), p. 117.

21. Albert L. Sturm, "State Constitutional Developments During 1982," *National Civil Review* 72 (January 1983):35.

22. For an example, see the *Constitution of the State of New York*, Art. 7, § 11.

23. Ibid., Art. 7, §§ 14 and 18-19.

24. *Measures Submitted to Voters under Amendments to the Constitution, Article XLVIII, General Provisions IV* (Boston: Secretary of the Commonwealth, 1964).

25. *Voters' Guide to Amendment Proposed to the Constitution of the State of New Hampshire* (Concord: State of New Hampshire, 1972).

26. Lawrence E. Davies, "California Faces Ballot Problem," *The New York Times*, July 8, 1962, p. 47.

27. Paul Guzzi, "Secretary of the Commonwealth Analysis of Election Day Poll" (Boston: Secretary of the Commonwealth, 1976, mimeographed), p. 2.

28. David B. Magleby, "Voter Pamphlets: Understanding Why Voters Don't Read Them" (paper presented at the 1981 Annual Meeting of the American Political Science Association, New York, N.Y.), pp. 10, 33.

29. *Oregon Laws of 1973*, chap. 744, § 36; *Oregon Laws of 1979*, chap. 667, § 2; and *Oregon Revised Statutes*, tit. 23, chap. 260-532.

30. "Cocoa Beach to Vote on Toplessness Ban," *The New York Times*, November 5, 1974, p. 24.

31. Fred Kaplan, "Mixed Results for the Freeze," *Boston Sunday Globe*, November 7, 1982, p. A69.

32. Ibid., p. A72.

33. Chris Pope, "Ballot Questions Give Voters Good Chance to Answer Back," *Worcester Telegram* (Massachusetts), November 3, 1982, p. 17A.

34. "Austin Votes Back a Nuclear Freeze," *The New York Times*, September 13, 1982, p. A16.

35. *San Jose City Charter*, § 1700.

36. *Constitution of Montana*, Art. 11, § 9(1).

37. Ibid., (2).

38. For details, see James J. Lopach and Lauren S. McKinsey, "Local Government Reform by Referendum: Lessons from Montana's Voter Review Experience," *State & Local Government Review* 11 (January 1979):35-39.

39. *Constitution of the Commonwealth of Massachusetts*, part the second, chap. 6, Art. 10.

40. *The Book of the States 1982–83*, p. 122.

41. *Constitution of California*, Art. 16, § 18.

42. *The Book of the States 1982–83*, p. 368.

43. For an example, see *New York Laws of 1961*, chap. 603 and *New York Private Housing Finance Law*, § 48 (McKinney 1962).

44. For details on the lease-purchase agreement entered into by the state of New York relative to the Empire State Plaza, an office complex in Albany, see *Schuyler v. South Mall Constructors*, 32 App.Div.2d 454 (1969). See also Joseph F. Zimmerman, "Lease-Purchase Fails," *National Civic Review* 48 (May 1959):1–6.

45. *New York Education Law*, § 2023 (McKinney 1969).

46. *Constitution of California*, Art. 13B, § 1.

47. Ibid., § 4.

48. *New Jersey Statutes Annotated*, §§ 52:9H-7 and 52:9H-10 (1984 Supp.).

49. *Minnesota Laws of 1983*, chap. 314 and *Minnesota Statutes*, § 275.125 subd. 2d (1969 and 1984 Supp.).

50. Ibid.

51. *Massachusetts General Laws Annotated*, chap. 59, § 5C (1984 Supp.).

52. "Harrison Moved Toward Village Status," *The New York Times*, June 22, 1974, p. 41.

53. For an example, see *Texas Acts of 1929*, chap. 110 and *Vernon's Annotated Revised Civil Statutes of the State of Texas*, Art. 970a, § 8 (1963).

54. *Minnesota Statutes*, chap. 414 (1984 Supp.).

55. *Indiana Acts of 1969*, chap. 67, and *Burns Indiana Statutes Annotated* § 29-1-3-3.

56. David A. Booth, *Metropolitics: The Nashville Consolidation* (East Lansing: Michigan State University Institute for Community Development and Services, 1963), pp. 84–85, and W. E. Lyons, *The Politics of City-County Merger: The Lexington-Fayette County Experience* (Lexington: The University Press of Kentucky, 1977), pp. 28–29, 138, 145, and 147.

57. For examples, see *Massachusetts General Laws Annotated*, chap. 138, § 11, and *New Hampshire Revised Statutes Annotated*, chap. 179, § 1 (1977).

58. See, for example, *Official Code of Georgia Annotated*, chap. 3, § 3-3-7 (1982).

59. *Southern Alameda Spanish Speaking Organization v. City of Union City* 424 F.2d 291 at 294 (1970).

60. *Constitution of the Commonwealth of Massachusetts*, articles of amendment, Art. 48, the referendum, § 2.

61. *Murray v. Secretary of Commonwealth*, 345 Mass. 23, 184 N.E.2d 336 (1962).

62. *Molesworth v. Secretary of Commonwealth*, 347 Mass. 47, 196 N.E.2d 312 (1974). See also *Massachusetts Laws of 1963*, chap. 506.

63. In Massachusetts, the General Court may attach an emergency preamble to a law or the governor may file an emergency statement with the secretary of the commonwealth. In either case, a law takes effect forthwith rather than at the end of 90 days and cannot be suspended by the protest

referendum. However, a referendum still may be held on the law if the requisite number of signatures is certified.

64. For an example, see the *Newport (Rhode Island) Charter*, § 2–14.

65. For details, see *The Book of the States* published biennially by the Council of State Governments.

66. *New Hampshire Revised Statutes*, § 31:64 (1983 Supp.). See also *Disco v. Board of Selectmen*, 115 N.H. 609 (1975).

67. *Connecticut General Statutes*, § 7–7 (1984 Supp.).

68. Ben A. Franklin, "Petitions Block a Maryland Law to Combat Bias," *The New York Times*, June 2, 1963, pp. 1 and 70.

69. "Petitions Filed for Referendum to Repeal Bay State Bottle Bill," *The Keene Sentinel* (New Hampshire), February 17, 1982, p. 15.

70. "San Diego, in a Mail Referendum, Rejects Convention Complex Plan," *The New York Times*, May 7, 1981, p. A20.

71. *Constitution of Georgia*, Art. 13, § 1 (1877). The current Georgia Constitution expressly authorizes the state legislature to propose a new constitution. See Art. 10, § 1.

72. *Wheeler v. Board of Trustees*, 200 Ga. 323, 37 S.E.2d 322 (1946).

73. *Illinois Annotated Statutes*, chap. 46, § 28–6 (1984 Supp.).

74. *Georges v. Carney*, 546 F. Supp. 469 (1982).

75. Ibid., at 477.

76. Linda Greenhouse, "Voters Can Be For and Against a Proposition One in Yonkers," *The New York Times*, November 4, 1972, p. 19.

77. *State ex rel. Bailey v. Celebrezze, Jr.*, 67 Ohio St.2d 516 at 520 (1981).

78. Ibid., at 519–20.

79. *Gormley v. Lan*, 88 N.J. 26, 438 A.2d 519 (1981). See also "Jersey High Court Upholds Ballot Bias Ruling," *The New York Times*, October 7, 1981, p. B5.

80. "Six in a Bond Drive Indicted for Forged Missouri Petitions," *The New York Times*, September 17, 1972, p. 46.

81. *Massachusetts Acts of 1963*, chap. 506.

82. The Massachusetts Constitution stipulates that no more than one-fourth of the certified signatures may be from any one county. *Constitution of the Commonwealth of Massachusetts*, articles of amendment, Art. 48. See also *Lincoln v. Secretary of Commonwealth*, 326 Mass. 313 (1950).

83. *Molesworth & Others v. State Ballot Law Commission*, 348 Mass. 23, 200 N.E.2d 583 (1964).

84. *Federal Election Campaign Act of 1971*, 85 Stat. 3, 2 U.S.C. §§ 431–41 (1971 supp.), and *Federal Election Campaign Act Amendments of 1974*, 88 Stat. 1263, 2 U.S.C. §§ 431–37 (1976 supp.).

85. *Buckley v. Valeo*, 424 U.S. 1 at 143 (1976).

86. Ibid., at 52. In 1978, the U.S. Court of Appeals voided a statute prohibiting corporate contributions to referendum campaigns. See *C & C Plywood Corporation v. Hanson*, 583 F.2d 421 (9th Cir. 1978). In 1980, the U.S. Court of Appeals struck down a Florida statute limiting contributions by an individual to a ballot committee to $3,000. See *Let's Help Florida v. McCrary*, 621 F.2d 195 (5th Cir. 1980).

87. *Citizens for Jobs and Energy v. Fair Political Practices Commission*, 16 Cal. 3d 671, 547 P.2d 1386 (1976).

88. *First National Bank of Boston et al v. Bellotti*, 435 U.S. 765 (1978).

89. *Election Reform Act of 1974*, Berkeley, California, ordinance number 4700–N.S., § 602.

90. *Citizens Against Rent Control v. City of Berkeley*, 102 S.Ct. 434 (1981).

91. Ibid., at 441.

92. Ibid., at 445.

93. *Massachusetts General Laws*, chap. 55, § 7 (1984 supp.), and *Michigan Consolidated Laws Annotated*, §§ 169.201 to 169.282 (1984 supp.).

94. *Lance v. Board of Education*, 153 WV 559, 170 S.E.2d 783 (1969). See also *Constitution of West Virginia*, Art. 10, § 8, and *West Virginia Code*, §§11–8–16 (1983).

95. *Gordon v. Lance*, 91 S.Ct. 1889 (1971).

96. *Constitution of New York*, Art. 9, § 1 (h) (1).

97. *Citizens for Community Action at the Local Level, Incorporated v. Ghezzi*, 386 F. Supp. 1 (1974).

98. *Town of Lockport v. Citizens for Community Action at the Local Level, Incorporated*, 423 U.S. 808 (1977).

99. *Cipriano v. City of Houma*, 395 U.S. 701 (1969).

100. *Application of Cohalan*, 71 Misc.2d 196, affirmed 41 A.D.2d 840 (1972). See also *Hill v. Stone*, 421 U.S. 289 (1975).

101. *New York Town Law*, § 84 (1) (McKinney 1965).

102. *Constitution of Ohio*, Art. 2, § 1.

103. *City of Eastlake et al. v. Forest City Enterprises, Incorporated*, 41 Ohio St.2d 187, 324 N.E.2d 740 (1975).

104. *City of Eastlake et al. v. Forest City Enterprises, Incorporated*, 426 U.S. 668 at 673. See also *Hunter v. Erickson*, 393 U.S. 385 at 392 (1969).

105. *City of Eastlake et al. v. Forest City Enterprises, Incorporated*, 426 U.S. 668 at 680 and 693 (1976).

106. "Court Invalidates Berkeley Rent Control Law," *The New York Times*, October 30, 1983, p. 32.

107. *Hunter v. Erickson*, 393 U.S. 385 (1969). See also *Akron City Charter*, § 137 (1969).

108. *Hunter v. Erickson*, 393 U.S. 385 at 391 (1969).

109. *James v. Valtierra*, 402 U.S. 137 (1971).

110. *Housing Authority v. Superior Court*, 35 Cal.2d 550 at 557–58, 219 P.2d 457 at 460–61 (1950).

111. *Constitution of California*, Art. 34, § 1.

112. *James v. Valtierra*, 313 F. Supp. 1 (N.D. Cal. 1970).

113. *James v. Valtierra*, 402 U.S. 137 at 141–42 (1971).

114. "North Carolina State Board Voids Referendum Due to FBI Involvement with Electoral Process," *Election Administration Reports* 14 (February 6, 1984):3–4.

115. Walter E. Weyl, *The New Democracy: An Essay on Certain Political*

and Economic Tendencies in the United States (New York: Macmillan, 1912), p. 308.

116. Richard S. Childs, *The Short Ballot: A Movement to Simple Politics* (New York: The National Short Ballot Organization, 1916), p. 4.

117. *Initiative and Referendum . . . "NO" for Minnesota* (Minneapolis: Citizens League, 1979), p. 26.

118. "Secretary of State: Foes of Bottle Bill Misleading Voters," *The Evening Gazette* (Worcester, Massachusetts), November 1, 1982, p. 18.

119. Weyl, *The New Democracy*, p. 309.

120. Edward Hudson, "Westchester Drums Beat Over Vote on Con Edison," *The New York Times*, October 9, 1979, p. B2.

121. Anthony Lewis, "Tyranny of a Majority," *The New York Times*, June 13, 1977, p. 29.

122. James R. Holland, "President's Message," *Georgia County Government*, 35 (December 1983):inside front cover.

Chapter **4**

CITIZEN-INITIATED LAW MAKING

The initiative, the petition process by which citizens place questions on the referendum ballot, is traceable in origin to the open town meeting in the New England states.[1] Voters in Massachusetts towns have been empowered to employ the initiative since December 22, 1715, when the General Court (state legislature) enacted a law requiring the selectmen to include in the warrant calling a town meeting any item accompanied by a petition signed by ten or more voters.[2] A second eighteenth-century example of employment of the initiative is found in the Georgia Constitution of 1777, which was framed and adopted by a convention but was not submitted to the electorate for ratification. The amending article of this document provided for the calling of a constitutional convention to revise the organic law only upon "the petitions from each county . . . signed by a majority of voters in each county. . . ."[3]

Development of the Initiative

Most writers attribute the initiative to Swiss cantons and to South Dakota where voters adopted a constitutional amendment in 1898 providing for the initiative and the petition referendum.[4] In the same year, San Francisco freeholders adopted a new city–county charter providing for the initiative and the petition referendum.[5] The former is a logical extension of the mandatory referendum for the adoption of constitutions, constitutional amendments, and pledging the "full faith and credit" of the state, which had become well established by the latter half of the nineteenth century, a subject examined in Chapter 3.

The early state constitutions were drafted by persons who placed great trust in legislative bodies and limited the role of the electorate primarily to the selection of representatives. State legislatures, however, did not always live up to the high expectations of the constitutional drafters in terms of responsiveness to public opinion. The initiative, as developed outside of New England towns, is rooted in agrarian discontent following the civil war; a period when railroads generally had a monopoly on bulk transportation. The agitation for control of railroad monopolies and reform of state legislatures started with the granger movement in the Midwest and continued with the development of the populist movement. In 1892, the People's party included a provision for direct legislation (initiative and petition referendum) in its national platform because "they saw legislatures fail repeatedly to enact reform laws. . . . "[6]

The direct legislation drive gained important support from the progressive movement during the first two decades of the twentieth century. In California, progressives were upset greatly by what they perceived to be control of the state legislature by corporations, and concluded the initiative and petition referendum could break monopoly control and machine politics.[7] Robert M. La Follette, a leading progressive, wrote:

> For years the American people have been engaged in a terrific struggle with the allied forces of organized wealth and political corruption. . . . The people must have in reserve new weapons for every emergency, if they are to regain and preserve control of their governments. . . .
>
> Through the initiative, referendum, and recall the people in any emergency can absolutely control.
>
> The initiative and referendum make it possible for them to demand a direct vote and repeal bad laws which have been enacted, or to enact by direct vote good measures which their representatives refuse to consider.[8]

Public enthusiasm in favor of law making by unassembled citizens was strong in the period 1898 to 1918 as 19 states adopted the initiative. All were west of the Mississippi River except Maine, Massachusetts, and Ohio. No state subsequently adopted the initiative until 1959 when Alaska entered the Union with a constitutional provision for the initiative. Wyoming adopted the initiative in 1968; Illinois in 1970 adopted a constitution providing for the initiative relative to the legislative article only of the constitution; and Florida adopted the constitutional initiative in 1972. The Illinois Supreme Court ruled in 1976 that only voter-approved initiated constitutional amendments proposing structural and procedural changes in the legislative article of the constitution are valid.[9]

The Initiative Today

The constitutions of 23 states contain provisions for one or more types of initiatives. Constitutional provisions for direct legislation in some states – Idaho, South Dakota, and Utah are examples – are brief and implementation of the provisions is the responsibility of the state legislature. On the other hand, the Colorado and Ohio constitutions contain detailed procedural provisions. In a number of states, the constitutional provisions for the initiative and the referendum are self-executing; that is, no implementing legislation is required.

In 17 states, the initiative may be employed in the process of amending the state constitution. In 1982, 12 constitutional amendments were proposed by the initiative and voters ratified three.[10] By way of contrast, state legislatures proposed 287 constitutional amendments and the electorate ratified 214, a 74.6 percent approval rate.[11]

The initiative in 21 states may be employed in the process of enacting ordinary statutes. The veto power of the governor does not extend to voter-approved initiated measures. Proponents, as well as opponents of the initiative, in several states recognized that certain sensitive matters should not be subject to an initiative campaign which might produce an emotional reaction by the majority of the voters.

The initiative, as authorized by the state constitution, state law, or local charter, may be employed in most states to adopt and amend local charters and ordinances.[12] A 1981 national study revealed that local government charters are not often drafted and adopted by means of the initiative and the referendum.[13] Furthermore, 20 percent of the reporting municipalities indicated the power to amend the local charter had never been employed and an additional 36 percent indicated the amending power seldom had been used.[14] Of municipalities reporting charter amendments, 73 percent noted the amendments generally were minor ones.[15]

Most initiative sponsors fail to secure the required number of valid signatures on petitions. To date, no initiative petition has qualified for the referendum ballot in Wyoming since the state constitution was amended in 1968 to authorize employment of the initiative.[16] When employed successfully to repeal a statute, the initiative serves the same function as the protest or petition referendum, which is examined in Chapter 3.

Restrictions on Use

Constitutional provisions for the initiative contain several restrictions. Alaska, California, Massachusetts, Missouri, Nebraska, Nevada, North Dakota, South Dakota, and Wyoming exempt certain subjects from the initiative or place restriction on its exercise. Appropriations, the judiciary, emergency measures, and support of the government typically are not subject to the initiative. The longest list of matters exempted from the initiative is contained in the Massachusetts Constitution.

The Nevada Constitution forbids the use of the initiative to appropriate funds unless the initiated measures provides for the levying of a tax to supply the funds.[17] The Maine Constitution stipulates that an initiated measure providing for expenditures exceeding the amount appropriated becomes invalid 45 days after the legislature convenes.[18]

The California and Missouri constitutions restrict the initiative to a single subject,[19] and the Illinois Constitution limits the number of propositions on the referendum ballot of a political subdivision to three.[20] By way of contrast, the Arkansas Constitution specifically stipulates "no limitations shall be placed upon the number of constitutional amendments, laws, or other measures which may be proposed and submitted to the people by either initiative or referendum petition. . . . "[21] The constitutions of Nebraska and Wyoming do not allow a defeated initiative proposition to be placed upon the ballot a second time for a period of three years and five years, respectively.[22]

In contrast to referred propositions, opponents of an initiated proposition can initiate an alternative proposition in the hope it may be more popular than the proposition they oppose. The anti-bottle deposit groups in particular have employed the initiative to place an alternative measure on the referendum ballot.

Petition Requirements

With the exception of Alaska, states authorizing the employment of the initiative on the state level require the preliminary filing of a proposed petition with the attorney general or the secretary of state (commonwealth) who checks for conformance with constitutional and statutory requirements. In Alaska, sponsors file the preliminary petition with the lieutenant governor who also receives all signed petitions filed by the deadline date. Three states require a deposit—$100 in Alaska and Wyoming and $1,000 in California—when an application for the initiative is filed. The deposit is refunded if the proposition qualifies for the ballot.

Conference with Sponsors

A major objection to the initiative over the years has been faulty draftsmanship which causes serious implementation problems if the initiated measure is ratified by the voters.

To avoid such problems, Colorado and Idaho statutes provide for conferences with initiative petition filers at which state officials explain wording problems, if any, and offer suggestions to overcome the problems. In Colorado, the directors of the legislative council and the legislative drafting office must, within two weeks of the filing of a petition, provide sponsors with comments and "the proponents may amend the petition in response to some or all of the comments . . . and resubmit the petition at a later date, or they may disregard the comments entirely."[23] In Idaho, the attorney general is directed by statute to provide petition submitters with advice which may be accepted or rejected "in whole or in part."[24]

In Washington, the secretary of state must transmit a copy of an initiative petition to the code reviser who has ten working days to recommend changes to the sponsor.[25]

Ballot Title

In most initiative states, the attorney general (lieutenant governor in Alaska) is directed to prepare a ballot title and a summary of the proposition which is printed at the top of each petition. The *Washington Revised Code Annotated* specifically stipulates that "the attorney general shall formulate . . . a concise statement posed as a question and not to exceed twenty words . . . it shall not be intentionally an argument, nor likely to create prejudice, either for or against the measure. Such concise statement shall constitute the ballot title."[26] Legal questions relative to ballot wording are examined in Chapter 3.

Estimate of Cost

The secretary of state, upon receiving a verified copy of a proposed constitutional amendment or state law proposing the levy of a tax or necessitating the expenditure of funds by the state or any local government, is directed by the *Ohio Revised Code* to request the state tax commissioner to prepare an estimate of proposed annual expenditures. The estimates of the cost of various propositions are included in the referendum pamphlets distributed to the voters.

Printing of Petitions

Upon approval of the proposed initiative petition, a designated state official (usually the secretary of state) is responsible for printing the petition forms at public expense. Idaho is an exception in that sponsors of an initiative are responsible for printing the petitions.[27]

Paid Circulators

Six states – Colorado, Idaho, Massachusetts, Ohio, South Dakota, and Washington – by statute restrict or prohibit organizers of initiative campaigns to pay petition circulators.[28] In 1976, the California Supreme

Court struck down a provision of a 1974 law limiting payment for petition signatures to 25 cents per signature as infringing "impermissably upon rights of free speech. . . . "[29] Signature collection firms commonly are employed in California where the charge for collecting a sufficient number of certifiable signatures can exceed a quarter of a million dollars.

Oregon repealed its ban on paid circulators of initiative petitions as the result of U.S. District Court Judge Helen Frye's ruling in 1982 that the law imposing the prohibition violated the right of free speech guaranteed by the First Amendment to the U.S. Constitution because the law "restricts the candidate's opportunity to get his views across to the public by circulating petitions; it restricts the discussion of issues that normally accompanies the circulation of petitions; and it restricts the size of the audience that can be reached."[30]

A study by *The Initiative News Report* in 1983 revealed that 76 percent of initiated propositions placed on state referenda ballots in 1980–82 were primarily the result of signatures collected by volunteers.[31]

Required Number of Signatures

All state constitutions authorizing the initiative require the filing of a specified minimum number of signatures of registered voters on petitions to validate the initiative. Each petition circular must sign an affidavit or jurat on each petition sheet attesting that the signatures contained thereon are those of eligible registered voters.

The number of required signatures is based on a percentage of the votes cast at the most recent general election or a percentage of the votes cast for governor (secretary of state in Colorado).[32] Signature requirements for constitutional amendment initiatives vary from 3 percent of the vote for governor in Massachusetts to 15 percent in Arizona and Oklahoma. The Massachusetts Constitution stipulates the petitions must be submitted to the General Court and will be placed on the referendum ballot only if approved by at least one-fourth of the members in two consecutive sessions. If placed on the ballot, the proposed amendment is ratified by a majority of the votes cast on the proposal provided the majority includes 30 percent of the total number of ballots cast in the election.[33]

Signature requirements for statutory initiatives range from 3 percent of the votes cast for governor in the preceding general election in Massachusetts to 15 percent of the electorate participating in the last general election and residing in at least two-thirds of the counties in Wyoming. Although North Dakota has a 2 percent petition requirement, the base is the state's population in the latest federal census which produces a higher signature requirement than the Massachusetts requirement.

Eight states have constitutional provisions relative to the distribution of signatures on petitions for constitutional amendments, ranging from 5 percent of the votes cast for governor in each of 15 counties in Arkansas to 10 percent of the registered voters in each of 40 percent of the legislative districts in Montana.

The Massachusetts Constitution stipulates that no more than 25 percent of the required number of signatures may be of registered voters in any one county.[34] Seven states have similar constitutional distributional requirements for petitions proposing ordinary laws. The purpose of this requirement is to ensure there is general support in various sections of the state for the initiative proposition. The petition signature threshold and/or distribution requirements affect significantly the relative ease or difficulty of employing the initiative.

Petition Verification

Arkansas, Colorado, and South Dakota do not require certification of filed initiative petitions unless an objection is made. In the other initiative states, petitions are submitted for verification to the secretary of state (commonwealth) except in Alaska where the duty is placed upon the lieutenant governor.

The secretary of state has a stipulated number of days — ranging from 25 days in North Dakota to 60 days in Wyoming — to complete the signature verification process. The *Oregon Revised Statutes* mandates that "the secretary of state shall use a statistical sampling technique or techniques for the verification of signatures. . . ."[35] Seven other states also provide for statistical sampling of petition signatures as part of the verification process.

If insufficient signatures are obtained on initiative petitions to meet the ballot deadline, the signatures may be employed in a future initiative petition campaign in Florida, Illinois, Ohio, Maine, and Montana. Maine, however, limits the carry-over of petition signatures to one year and Illinois stipulates the petitions must have been signed during the two years preceding the date of the referendum.[36]

Opponents of initiative petitions often challenge the validity of filed signatures. If either the proponents or opponents are dissatisfied with the verification ruling, it may be appealed to the courts. As discussed in Chapter 3, charges of fraudulent signatures on petitions are common and questions have been raised in court as to whether one fraudulent signature or jurat on a petition sheet invalidates all signatures on the sheet.

Voter Pamphlets

The states currently distribute an official pamphlet to voters describing the propositions on the forthcoming ballot and the arguments pro and con relative to each proposition. The Ohio secretary of state is required to include in the voter pamphlets the estimates of proposed annual expenditures and annual yield of proposed taxes, if any, prepared by the state tax commission.[37]

Voter pamphlets are expensive to print and distribute, with costs exceeding $1 million in California. Studies by Professor David B. Magleby of Brigham Young University reveal that California voters obtain most of their information on propositions from the media rather than from the voter pamphlets which tend to be written in language beyond the comprehension of most voters.[38]

Approval Requirements

The constitutions of 13 states provide that a constitutional amendment proposed by the initiative becomes effective if ratified by a majority of those voting on the proposition. Four other state constitutions have additional ratification requirements. In Illinois, an amendment proposed by the initiative becomes effective if approved by either a majority of those voting in the election or 60 percent of those voting on the proposal.[39] The Massachusetts ratification requirement is an affirmative majority vote provided it includes 30 percent of the ballots cast at the election.[40] The Nebraska Constitution contains a provision similar to the Massachusetts one except that the affirmative majority must include a minimum of 35 percent of the votes cast at the election.[41] The ratification requirement in Nevada is the affirmative majority vote on the proposed constitutional amendment in two consecutive general elections.[42]

Relative to the statutory initiative, propositions are approved by a simple affirmative majority vote except in Massachusetts where the affirmative majority also must include at least 30 percent of the ballots cast at the election.

If two or more conflicting propositions concurrently receive the required affirmative majority, the proposition receiving the largest vote is approved.[43]

Legislative Amendment or Repeal

Arizona and Washington do not allow the state legislature to amend or repeal initiated statutes under any circumstance. In California, an amendment or repeal of an initiated measure becomes effective only if approved by the voters in a referendum.[44] Alaska and Nevada do not allow an amendment or repeal for two years and three years, respectively, after an initiated measure is approved.[45] The North Dakota Constitution forbids legislative amendment or repeal of an initiated statute for a period of seven years except by a two-thirds vote of the members elected to each house of the state legislature.[46] The Michigan Constitution allows the state legislature to amend or repeal an initiated statute only if provided by the statute or by a three-fourths vote of the members elected to the state legislature.[47] In Wyoming an initiated statute may be amended at any time by the state legislature, but may not be repealed for a period of two years.[48]

Types of Initiatives

Initiatives may be classified as (1) state or local, (2) constitutional or statutory, (3) direct or indirect, and (4) advisory. The first two categories are self-explanatory.

Direct or Indirect

Under the direct initiative, the entire legislative process is circumvented as propositions are placed directly on the referendum ballot if the requisite number and distribution of valid signatures are collected and certified.

On the substate level, the direct initiative commonly is employed to place local charters or charter amendments on the referendum ballot as illustrated by voters in Summit County, Ohio, in 1980, successfully placing on the ballot a proposed home rule county charter that was ratified by the voters. In 1982, Leominister, Massachusetts voters approved an initiative proposition creating a city charter revision commission. Although the New York City Charter authorizes the use of the initiative to propose charter amendments, the initiative has not been employed to date.[49]

The indirect initiative, employed in eight states, involves a more cumbersome process as a proposition is referred to the legislative body upon the filing of the required number of certified signatures. Failure of the legislative body to approve the proposition within a stipulated number of days, varying from 40 days in Michigan to adjournment of the Maine legislature, leads to the proposition being placed automatically on the referendum ballot. In three states, additional signatures must be collected to place the proposition on the ballot as follows: one-half of 1 percent and 10 percent of the votes cast for governor in the last general election in Massachusetts and Utah, respectively, and 3 percent of the registered voters in Ohio.

Only the Massachusetts Constitution authorizes the indirect initiative for constitutional amendments. To be placed upon the referendum ballot, the initiative proposal must be approved by each of two successive joint sessions of a successively elected General Court or receive the affirmative vote of 25 percent of all members in each of two successive joint sessions.[50]

The state legislature in five states – Maine, Massachusetts, Michigan, Nevada, and Washington – is authorized to place a substitute proposition on the referendum ballot whenever an initiative proposition appears on the ballot.[51] The Maine Supreme Court in 1948 issued a decision interpreting the legislative substitute provision. Specifically at issue was the question whether a law enacted by the state legislature banning "closed shops" was a statute or a legislative substitute for a proposition requiring an "open shop" initiated by the voters and pending in the state legislature.[52] The court ruled a bill dealing with the same subject but "in a manner inconsistent with the initiated measure" is a legislative substitute.[53]

Although the constitution of Alaska provides only for the direct initiative and contains no provision for an indirect initiative, a section of the constitution allows the state legislature to enact a legislative substitute that voids the initiative petition provided the substitute is "substantially the same."[54] An important court case involved a legislative substitute for an initiative petition proposing a campaign finance law limiting contributions and expenditures, establishing reporting requirements, and providing for an enforcement committee and private court actions. The substitute measure was narrower in terms of its coverage of elected officials than the initiative proposition and did not provide for private court action. The Alaska Supreme Court ruled the legislative substitute was essentially the same as the initiative proposition.[55]

The Massachusetts Constitution does not define the terms "alternative" or "substitute" and the Supreme Judicial Court in 1976 ruled off the referendum ballot a General Court–approved "legislative substitute" because it must retain the sense of the proposition in editing, polishing, or amending it.[56] In the same year, the Supreme Judicial Court advised that a law proposed by initiative petitions and approved by the General Court was subject to the gubernatorial veto.[57] The justices concluded the framers of the initiative amendment did not intend that a measure proposed by petitions signed by 3 percent of the electorate and approved by the General Court should become law without the "important constitutional requirement that the governor approved all laws. . . . "[58]

Relative to proposed statutes, Maine, Massachusetts, and Wyoming provide only for the indirect initiative. Michigan, Nevada, Ohio, South Dakota, Utah, and Washington authorize the employment of both the indirect and the direct initiative.

The National Municipal League, a leading reform group since 1894, recommended the direct initiative at the state level until 1948 because many state legislatures met only for short periods of time biennially. Today, the League favors employment of the indirect initiative for the following reasons:

> All too often, direct initiative measures are ambiguously worded, violate either the state or federal constitution, or involve side effects their authors may not have intended. This happens because the language has not been subject to the scrutiny, debate, and compromise typical of the legislative process. . . .
>
> The League . . . believes that this process [indirect initiative] preserves sovereignty but also strengthens rather than weakens representative democracy.[59]

Advisory

This type of initiative allows voters to circulate petitions to place non-binding question on the ballot at an election. As explained in Chapter 3, legislative bodies also may place nonbinding questions on the ballot.

The advisory initiative is a mechanism citizens and groups can employ to place pressure on legislative bodies to take a certain course of action. If petition circulators are successful in collecting the required number of verified signatures for a referendum, a large favorable vote on the question exerts great pressure on the legislative body to accede to the desire of the electorate.

Until the late 1970s, the advisory initiative was employed relatively infrequently and attracted generally only local notice. The growth of the environmental and nuclear freeze movements, along with movements opposing U.S. involvement in Central America, has resulted in media attention being focused upon advisory referenda as national and regional groups employ the initiative to place questions on election ballots. In 1983, for example, voters approved advisory initiative Proposition 0 directing the mayor and board of supervisors of the city and county of San Francisco to notify President Ronald Reagan and Congress that the voters favor the repeal of the provisions of the federal Voting Rights Act requiring the city and county to provide ballots, voter pamphlets, and other materials on voting in Chinese and Spanish as well as in English.[60]

Legal Issues

The major constitutional challenge to the initiative was the allegation that direct legislation violated the U.S. Constitution which guarantees each state a republican form of government.[61] In 1903, the Oregon

Supreme Court ruled direct legislation "does not abolish or destroy the republican form of government or substitute another in its place. The representative character of the government still remains. The people simply reserved to themselves a larger share of legislative power."[62]

Nine years later, the U.S. Supreme Court upheld the constitutionality of direct legislation in Oregon by pointing out Congress in effect had recognized a republican form of government in Oregon when the state's representatives and senators were admitted into Congress.[63]

The Mississippi Constitution of 1890 provides: "If more than one amendment shall be submitted at one time, they shall be submitted in such manner and form that the people may vote for or against each amendment separately."[64] Voter ratification of a constitutional amendment authorizing the initiative and referendum was challenged on the ground the amendment had three separate purposes and the voters should have been permitted to vote on ratification of each purpose. Nevertheless, the Mississippi Supreme Court in 1917 upheld voter ratification of the amendment.[65] In 1922, however, the court ruled the amendment was unconstitutional because each of the three purposes or subjects contained therein had not been submitted to the voters separately.[66]

Chapter 3 examines ten legal issues involving the referendum — number of ballot questions, ballot language, petition fraud, referendum campaign finance, extra-majority approval requirements, concurrent vote requirements, property voting requirements, zoning changes, preemption by state law, and public housing. Not all of these issues involve the initiative although most legal issues involving the initiative also involve the referendum since the former is linked closely to the latter.

Number of Issues

As noted in Chapter 3, the United States District Court upheld the constitutionality of an Illinois law limiting to three the number of questions that may appear on any local government referendum ballot. In 1976, the Ohio Supreme Court ruled that multiple questions on a single initiative petition were legal.[67]

California voters in June 1982 approved initiative Proposition 8 entitled the "Victims Bill of Rights." Its validity was challenged on the ground the proposition violated a state constitutional provision restricting an initiative proposition to a single subject.[68] The California Supreme Court, by a four to three vote, upheld the validity of the proposition even though it dealt with several subjects, including school safety, elimination of plea bargaining, restrictions of the insanity defense, and provisions for longer prison terms for recidivists.[69] The majority wrote:

We are reinforced in our conclusion that Proposition 8 embraces a
single subject by observing that the measure appears to reflect
public dissatisfaction with the several prior judicial decisions in the
area of criminal law. In our democratic society, in the absence of
some compelling, overriding constitutional imperative, we should
not prohibit the sovereign people from either expressing or implementing their own will on matters of such direct and immediate importance as their own perceived safety.[70]

Solicitation of Signatures on Private Property

Can initiative petition proponents solicit voter signatures on private
property such as a shopping mall? The Washington State Supreme
Court addressed this issue in 1981 and held "signature gathering in a
shopping mall furthers the exchange of ideas and the initiative process. . . . To bar this activity would significantly undermine free speech
and particularly the effectiveness of the initiative process."[71]

Validity of Signatures

The 1980 Illinois constitutional initiative proposition reducing the size
of the House of Representatives from 177 to 120 members and abolishing cumulative voting was challenged on the grounds of petition signatures insufficiency and violation of the constitutional prohibition of
two separate and unrelated questions.[72]

The Illinois State Board of Elections, by a five to three vote, invalidated all signatures on a petition page containing the signature of
a person who was not from the same election jurisdiction as the other
persons who had signed the page. The Illinois Supreme Court in 1980
reversed the board's decision, invalidated the statutory requirement
that all signatures on a petition sheet must be those of registered voters
of the same election jurisdiction, and held the initiative proposition con-
sisted of related questions and did not violate the constitutional prohibition of multiple questions in a single proposition as the two questions were related.[73]

The Arizona Supreme Court in 1983 invalidated an initiative proposition requiring voter approval for freeway and parkway construction
in Tucson on the ground that the bulk of the petitions were notarized improperly.[74]

Federal Preemption

The U.S. Constitution expressly forbids states to take certain actions
and allows states to take other specified actions only with the permission of Congress.[75] The Constitution also provides for two types of

concurrent powers; ones that may be exercised by both Congress and states. The first type, including the power to tax, is not subject to formal federal preemption. Concurrent powers of the second type are ones granted to Congress by the Constitution and not prohibited to states. Should a direct conflict between a state law and a federal law occur involving the second type of concurrent power, the Constitution's supremacy clause ensures the prevalence of the federal law by invalidating the state law.[76]

In exercising the second type of concurrent power, Congress often has failed to include an explicit preemption provision.[77] Hence, opponents of state laws based upon this type of concurrent power — including initiated ones — challenge them in the United States District Court on the ground they are inconsistent with federal law.

In 1982, the U.S. Department of Justice filed suit against the state of Washington challenging the constitutionality of initiative Proposition 394, ratified by the voters in 1981, requiring the approval of the electorate for the issuance of bonds by the Washington Public Power Supply System to obtain revenue to complete construction of three power plants. The suit alleged the initiative violated the contract clause of the U.S. Constitution by impairing contracts entered into a decade ago by the Bonneville Power Administration, a unit of the U.S. Department of Energy, and its preference customers for the construction and operation of the power plants. The suit also alleged the initiative violated the supremacy clause of the U.S. Constitution and effectively disenfranchised the majority of Bonneville Power Administration's ratepayers throughout the Pacific Northwest.

On June 30, 1982, the United States District Court for the Western District of Washington found that the initiative, as applied to the System's projects 1, 2, and 3, violated the contract clause and therefore was invalid.[78] The court's decision was upheld by the United States Court of Appeals for the Ninth Circuit and a petition for the issuance of a writ of certiorari was denied by the U.S. Supreme Court.[79]

Civil Rights

California voters in 1964 approved initiative Proposition 14 repealing the Unruh and Rumford Acts prohibiting racial discrimination in the sale or rental of private housing containing in excess of four units. Each owner of real property specifically was guaranteed the right to refuse to sell or rent "property to such person or persons as he, in his absolute discretion, chooses."

The constitutionality of the proposition was challenged as violating the equal protection of the laws clause of the Fourteenth Amendment to the U.S. Constitution. In 1967, the U.S. Supreme Court affirmed the judgment of the California Supreme Court in striking down the proposition as unconstitutional.[80]

An action initiated in the California Superior Court in 1963 led to a finding in 1970 of de jure segregation in the public schools of the city of Los Angeles. While the court was examining alternative pupil reassignment and busing plans, California voters approved Proposition 1 in 1979 stipulating that a state court shall not order mandatory pupil reassignment or busing unless a United States Court "would be permitted under federal decisional law" to take such action to remedy a violation of the equal protection of the laws clause of the Fourteenth Amendment to the U.S. Constitution. Subsequent to the approval of Proposition 1, the school district requested the court to end mandatory reassignment and busing. In 1980, the court rejected the district's application on the ground the proposition was not applicable to the Los Angeles case that involves de jure segregation, but the California Court of Appeals reversed the lower court's decision.[81]

The California Supreme Court denied a petition for the issuance of a writ of certiorari and the decision was appealed to the U.S. Supreme Court which ruled in 1982 that Proposition 1 does not violate the equal protection of the laws clause.[82] The majority opinion held:

> Proposition 1 does not inhibit enforcement of any federal law or constitutional requirement. Quite the contrary, by its plain language the proposition seeks only to embrace the requirements of the federal constitution with respect to mandatory school assignments and transportation. It would be paradoxical to conclude that by adopting the equal protection clause of the Fourteenth Amendment, the voters of the state thereby violated it.[83]

Justice Marshall entered a strong dissent:

> Because I fail to see how a fundamental redefinition of the governmental decision making structure with respect to the same racial issue can be unconstitutional when the state seeks to remove the authority from local school boards, yet constitutional when the state attempts to achieve the same result by limiting the power of its courts, I must dissent from the court's decision to uphold proposition 1.[84]

In 1966, the California Supreme Court upheld a superior court ruling that the voter-approved 1964 initiative declaring pay television to be contrary to the public policy of the state violates freedom of speech as guaranteed by the First and Fourteenth Amendments to the U.S. Constitution.[85]

State Preemption

State law can prevent the employment of direct law making by voters of a local government if the statute contains restrictions relative to the use of the initiative and the referendum.

In 1983, voters in Hinsdale, Illinois, were prevented from employing the initiative to place on the November school board election ballot the question of removing the ban on the sale of alcoholic beverages because state law requires that a liquor referendum question must appear either on a general election or a municipal election ballot.[86] The refusal of the Du Page County Board of Election Commissioners to place the proposition on the referendum ballot was supported by the Illinois Board of Elections.

In 1983, the California Superior Court ruled invalid a Tehama County initiative proposition, approved by the voters in 1982, stripping the county of its power to regulate land use on the ground an initiated local ordinance cannot preempt the state zoning statute.[87]

Limited Constitutional Convention

A 1968 initiative proposition, approved by Massachusetts voters, providing for placing the question of calling a limited constitutional convention on the 1970 referendum ballot was ruled unconstitutional by the Massachusetts Supreme Judicial Court.[88] The General Court did not approve the indirect initiative petition and proponents collected an additional 95,000 signatures on petitions of which more than 77,700 were certified. The Supreme Judicial Court interpreted the words "law" or "laws" in the constitutional provision authorizing the initiative as not including a proposition that could result in the calling of a constitutional convention.

Excluded Subjects

In 1983, Massachusetts Attorney General Francis X. Bellotti disqualified 8 of 20 submitted initiative petitions on the ground the petitions dealt with powers of the courts specifically excluded from the initiative by the Constitution.[89]

In the same year, the Supreme Judicial Court invalidated initiative petitions, sponsored by the Coalition for Legislative Reform, to place on the referendum ballot a proposal to change the rules of the General Court. Initiated procedural statutes, according to the Supreme Judicial Court, "are not binding upon the houses; consequently they are not laws in the sense contemplated in article 48. Either branch, under its exclusive rule-making constitutional prerogatives, is free to disregard or supersede such statutes by unicameral action."[90]

Legislative Reapportionment

Unhappiness with the legislative and congressional reapportionment plans enacted into law by the state legislature controlled by Democrats led California Republican Assemblyman Don Sebastiani, without the support of his party, to conduct a $1 million initiative petition drive to place new reapportionment plans on the referendum ballot.

When sufficient signatures were collected and verified, Republican Governor George Deukmejian on July 17, 1983, called a special election for December 13, 1983; Democrats filed suit challenging the constitutionality of the initiative petition.[91] On September 15, 1983, by a six to one vote, the California Supreme Court ruled the statutory congressional and legislative initiative proposition violated the state constitution which authorizes reapportionment only once every ten years and the December 1982 reapportionment was valid.[92] This invalidation was the first one in 35 years of an initiative proposition before it was submitted to the electorate.

Legislative Organization and Rules

In 1983, Massachusetts Attorney General Francis X. Bellotti refused to certify an initiative petition relating to the selection of the legislature's presiding officers, appointment of leaders and committee chairpersons, and limits on the salaries of members. The attorney general maintained the initiative petition was not a law and his opinion was upheld by the Supreme Judicial Court which ruled the petition infringed upon the exclusive unicameral powers of each house of the legislature.[93]

Voter-approved California Proposition 24 of 1984 limits the majority party control of the state legislature, divides the legislature's appropriations between the two parties according to their respective membership, and curbs the power of the speaker of the assembly by removing his authority to assign members to committees and appoint committee chairpersons.

On November 29, 1984, the Superior Court ruled the initiated measure was unconstitutional on the ground the state constitution stipulates each house of the state legislature may elect its own officers and adopt procedural rules.[94]

Balanced Federal Budget

In 1984, the California Supreme Court removed from the November referendum ballot initiative Proposition 35 directing the state legislature to memorialize Congress to hold a constitutional convention for the purpose of proposing a balanced federal budget amendment to the U.S. Constitution.[95] The court's majority ruled the proposition violates Ar-

Citizen-Initiated Law Making   85

ticle 5 of the U.S. Constitution which stipulates that only state legislatures, and "not the people through the initiative," can memorialize Congress to call a constitutional convention to propose amendments to the U.S. Constitution. A similar initiated measure was ruled off the Montana ballot for the identical reason by the state supreme court in 1984.[96]

The Tax Revolt

Voters in New England towns with the open town meeting always have had the direct opportunity to reject borrowing and spending proposals as explained in Chapter 2. In 1842, Rhode Island voters amended their state constitution to include the first requirement for a referendum on state borrowing, a subject explored in greater detail in Chapter 3. Today, voters in numerous political jurisdictions have the opportunity to demonstrate their opposition to government spending and taxation by means of the mandatory or protest referendum.

With the exceptions of the open town meetings in New England, the initiative dates only to 1898 and was not employed on a regular basis to restrict state and local government spending until the 1970s. The success at the polls of California Proposition 13 on June 6, 1978, stimulated national interest in the employment of the initiative to limit the property tax. Similar propositions were approved by Idaho and Nevada voters on November 8, 1978, and Massachusetts voters in 1980 approved initiative Proposition 2½ which is discussed in Chapter 2. California voters in 1979 approved the Gann-sponsored Proposition 4 limiting increases in spending by the state and its political subdivisions to the percentage increases in the cost of living and population. Voters in Anchorage, Alaska, in 1983 approved a proposal similar to the Gann's proposition.

The tax revolt began to evidence loss of momentum in the 1980s as Oregon voters in 1982 defeated initiated ballot Measure 3 which would have limited local property taxes to 1½ percent of the full value of property in 1979, and Ohio voters in 1983 defeated propositions to cut nearly in half the state income tax and require a three-fifths vote of each house of the state legislature to approve a tax increase.[97] In 1985, tax limitation initiatives were defeated in California, Louisiana, Michigan, Nevada, and Oregon.[98]

Proposition 13

Proposition 13, a constitutional initiative, was sponsored by Howard A. Jarvis and Paul Gann. The former had been working actively to lower property taxes for fifteen years and stated in 1978 "government is the biggest growth industry in this country" and "the only way to cut the cost of government is not to give them money in the first place."[99] The latter commented: "The thing I am the proudest of is that the voters have turned out and told the government that we have had enough. The government has tried to become uncle, mother, and father and we simply can not afford it any more."[100]

The most common explanations for the affirmative vote for Proposition 13 are the sharp increase in the property tax, a highly visible tax, and voter distrust of government. David O. Sears and Jack Citrin maintained that the early part of the Proposition 13 movement "incorporated important elements of a populist crusade against established political and economic institutions. . . . Whatever mass character the tax revolt possesses, then, appears to be largely a function of generalized political cynicism."[101]

Provisions

Proposition 13 stipulates "the maximum amount of any ad valorem tax on real property shall not exceed one percent (1%) of the full cash value of such property."[102] However, the restriction does "not apply to ad valorem taxes or special assessments to pay the interest and redemption charges of any indebtedness approved by the voters prior to the time this section becomes effective."[103]

The authority of the state legislature to levy taxes also is limited by Proposition 13. Changes in tax laws designed to increase revenues require the approval of two-thirds of all members elected to each house. No new real property tax or property sales transaction taxes, however, may be levied. Cities, counties, and special districts also are restricted in their taxing powers as they, "by a two-thirds vote of the qualified electors of such district, may impose special taxes on such district, except ad valorem taxes on real property or a transaction tax or sales tax on the sale of real property within such city, county, or special district."[104]

Relatively minor amendments to the proposition were made by Proposition 8 (November 7, 1978); Proposition 7 (November 4, 1980); and Proposition 3 (June 9, 1982). These amendments deal with assessment of property and the definition of the term "change of ownership" of property.

In 1978, the California Supreme Court upheld the constitutionality of Proposition 13.[105] Proposition proponents, however, have been disturbed by several court decisions. In 1979, the California Court of Appeals ruled the 1 percent tax limitation on property taxes does not apply to various special assessments authorized by state law.[106] The following year, the same court held that "special taxes" referred to in Proposition 13 do not include fees for various land use regulatory activities.[107] In 1981, the Court of Appeals upheld the validity of a City of Oxnard ordinance levying a school impact fee by ruling the fee was not a prohibited "special tax."[108]

The California Supreme Court in 1982 upheld the imposition of a sales tax levied by the Los Angeles County Transportation Commission and approved by 54 percent of the voters in 1980 on the ground the sales tax was adopted by a body lacking the authority to impose property taxes and which was not seeking to replace lost property tax revenue.[109] Hence, the sales tax imposition did not violate the provision of Proposition 13 banning the levy of a "special tax" by a "special district" without the affirmative vote of two-thirds of the qualified electors. Critics charged that the series of court decisions weaken the effectiveness of Proposition 13. Harly Cole, vice president of the American Tax Reduction Movement and an associate of Howard Jarvis, described the decision as "an end run," and predicted "they'll come up with special taxes for police and fire protection in high-crime areas."[110]

Impact

In common with Proposition 2½ in Massachusetts, described in Chapter 2, Proposition 13 has had intended and unintended effects.

Although the property tax revenue of local governments decreased by approximately $7 billion during the first year Proposition 13 was in effect, local governments were not affected as dramatically as had been predicted for two major reasons. First, municipalities reduced personnel and relied more heavily upon user charges to raise revenue. Second, the state government distributed in excess of $4 billion of its approximately $7 billion surplus to local governments with the result that their loss of revenue due to the limit placed upon the property tax was reduced to approximately $3 billion. In the period to June 1984, the state government distributed $32 billion in extra financial assistance to local governments.[111] Furthermore, the statewide revenue total produced by the property tax increased relatively sharply subsequent to the approval of the proposition because of new construction. Nevertheless, California faced a serious budgetary problem in 1983, largely because of the recession of 1981 to 1983 and indexing the state's income tax to the cost of living. In January 1983, incoming Governor George Deukmejian was faced with an estimated state deficit of nearly $2 billion.[112]

The principal unintended result of Proposition 13 has been the levying of new user charges and the increasing of existing user charges. A corollary effect has been the greater reliance placed upon special districts to provide service. These districts typically are not subject to the same degree of citizen control as municipalities.

Initiative Campaign Finance

Statewide initiative and referendum campaigns are expensive because of the difficulties of obtaining the requisite number of certifiable signatures on petitions and the high cost of persuading voters to support or reject ballot propositions. Proposition 15 on the 1982 California ballot would have placed controls on handguns and resulted in approximately $10 million being spent by interest groups to secure its approval or defeat with the largest contribution, approximately $2½ million, coming from the National Rifle Association.[113] This proposition campaign holds the record as the most expensive one in the history of the United States if the effect of inflation is not considered.

Not surprisingly, initiative propositions affecting business and industry generate the most extensive and expensive campaigns. A study by the Council of Economic Priorities of 18 initiative and referendum campaigns affecting the interests of corporations revealed that corporations contributed funds to both proponents and opponents in only one campaign – the Colorado proposition to permit branch banking.[114] The study also reported that in the 14 campaigns in which "corporate funds dominated, the side with business backing won in eleven cases."[115]

A study by *The Initiative News Report* of campaign spending in the period 1976–83 revealed clearly the importance of money in such campaigns as 80 percent of the propositions were defeated when the opponents outspent the proponents.[116]

A most unusual financial arrangement covered the cost of holding the February 4, 1984, public referendum in Lihue, Hawaii. Hasegawa Komuten (USA), a developer of a resort project at Nukolii Beach, paid the estimated $50,000 cost of the referendum.[117] The initiative campaign originated with the decision of the Kauai County Council to change the zoning of the shore area from "agricultural" to "resort."[118] An initiative proposition rescinding the zoning ordinance was sponsored by the Save Nukolii Committee, an anti-development citizens committee, and approved by the voters in 1980.

On the basis of the zoning change to "resort," the developer with the support of Mayor Eduardo Malapit and a favorable Circuit Court decision commenced construction of 150 condominium units and a hotel.

On October 14, 1982, the Hawaiian Supreme Court upheld the appeal of the Save Nukolii Committee and ordered the construction of the resort project to be halted.[119] Chief Justice William Richardson wrote the court's decision that "subject to certain exceptions, all ordinances, including zoning changes, enacted after January 2, 1977, are subject to referendum power."[120] The decision prompted the developer to circulate a petition reenacting the zoning ordinance. Voters, by a margin of

8,476 to 5,917, approved the land use change initiative necessary for the development of the resort.[121] Reports filed by the pro-development group indicate Hasegawa Komuten (USA) contributed the bulk of the approximately $200,000 spent by the group in its sophisticated campaign.[122]

Can federal monies be employed to support a campaign for or against an initiated proposition? The answer clearly is no. The Legal Services Corporation Act of 1974, for example, specifically prohibits the use of federal funds to finance a pro or con campaign against a ballot proposition.[123] Nevertheless, a federally financed legal services corporation used federal funds to help defeat California initiative Proposition 9 in 1980 which would have reduced state income sharply.[124] The comptroller general of the United States reported:

> the Western Center for Law and Poverty and certain other unidentified California Legal Services grantees, violated the provision of 42 U.S.C. § 2996e(d) (4) in providing funds and personnel support for the Proposition 9 Task Force that operated a large scale opposition campaign to the Proposition 9 ballot measure during the first half of calendar year 1980.[125]

An Evaluation

The arguments for and against the initiative analyzed in this section to a large extent apply as well to the referendum and the recall, subjects examined in detail in Chapters 3 and 5, respectively. In assessing the arguments, the reader should bear in mind that the initiative and the petition referendum were promoted by many governmental reformers in the late nineteenth and early twentieth centuries as devices to enable voters directly to initiate the process of law making and to repeal laws whenever they were deemed to be the product of the influences of bosses and special interests. In addition, the reader must recognize the several arguments for and against the initiative apply more fully to the direct as opposed to the indirect initiative.

Arguments in Favor

The early supporters of the initiative were convinced that the collective wisdom of the common citizenry was superior to that of elected representatives, but recognized that not all needed laws should be enacted by the initiative and the referendum. In theory, the initiative would be exercised only when elected bodies failed to enact needed bills on im-

portant subjects or enacted laws not responsive to the wishes of the electorate. In other words, the initiative is based upon the proposition that
legislative bodies are not sufficiently open and responsive. Six principal
arguments are advanced in support of the initiative.

1. *The citizen is sovereign and popular law making is the most legitimate
form of law making.* Furthermore, the ability of the electorate directly to make
needed laws is a *sine qua non* of good government.

The progressives' arguments in favor of direct legislation were set forth
clearly by Robert M. La Follette of Wisconsin:

> The forces of special privileges are deeply entrenched. Their re-
> sources are inexhaustible. Their efforts never are lax. Their political
> methods are insidious. It is impossible for the people to maintain
> perfect organization in mass. They are often taken unaware and are
> liable to lose at one stroke the achievements of years of effort. In
> such a crisis, nothing but the united power of the people expressed
> directly through the ballot can overthrow the enemy.[126]

Similarly, U.S. Senator Mark O. Hatfield of Oregon in 1979 argued "the initiative
is an actualization of the citizens' first amendment right to petition the Government for redress of grievances; . . ."[127]

2. *The initiative places pressure on legislators to be representative of the
citizenry rather than of the bosses and special interest.* The initiative allows the
electorate to help establish the legislative agenda and can be employed to cir-
cumvent inertia and make legislative bodies more sensitive to voters' concerns.
Professor William B. Munro in 1937 wrote:

> The people want their laws to fit the age, and they grow impatient
> with legislatures which move haltingly because of constitutional
> restrictions, checks and balances, long debates, the retarding influ-
> ence of vested interests, the blight of bossism, and the wariness of
> the lawmakers.[128]

The indirect initiative may have the salutary effect of prodding the legislature to take action to solve a major problem. Within a fortnight of the filing
of 145,170 signatures on initiative petitions prohibiting the use of cats and dogs
from pounds for medical research, the Massachusetts General Court approved
the petition.[129] The New York State Senate Subcommittee on the Initiative and
Referendum reported in 1980 that 18 of 29 respondents in states with the initiative were convinced "the legislature does often or occasionally act on various
issues because of pressure resulting from a possible initiative."[130]

3. *The initiative broadens the opportunities for citizen participation in
public decision making.* In 1912, Lewis J. Johnson wrote direct legislation offers
"an attractive field of usefulness for citizens [who] do not care to give up their
whole time to public life."[131]

4. *The initiative increases citizen interest in government affairs and reduces alienation.* Shockley reported his study of initiated propositions in Colorado in 1976 "did not find citizens apathetic, cynical, or ignorant in their approach to the initiatives. The majority of the people were interested in the issues and did have ideas on them, and turnout figures revealed their concern. . . . "[132] He also reported "in all areas of Colorado fewer people voted for state legislative candidates than for the more controversial initiatives."[133] Similarly, Professor Eugene C. Lee of the University of California, Berkeley reported, relative to his state "the vote on initiatives—reflecting their more controversial nature—almost always exceed by several percentage points the vote for constitutional amendments proposed by the legislature."[134]

The Citizens League of the Twin Cities of Minnesota, however, stressed "voters in states that have initiative/referendum are no more likely to feel in control of government than are those in states without initiative/referendum" and reported "the tendency of initiatives to present more extreme positions than those found in bills debated by the legislature is also more likely to leave persons on the 'losing' side even more disappointed than they would be by legislative action (or inaction) on that issue."[135]

In 1978, *The New York Times* editorialized:

> Direct democracy offers another benefit: It is a powerful stimulus to political participation. Nobody said democracy has to be dull. People are more likely to vote when issues capture their interest. Consider Oregon's experience. Elsewhere there were complaints of voter turnout as low as 30 percent. In Oregon, which had a half-dozen hot ballot measures, the turnout was 65 percent. Use of the referendum and initiative is not the only explanation, but it's a good one.[136]

5. *The initiative, in common with the mandatory and petition referenda, generates voter support for state constitutions and local government charters that are brief and confined to fundamentals because voters know that they can initiate action as well as reverse the decisions made by legislative bodies.* Armed with the initiative, the referendum, and the recall, voters do not need restrictive provisions in the state constitution to protect the public's interest.

6. *The initiative performs an important civic educational function.* As with the referendum, the public can be misinformed as well as informed. Some groups utilize the initiative aware that the proposition will not receive voter approval but convinced that the proposition and its associated campaign will have a long-term beneficial educational effect leading to legislative action.

Arguments in Opposition

Opponents of the initiative advanced 17 arguments to demonstrate its undesirability.

1. *The initiative establishes two coordinate bodies with law-making powers — the legislature and voters who mark their choices on ballot questions.* Whereas

92   Participatory Democracy

elected public representatives have a continuing responsibility to the general
public, citizens voting on propositions do not. Energetic and innovative individuals may be discouraged from seeking office as legislators since their law-
making function can be superseded by voters employing the initiative and the
referendum. Writing in 1912, Walter E. Weyl contended:

> A high-spirited statesman, placed in a position where he may be
> checked, halted, thwarted – often most unreasonably – where an ap-
> peal lies from his every action, where even his tenure depends upon
> his "giving satisfaction," is tempted to withdraw from the important
> eminence of office; if, he remain, he may suffer in initiative, courage,
> and self-esteem.[137]

Experience in California, a state in which the initiative is employed frequently, refutes the above argument as the California legislature was ranked
the most effective state legislature in the nation in 1971 by the Citizens' Conference on State Legislatures.[138]

   2. *Elected legislators produce better laws than initiated ones in part because the legislators in time become experts in various areas of the law.*[139]

   3. *Initiated laws often are poorly drafted by amateurs and create problems
of implementation.* An editorial in *The New York Times* in 1978 explained the
defeat of a California proposition limiting smoking in public places in the following terms:

> It lost heavily, people on both sides agree, not simply because of an
> expensive campaign by the tobacco industry but because it was
> poorly drafted. Opponents were able, with reason, to ridicule the
> proposition for permitting smoking at rock concerts but not at jazz
> concerts. A legislature could have clarified or compromised on lan-
> guage. But the terms of a proposition are frozen and must be voted
> on, yes or no.[140]

State legislatures, however, also approved poorly drafted bills as well as
conflicting laws in the same session.[141] A New York State Senate Subcommittee, after conducting a national study of the initiative, concluded "initiatives
are at least as well drafted as bills produced within state legislatures; . . . "[142]

   4. *Initiated measures may not be coordinated with other related statutes,
thereby causing implementation problems for the latter.* The Citizens League
in the Twin Cities area of Minnesota pointed out in 1979:

> Minnesota's tax policy is expressed through many laws, including
> those governing income tax rates, deductions and credits, property
> classification, sales tax rates, school aids, tax base sharing and tax
> increment finance. An initiative or referendum could address any one
> of these items singly, and throw the whole system out of balance.[143]

A Virginia study group in 1981 recommended against the adoption of the initiative and the referendum because in the legislative process "proposed statutes are subject to extensive scrutiny. This scrutiny often results in the refining of the language in a measure so as to better reach a consensus and protect the interests of all involved."[144]

To overcome this objection, initiative provisions in Colorado and Idaho provide for conferences between initiative sponsors and state officials, as explained in an earlier section.

5. *V. O. Key, Jr. and Winston W. Crouch in 1939 wrote the process of formulating initiated measures "is deficient as a legislative device in that there is no opportunity for its opponents to be heard."*[145]

6. *Elected legislators are better informed than voters, in part because the legislators are supported by professional staff who conduct factual research on complex issues leading to improvements in bills passing through the legislative process.* Professor William B. Munro in 1937 described the submission of a "complicated or technical" issue to the voters as referring "the decision to a supreme court of ignorance." [146] The Citizens League of the Twin Cities area concluded "a 'saturation point' is quickly reached, after which the number of persons who inform themselves on the issues does not increase, regardless of the length or intensity of the education campaign."[147]

Proponents of the initiative reject this argument on the ground the argument undermines the principle upon which democratic government is based; that is, the ability of the average citizen to make wise decisions. Furthermore, proponents agree with Joseph G. LaPalombara, who maintained in 1950 when referring to the Oregon legislature, that "the great bulk of legislation passed in the state legislature is unknown in detail to most of the representatives."[148]

In 1979, Marcia Molay, director of elections in Massachusetts, testified that

> voters have acted responsibly – in general, they have disagreed with the elected Legislature in recent years mostly when some entrenched political interest was at stake (legislative compensation, reducing the power of Executive Council, cutting the size of the Massachusetts House of Representatives, breaking the state highway trust fund, campaign finance).[149]

7. *Proponents and opponents of initiated propositions may be unethical in their media campaigns and mislead the electorate.* There is no denying the possibility that media campaigns may misrepresent the nature of an issue. In Oregon, a citizen can sue in court for damages if there is false advertising connected with an initiative campaign.

8. *The wording of the initiated proposition on the ballot may confuse voters who cast affirmative votes believing they voted in favor of a given policy whereas in fact a "yes" vote is against the policy.* Careful wording of propositions by responsible state officials should avoid this problem.

9. *The initiative produces an oversimplification of issues.* In the view of its detractors, it is based upon the unrealistic assumption there is a simple "yes" or "no" answer to each complex question, and sets up a confrontation between supporters and opponents of a proposition who through the legislative process might be able to develop a compromise bill agreeable to all concerned parties.

10. *Special interests are afforded the opportunity with the initiative to obtain laws favorable to their interest and repeal unfavorable laws.* In 1914, Herbert Croly recognized a potential danger relative to the initiative.

> The ordinary mechanism of the initiative operates so as to give to a small percentage of the voters the right to force the electorate either to accept or reject a specific legislative measure. This is an extremely valuable privilege, because the right to force a vote on specific legislative projects . . . places an enormous power in the hands of a skillful and persistent minority. The initiators might frequently be able to wear down or circumvent the opposition of a less able and tenacious majority.[150]

A New York State Senate Subcommittee in 1980 concluded "fears by opponents of out and out domination of the initiative process by various groups simply do not bear up when the actual use of the initiative in other states is closely examined."[151]

The fear is expressed that well-financed special interest groups will overwhelm the voters with a sophisticated media campaign, particularly in view of the decisions of the U.S. Supreme Court striking down state laws prohibiting or limiting corporate financial involvement in initiative and referenda campaigns. As pointed out in an earlier section, corporations in most instances react to rather than initiate propositions. Opponents of propositions often contend the proposals were rejected by the voters because they were drafted poorly or would institute an undesirable policy and the amount of funds expended by opponents alone did not cause the rejections.

John S. Shockley reported that Colorado opponents of "four liberal or consumer oriented initiatives in 1976 received contributions of $1,292,000 whereas proponents received only $169,000 in contributions."[152] He also noted "every single one of the ballot propositions which had strong corporate opposition had been defeated."[153] In 1978, the tobacco industry spent $5.6 million in a successful campaign to defeat an initiative proposition prohibiting smoking in most enclosed places in California, and out-of-town developers contributed a major part of the $550,000 raised to help defeat San Francisco's 1983 Proposition M requiring developers to share benefits of the building boom with city residents.[154] Nevertheless, the reader should bear in mind that special interest groups spend large sums of money attempting to influence decisions made by legislative bodies.

11. *Minorities and low-income persons may be affected adversely by the successful employment of the initiative and lack the resources to protect them-*

selves. Federal courts, however, generally have been effective in protecting the rights of minorities as pointed out in the section on legal issues.

12. *The initiative underrepresents groups with low rates of turnout at the polls and citizens below the legal voting age*.[155] These groups, of course, also have relatively little influence in electing legislators.

13. *An associated objection is the "tyranny of the majority" argument — the initiative may be employed to deprive minorities of some of their basic rights.* The record to date proves this argument to be invalid.

14. *The ballot will be cluttered with minor propositions as well as emotional ones.* A study by the Massachusetts Legislative Research Council refuted the charge that the ballot has been cluttered with minor issues.[156] Marcia Molay in 1979 reported that the initiative in Massachusetts "has not been used to place volatile 'social' issues . . . on the ballot" and "in general has not been overused; . . ."[157] In Massachusetts, only 29 propositions were placed on the referendum ballot in the period 1919–82.

15. *The initiative, in conjunction with the referendum, weakens political parties.* While provisions for the initiative tend to be found most commonly in states with weak political parties, a *post hoc, ergo propter hoc* situation apparently is not involved as the concerned states had weak political parties at the time of the adoption of the initiative.

16. *A successful initiative campaign produces inflexibility as matters approved by the electorate may not be amended or repealed by the state legislature in several states or there are time or other restrictions on amendment or repeal as pointed out in an earlier section.* Even if empowered to do so, the state legislature is reluctant to amend or repeal an approved initiated statute.

17. *Taxpayer costs may be increased significantly if the initiative necessitates a special election.* Such costs also are increased by the requirement that a voter information pamphlet be prepared and distributed.

Conclusions

Whereas few citizens question the desirability of submitting proposed state constitutions, constitutional amendments, local charters, and local charter amendments to the voters for their decision, there is strong political opposition in many states to a constitutional provision authorizing the electorate to place proposed constitutional amendments and statutes on the referendum ballot by means of petitions.

Circulation of a large number of initiative petitions is an indicator of voter discontent and protest of the unresponsiveness of legislative bodies to the concerns of certain groups of citizens. Legislative sins of omission are correctable by the successful employment of the initiative. We agree with Professor Hugh A. Bone's conclusion:

> The persistence of initiatives as against demanded referenda appears
> to be a reflection of legislative inaction. This is especially true in

areas of reapportionment, liquor policies, and political-governmental
reform. Special interests have frequently been successful in bottling
up proposals for change in committees or defeating them on the floor
of the legislature.[158]

Although the initiative represents a patchwork approach to law
making, initiated statutes in general have not caused serious problems
in part because they account for only a minute fraction of the statutes
enacted in the state. Similarly, initiated constitutional amendments constitute a small fraction of all ratified amendments.

We conclude that the initiative generally has been a salutary adap-
tation of the legislative process which has educated citizens with respect
to important public policy issues.

Voters tend to be perspicacious even on Daedalian issues. In 1912,
Ellis P. Oberholtzer examined 32 initiated propositions in Oregon and
concluded that

> despite the confusion which must have possessed the minds of 99
> out of every 100 voters of the state because of the great number and
> conflicting variety of the submitted measures, the result indicates
> a checking of the current of folly.[159]

Critics notwithstanding, the general electorate has been discrimi-
nating in examining the pro and con arguments for an initiated proposition prior to deciding upon how to vote. Experience with the initiative
and the referendum supports the Aristotelian concept of the collective
wisdom of the voters. Furthermore, voters have not been enthralled
with the rhetoric of ideologues on the "right" or the "left." We agree with
a *New York Times* editorial:

> If California voters show themselves to be conservative by reviv-
> ing the death penalty, then what do they show themselves to be
> upholding the right of homosexuals to teach in public schools? Such
> mixed results are evident in other states and in other years and
> nullify fears that the process would invite ideological triumph for
> the right — or the left.[160]

Nevertheless, the older, better educated, and wealthier voters participate to a greater extent in initiated referenda with the result that
decisions tend to be made by what can be labeled an elite group.

Would the populists and progressives of the late nineteenth and
early twentieth centuries be pleased with their initiative legacy? While
they probably still would espouse faith in the average voter, they undoubtedly would be disturbed by the large sums spent by corporate in-

terests in attempts to defeat initiatives. Yet their trust in the common sense of the average citizen would be undaunted.

On balance, the indirect initiative strengthens the governance system. This type of initiative has the benefit of the legislative process, including public hearings and committee review, study, and recommendations. Should the legislative body fail to approve the proposition, voters have been advantaged in their decision-making capacity by the information on the proposition generated by the legislative process.

The indirect initiative is a useful adjunct or complement to the conventional law-making process and offers no threat to basic civil rights as all initiated propositions, statutory and constitutional, are subject to federal constitutional standards. The indirect initiative can be an effective counterbalance to an unrepresentative legislative body and no more undermines representative government than the executive veto and the judicial veto. A major advantage of the initiative is the fact it makes the operation of interest groups more visible in comparison with their lobbying activities in a state legislature and a local legislative body. Furthermore, the availability of the initiative increases the citizen's stake in the government.

Support for the indirect initiative does not suggest that it should be employed frequently. It should be a reserve power or last-resort weapon and the relative need for its use depends upon the degree of accountability, representativeness, and responsiveness of legislative bodies.

A model constitutional provision for the initiative should contain the following elements: The attorney general and/or community affairs department should be directed to provide petition drafting services to sponsors of initiatives. Upon submission of a certified petition, a conference should be held at which the attorney general or community affairs department explains initiative wording problems, if any, to sponsors and suggests amendments if needed. If a defeated proposition is resubmitted to the voters within two years, sponsors should be required to obtain additional signatures on petitions equal to 2 percent of the votes cast for governor in the last general election in the affected jurisdiction. The state constitution should authorize the employment of the initiative for purposes of placing the question of calling a constitutional convention on the ballot.

The indirect initiative attempts to make legislative bodies more responsive to voter concerns by forcing the bodies to consider propositions and the direct initiative allows the electorate to bypass the legislative process and directly to make decisions on issues. A companion device – the recall – seeks to make public officers continuously responsible to the voters by threatening to remove unresponsive officers

— as well as those guilty of malfeasance, misfeasance, and nonfeasance —
from office.

Notes

1. The New England town meeting is described and analyzed in Chap. 2.
The advisory referendum bears resemblance to the initiative in that a proposition is advanced for consideration by voters by means of petitions, but differs
in that voter approval of the advisory proposition does not make it law.

2. *The Acts and Resolves of the Province of the Massachusetts Bay*, vol.
2 (Boston: Wright and Potter, 1874), p. 30.

3. *Constitution of Georgia*, Art. 63 (1777).

4. *Constitution of South Dakota*, Art. 3, § 1 (1898). The referendum is examined in detail in Chap. 3.

5. *Charter for the City and County of San Francisco*, Art. 2, Chap. 1, §§
20–22.

6. John D. Hicks, *The Populist Revolt: A History of the Farmers' Alliance
and the People's Party* (Lincoln: University of Nebraska Press, 1961), pp. 406–7.

7. George E. Mowry, *The California Progressives* (Berkeley: University
of California Press, 1951), p. 289.

8. Ellen Torelle, comp., *The Political Philosophy of Robert M. LaFollette*
(Madison, Wis.: The Robert M. LaFollette Company, 1920), pp. 173–74.

9. *Coalition for Political Honesty v. State Board of Elections*, 65 Ill.2d
453, 359 N.E.2d 138 (1976).

10. Albert L. Sturm, "State Constitutional Developments During 1982,"
National Civic Review 72 (January 1983): 38–39.

11. Ibid.

12. See Ross H. Hoff, "Mayor, Council, and Electoral Characteristics in
Cities under 25,000 Population," *Urban Data Service Report* 13 (December 1981):
1–25.

13. Joseph F. Zimmerman, *Measuring Local Discretionary Authority*
(Washington, D.C.: United States Advisory Commission on Intergovernmental
Relations, 1981), pp. 26–27.

14. Ibid., p. 27.

15. Ibid.

16. *Constitution of Wyoming*, Art. 3, § 52.

17. *Constitution of Nevada*, Art. 19, § 6.

18. *Constitution of Maine*, Art. 4, part 3, § 19.

19. *Constitution of California*, Art. 2, § 8 (d), and *Constitution of Missouri*,
Art. 3, § 50.

20. *Constitution of Illinois*, Art. 14, § 28–1.

21. *Constitution of Arkansas*, Amendment 7.

22. *Constitution of Nebraska*, Art. 3, § 2, and *Constitution of Wyoming*,
Art. 2, § 52 (d).

23. *Colorado Revised Statutes*, § 1–40–101 (1980 and 1983 supp.).

24. *Idaho Code*, § 34–1809 (1981).

25. *Washington Revised Code*, § 29.79.105 (1965 and 1984 supp.).

26. Ibid., § 19.79.040.

27. *Idaho Code*, § 34–1805 (1981).

28. David D. Schmidt, *Initiative Procedures: A Fifty-State Survey* (Washington, D.C.: Initiative News Service, 1983), p. 7. A provision of a 1974 California law restricting the maximum payment per petition signature to 25 cents was invalidated by the California Supreme Court as violating the guarantee of freedom of speech. See *Hardie v. Eu*, 18 Cal. 3rd 1971 (1976).

29. *Hardie v. Eu*, 18 Cal. 3rd 1971, 556 P.2d 301 (1976).

30. *The Libertarian Party of Oregon v. Paulus*, civil case number 82–521–FR, United States District Court, District of Oregon (1982).

31. *The Initiative News Report*, February 11, 1983, p. 2.

32. For details, see *The Book of the States* published biennially by the Council of State Governments.

33. *Constitution of Massachusetts*, Articles of amendment, Art. 48.

34. Ibid. See also *Lincoln v. Secretary of Commonwealth*, 326 Mass. 313 (1950).

35. *Oregon Laws of 1979*, Chap. 190, and *Oregon Revised Statutes*, § 249.865 (1983).

36. *Constitution of Maine*, Art. 4, part 3, § 18 (2), and *Constitution of Illinois*, Art. 14, § 3.

37. *Ohio Revised Code*, §§ 3519.04 and 3519.19 (1972 and 1983 supp.).

38. David B. Magleby, "Voter Pamphlets: Understanding Why Voters Don't Read Them" (paper presented at the 1981 Annual Meeting of the American Political Science Association, New York, N.Y.), p. 10.

39. *Constitution of Illinois*, Art. 14, § 3.

40. *Constitution of Massachusetts*, Articles of amendment, Art. 48, § 5.

41. *Constitution of Nebraska*, Art. 3, § 4.

42. *Constitution of Nevada*, Art. 19, § 2 (4).

43. See for example, *Constitution of Missouri*, Art. 3, § 51.

44. *Constitution of California*, Art. 4, § 24 (c).

45. *Constitution of Alaska*, Art. 9, § 6, and *Constitution of Nevada*, Art. 19, § 2 (3).

46. *Constitution of North Dakota*, Art. 105, § 8.

47. *Constitution of Michigan*, Art. 2, § 9.

48. *Constitution of Wyoming*, Art. 2, § 52 (f).

49. *Charter of the City of New York*, § 42.

50. *Constitution of Massachusetts*, Articles of amendment, Art. 48, § 5.

51. *Constitution of Maine*, Art. 4, part III, § 18; *Constitution of Massachusetts*, Articles of amendment, Art. 48, the initiative, part III, § 2; *Constitution of Michigan*, Art. 2, § 9; *Nevada Revised Statutes*, § 295.025–3; and *Constitution of Washington*, Art. 2, § 1 (a).

52. *Farris ex rel Dorsky v. Goss*, 143 Me. 227, 60 A.2d 909 (1948).

53. Ibid., 143 Me. 227 at 232, 60 A.2d 909 at 911 (1948).

54. *Constitution of Alaska*, Art. 11, §4.

55. *Warren v. Boucher*, 543 P.2d 731 at 738–39 (1975).

56. *Constitution of Massachusetts*, Articles of amendment, Art. 48, part 3, § 2, and *Buckley v. Secretary of the Commonwealth*, 371 Mass. 195 at 201, 355 N.E. 806 at 811 (1976).

57. *Opinion of the Justices*, 370 Mass. 869, 347 N.E.2d 671 (1976).

58. Ibid., 370 Mass. 869 at 876, 347 N.E.2d 671 at 674 (1976).

59. "The Indirect Initiative," *National Civic Review* 68 (May 1979): 232–33.

60. Judith Cummings, "San Francisco's Absentees Decide Smoking and Building Measures," *The New York Times*, November 10, 1983, p. D26. See also Joseph F. Zimmerman, "The Federal Voting Rights Act and Alternative Election Systems," *William & Mary Law Review* 19 (Summer 1978): 621–60.

61. *Constitution of the United States*, Art. 4, § 4.

62. *Kadderly v. Portland*, 44 Or. 118 at 145, 74 P. 710 at 737 (1903).

63. *Pacific States Telephone and Telegraph Company v. Oregon*, 223 U.S. 118 (1912). See also *Luther v. Borden*, 7 Howard 1 (1849).

64. *Constitution of Mississippi*, Art. 15 (1890).

65. *State v. Brantley*, 113 Miss. 786, 74 So. 662 (1917).

66. *Power et al. v. Robertson*, 130 Miss. 188, 93 So. 769 (1922).

67. *State ex rel. O'Grady v. Brown*, 47 Ohio St.2d 265 (1976).

68. *Constitution of California*, Art. 2, § 8 (d).

69. *Brosnahan v. Brown*, 32 Cal.3d 236, 186 Cal. Reptr. 30, 651 P.2d 274 (1982).

70. Ibid., 651 P.2d 274 at 281 (1982). See also Rosaline Levenson, "California Supreme Court Upholds Crime Initiative," *National Civic Review* 72 (February 1983): 105.

71. *Alderwood Associates v. Washington Environmental Council*, 96 Wn.2d 230 at 245–46; 635 P.2d 108 at 116–17 (1981).

72. For information on cumulative voting, see Joseph F. Zimmerman, *The Federated City: Community Control in Large Cities* (New York: St. Martin's Press, 1972), pp. 72–74.

73. *Coalition for Political Honesty v. State Board of Elections*, 83 Ill.2d 236 (1980). See also *Constitution of Illinois*, Art. 3, § 3 and *Illinois Revised Statutes*, § 28–3 (1965 and 1984 Supp.).

74. "Tucson Initiative Fails to Make Ballot," *Public Administration Times* 6 (December 15, 1983): 1.

75. *United States Constitution*, Art. 1, § 10.

76. Ibid., Art. 6, § 2.

77. For details, see Joseph F. Zimmerman, *State–Local Relations: A Partnership Approach* (New York: Praeger, 1983), pp. 204 and 133–45.

78. *Continental Illinois National Bank & Trust Company v. Sterling National Bank*, 565 F. Supp. 101 (1983).

79. *Continental Illinois National Bank & Trust Company v. State of Washington*, 696 F.2d 692 (1983), and *Don't Bankrupt Washington Committee v. Continental Illinois National Bank and Trust Company*, 103 S.Ct 1762 (1983).

80. *Reitman v. Mulkey*, 387 U.S. 369 at 373 (1967).

81. *Crawford et al. v. Los Angeles Board of Education*, 113 Cal. App.3d 633 (1981).

82. *Crawford et al. v. Los Angeles Board of Education*, 102 S.Ct. 3211 (1982).

83. Ibid., at 3216–217.

84. Ibid., at 3223.

85. *Weaver v. Jordan*, 64 Cal.2d 235, 49 Cal. 537, 411 P.2d 289 (1966).

86. "Hinsdale Won't Vote on Liquor Sales," *Chicago Tribune*, September 2, 1983, sec. 2, p. 2.

87. Rosaline Levenson, "Zoning Initiative Overturned in Cal.," *National Civic Review* 72 (September 1983): 442.

88. *Cohen v. Attorney General*, 357 Mass. 564, 259 N.E.2d 539 (1970).

89. *Constitution of Massachusetts*, Articles of amendment, Art. 48, the initiative, § 2.

90. *Paisner v. Attorney General*, 390 Mass. 593 at 601–2 (1983).

91. Philip Hager, "Remapping Vote Voided by High Court," *Los Angeles Times*, September 15, 1983, pp. 1 and 20. See also Richard W. Gable, "The Sebastiani Initiative," *National Civic Review* 73 (January 1984): 16–23.

92. *Assembly of the State of California v. Deukmejian*, 180 Cal. 297, 639 P.2d. 939 (1982). The U.S. Supreme Court denied the petition for issuance of a writ of certiorari. See *Republican National Committee et al. v. Burton*, 456 U.S. 941 (1982). See also *Constitution of California*, Art. 21.

93. *Paisner v. Attorney General*, 390 Mass. 593. See also *United States v. Ballin*, 144 U.S. 1 (1892).

94. "California Court Upsets Legislative Initiative," *Public Administration Times* 8 (January 1, 1985): 6.

95. "U.S. Balanced Budget Measure Taken Off Ballot," *The New York Times*, August 28, 1984, p. B20.

96. "Courts Intervene in Initiative Process," *Public Administration Times* 8 (March 1, 1985): 3.

97. "Ohio Rejects Tax Repeal," *The New York Times*, November 10, 1983, p. D26. See also "Tax Revolt Measures Defeated by Ohio Voters," *State Legislatures* 10 (January 1984): 5–6.

98. William C. Mathewson, "Michigan, Five Other States Reject Rollback Proposals," *Michigan Municipal Review* (March 1985): 35.

99. "Generals of the California Taxpayers' Revolt," *The New York Times*, June 8, 1978, p. 25.

100. Ibid.

101. David O. Sears and Jack Citrin, *Tax Revolt: Something for Nothing in California* (Cambridge: Harvard University Press, 1982), p. 8.

102. *Constitution of California*, Art. 13A, § 1.

103. Ibid., § 3.

104. Ibid., § 4.

105. *Amador Valley Joint Union High School District v. State Board of Equalization*, 22 Cal.3d 208, 583 P.2d 1281 (1978).

106. *County of Fresno v. Malmstrom*, 94 Cal.App. 3d 974 (1979). See also *California Streets and Highway Code*, §§ 5,000 *et seq.* and 10,000 *et seq.*

107. *Mills v. County of Trinity*, 108 Cal. App.3d 656 (1980).

108. *Trent Meredith, Incorporated v. City of Oxnard*, 114 Cal. App.3d 317 (1981).

109. *Los Angeles County Transportation Commission v. Richmond*, 31 Cal.3d 197, 643 P.2d 941 (1982).

110. Judith Cummings, "Ruling on Transit Stirs Coast Hopes," *The New York Times*, May 8, 1982, p. 8.

111. Charles Bell, "California's Continuing Budget Conflict," *Comparative State Politics Newsletter* 4 (October 1983): 9.

112. Wallace Turner, "Effects of Proposition 13 to Strike California Cities," *The New York Times*, January 24, 1983, p. A15.

113. Tom Wicker, "Tale of Two Initiatives," *The New York Times*, October 29, 1982, p. A27.

114. Steven D. Lydenberg, *Bankrolling Ballots Update 1980* (New York: Council on Economic Priorities, 1981), pp. 1–2.

115. Ibid., p. 2.

116. "INR Campaign Spending Study: Negativism Effective," *The Initiative News Report* 4 (December 2, 1983): 1.

117. Wallace Turner, "Developer Pays Expenses for Voting on Zoning on Little Hawaiian Island," *The New York Times*, January 12, 1984, p. A22. See also "Hawaii Court Says Work on Resort Must End," *The New York Times*, October 25, 1982, p. B12.

118. *Kauai County Charter*, §§ 5.01.11.

119. *County of Kauai v. Pacific Standard Life Insurance Company*, 65 AH 8267, 653 P.2d 766.

120. Ibid., 653 P.2d 766 at 772.

121. "Islanders Back Zoning for Resort in Hawaii," *The New York Times*, February 6, 1984, p. A14.

122. "Private Financing of Public Election Issue in Kauai, Hawaii Initiative Vote," *Election Administration Reports* 14 (February 20, 1984): 3–4.

123. *Legal Services Corporation Act of 1974*, 88 Stat. 378, 42 U.S.C. 2996e (d) (4) and 2996f (b) (7) (1973 and 1983 Supp.).

124. *Letter Report B-210228/B-202116*, dated September 1983, to Representative F. James Sensenbrenner of Wisconsin from the Comptroller General of the United States, pp. 12–16.

125. Ibid., p. 15.

126. Torelle, *The Political Philosophy of Robert M. La Follette*, p. 173.

127. Mark O. Hatfield, "Voter Initiative Amendment," *Congressional Record* 125 (February 5, 1979): S. 1062.

128. William B. Munro, *The Government of the United States*, 4th ed. (New York: Macmillan, 1937), p. 610.

129. *Massachusetts Laws of 1983*, Chap. 631.

130. *Report of the Subcommittee on Initiative and Referendum to the Majority Leader of the New York State Senate* (Albany: New York State Senate, 1980), p. 23.

131. Lewis J. Johnson, "Direct Legislation as an Ally of Representative

Government," in *The Initiative, Referendum, and Recall*, ed. William B. Munro (New York: D. Appleton, 1912), p. 151.

132. John S. Shockley, *The Initiative Process in Colorado Politics: An Assessment* (Boulder: Bureau of Governmental Research and Service, University of Colorado, 1980), p. 45.

133. Ibid., p. 47.

134. Eugene C. Lee, "California," in *Referendums: A Comparative Study of Practice and Theory*, ed. David Butler and Austin Ranney (Washington, D.C.: American Enterprise Institute for Public Policy Research, 1978), p. 108.

135. *Initiative and Referendum . . . "NO" for Minnesota* (Minneapolis: Citizens League, 1979), pp. 21–22.

136. "Making Democracy More Interesting," *The New York Times*, November 27, 1978, p. A18.

137. Walter E. Weyl, *The New Democracy: An Essay on Certain Political and Economic Tendencies in the United States* (New York: Macmillan, 1912), p. 307.

138. The Citizens' Conference on State Legislatures, *State Legislatures: An Evaluation of their Effectiveness* (New York: Praeger, 1971), p. 88.

139. Priscilla F. Gunn, "Initiatives and Referendums: Direct Democracy and Minority Interests," *Urban Law Annual* 22 (1981): 136.

140. "Making Democracy More Interesting," *New York Times*, p. A18.

141. Charles A. Beard, *American Government and Politics*, 7th ed. (New York: Macmillan, 1935), pp. 538–39.

142. *Report of the Subcommittee on Initiative and Referendum*, p. 46.

143. *Initiative and Referendum . . . "NO" for Minnesota*, p. 27.

144. *Report of the Joint Subcommittee Studying the Initiative and Referendum to the Governor and General Assembly of Virginia* (Richmond: The Senate, 1981), p. 3. (Published as Senate Document No. 4.)

145. V. O. Key, Jr. and Winston W. Crouch, *The Initiative and Referendum in California* (Berkeley: University of California Press, 1939), p. 568.

146. Munro, *The Government of the United States*, p. 617.

147. *Initiative and Referendum . . . "NO" for Minnesota*, p. 10.

148. Joseph G. LaPalombara, *The Initiative and Referendum in Oregon: 1938–1948* (Corvallis: Oregon State College Press, 1950), pp. 111–12.

149. "Testimony of Marcia Molay, Massachusetts Director of Elections, before the New York State Subcommittee on Initiative and Referendum," September 17, 1979, p. 2 (mimeographed).

150. Herbert Croly, *Progressive Democracy* (New York: Macmillan, 1914), p. 307.

151. *Report of the Subcommittee on Initiative and Referendum*, p. 43.

152. Shockley, *The Initiative Process in Colorado Politics*, p. 9.

153. Ibid., p. 10.

154. John Herbers, "13 States Curb Taxes or Spending: A Variety of Other Initiatives Fail," *The New York Times*, November 9, 1978, p. A20, and Judith Cummings, "San Francisco's Absentees Decide Smoking and Building Measures," *The New York Times*, November 10, 1983, p. D26.

155. "A Tool of Democracy?" *National Civic Review* 67 (September 1978): 353.

156. *Report Relative to Revising Statewide Initiative and Referendum Provisions of the Massachusetts Constitution* (Boston: Legislative Research Council, 1975), p. 92.

157. Molay, "Testimony," p. 2.

158. Hugh A. Bone, "The Initiative in Washington: 1914–1917," *Washington Public Policy Notes* 2 (October 1974): 2.

159. Ellis P. Oberholtzer, *The Referendum in America Together with Some Chapters on the Initiative and the Recall* (New York: Charles Scribner's Sons, 1912), p. 405.

160. "Making Democracy More Interesting," *New York Times*, p. A18.

Chapter **5**

THE RECALL:
Citizen Removal of
Public Officers

Whereas the petition referendum and the initiative attempt to reverse legislative errors of commission and omission, respectively, the recall is designed to remove public officers from office prior to the expiration of their terms. In common with the petition referendum and the initiative, the process of removing an officer is commenced by the circulation of petitions for voter signatures.

The concept of the recall was incorporated into Article 5 of the Articles of Confederation and Perpetual Union which provided that states were authorized to replace their delegates to Congress. However, the voters only indirectly participated in this type of recall since the state legislature possessed the power of the recall.

The reasons for the use of the recall in most states are not limited to a *scandalum magnatum* as the recall can be employed for any reason, including disagreement on a policy issue. The Michigan Constitution stipulates "the sufficiency of any statement of reasons or grounds procedurally required shall be a political rather than a judicial question."[1]

The recall is a natural extension to the petition referendum and the initiative which, as explained in Chapters 3 and 4, first were authorized by a South Dakota constitutional amendment ratified by the electorate in 1898. Although the 1892 and 1896 national platforms of the Socialist Labor Party and the platform of the Populist Party in a number of states called for adoption of the recall (also known as "the imperative mandate"), no government adopted the recall until voters approved a new city charter for Los Angeles on January 22, 1903.[2]

Continuous voter control of public officers is the goal sought by promoters of the recall. If carried to the extreme, the recall would establish the principle that officers are agents of the voters who have the right at any time to replace their agents.

On August 15, 1911, President William H. Taft vetoed, by returning to the House of Representatives without his signature, House Joint Resolution Number 14 admitting the Arizona and New Mexico territories into the Union conditional upon Arizona submitting to the voters the question of the wisdom of the provision in the state constitution authorizing the employment of the recall to remove judicial officers.[3] The president, reflecting the thinking of many citizens at the time, added:

> This provision of the Arizona constitution, in its application to county and state judges, seems to me so pernicious in its effect, so destructive of independence in the judiciary, so likely to subject the rights of the individual to the possible tyranny of a popular majority, and, therefore, to be so injurious to the cause of free government, that I must disapprove a constitution containing it.[4]

Earlier, the New Mexico territory removed the provision for the recall in its proposed state constitution at the insistence of President Taft. Interestingly, the United States Supreme Court in 1919 ruled that conditions for admission to the Union affecting the internal organization and government of a state are not binding upon a state.[5]

The recall was a product of the populist and municipal reform movements that were in sympathy with the Jacksonian distrust of government officials. Jacksonian democracy attempted to keep public officials continuously responsible to the electorate by providing that most public officials should be elected and their terms of office should be short; that is, six months to one year.

Walter E. Weyl, writing in 1912, pointed out the reformers were seeking "to break the power of a politically entrenched plutocracy" and to hold the elected officer continuously responsible.[6] He added:

> The old solution of this difficulty is to threaten the representative that if he betrayed his trust he would *never* be reelected. This method was not efficacious. The legislator shrewdly interpreted the word "never" in a Gilbertian sense, as meaning "hardly ever."[7]

Supporters of the recall were convinced that the existence of the recall would be a sufficient deterrent to unrepresentative behavior that there would be little need to employ the recall.[8]

The Recall Today

The constitutions of 14 states authorize the employment of the recall to remove state officers from office.[9] The Arizona provision, adopted in 1912, stipulates that

every public officer in the state of Arizona, holding an elective office, either by election or appointment, is subject to recall from such
office by the qualified electors of the electoral district from which
candidates are elected to such office. Such electoral district may include the whole state. Such number of said electors as shall equal
twenty-five per centum of the number of votes cast at the last
preceding general election for all of the candidates for the office held
by such officer, may by petition, which shall be known as a Recall
Petition, demand his recall.[10]

The newest constitution with a recall provision – Alaska – simply provides "all elected public officials in the state, except judicial officers, are
subject to recall by voters of the state or political subdivision from
which elected. Procedures and grounds for recall shall be prescribed by
the legislature."[11]

The states with a constitutional recall provision also authorize, by
statute, all or certain local governments to employ the recall against
all or specified local government officers. In addition, 17 states authorize
the recall of local officers by general law, special law, or a locally drafted
and adopted charter.[12] Although the California Constitution directs the
state legislature to provide for the recall of local officers, this directive
does not affect cities and counties with "home rule" charters providing
for the recall.[13]

The New Jersey Optional Municipal Charters Law stipulates "any
elective officer shall be subject to removal from office for cause connected with his office, after he has served at least one year, upon the
filing of a recall petition and the affirmative vote of a majority of those
voting on the question of removal at any general, regular municipal, or
special election."[14]

In Massachusetts, 52 locally drafted charters provide for the recall. The Billerica town charter stipulates "any person who holds an
elected town office, but not including an elected town meeting member,
with more than six months remaining of the term of office, may be recalled from office by the voters, . . . "[15] The Oxford town charter simply provides "any elective officer of the town may be recalled and removed from public office by the voters of the town as herein provided."[16]
In Connecticut 20 towns have recall provisions in their charters; 15 are
contained in locally drafted and adopted charters and 5 are special law
provisions.

The Wisconsin Constitution authorizes the voters in each congressional district to petition to recall any elected officer which implies the
recall of a member of the United States House of Representatives is
possible.[17] In 1979, the Wisconsin attorney general issued an opinion,
in response to a request of the executive secretary of the state election

board, that "in the event petitions for the recall of a United States
Senator are presented to the election board, you should proceed to carry
out your responsibilities under Wis. Const. art. XIII, sec. 12, and sec.
9.10, Stats., unless and until directed otherwise by a court of law."[18]
The attorney general admitted there is a question as to whether the
recall provision violates the U.S. Constitution, but pointed out that the
Wisconsin Supreme Court has issued decisions directing administrative
bodies and officers to perform ministerial duties even if the result is of
questionable constitutional validity.[19] The Michigan recall statute specifically makes members of the U.S. Senate and House of Representatives subject to the recall.[20]

It is clear, however, that the recall cannot be employed against
a member of the U.S. Congress without a constitutional amendment
authorizing the recall.[21] The Arizona statutes contain a provision for
a "moral obligation" resignation by stipulating candidates for the U.S.
House of Representatives and Senate may file a preprimary pledge to
resign their seats should they lose a recall election.[22]

The locally drafted and adopted charters providing for a professional manager often include authorization for the recall because opponents of the manager plan of administration hold that a non-elected officer should not possess the amount of authority typically delegated to
a manager. When proponents of the plan pointed out the manager can
be removed at any time by a simple majority vote of the local legislative
body, the opponents often replied all the manager has to do to stay in
office is to perform favors to keep a majority of the members of the
governing body satisfied and they will vote to retain him. In response
to this objection, proponents suggested the incorporation of a recall provision in the charter to allow voters to remove local legislators who do
not vote to discharge an incompetent manager.

In practice, the recall in manager municipalities generally has been
employed to remove local legislators who voted to discharge the manager. Voters in Norwood, Massachusetts, in 1939 recalled the selectmen
who, in the minds of the voters attempted to fire the town manager without sufficient cause.[23] Voters of Mansfield, Massachusetts, in 1982 recalled three selectmen who had voted to fire the town manager.[24] A
fourth selectman who had voted to fire the manager also was recalled,
but was reelected on the same ballot. And voters in the City of Benton
Harbor, Michigan, in 1976 recalled the mayor and three members of the
city commission who had voted not to renew the contract of the city
manager.[25]

The constitutional recall provision in Washington requires petitioners for a recall of an officer to recite "that such officer has committed
some act or acts of malfeasance or misfeasance while in office, or who

has violated his oath of office, stating the matters complained of, . . . "[26] The Revised Code of Washington expands upon the constitutional reasons for the recall in the following terms:

> Whenever any legal voter or committee or organization of legal voters of the state or of any political subdivision thereof shall desire to demand the recall and discharge of any elective public officer of the state or of such political subdivision . . . he or they shall prepare a typewritten charge, reciting that such officer, has committed an act or acts of malfeasance, or an act or acts of misfeasance while in office, or has violated his oath of office, or has been guilty of any two or more of the acts specified in the Constitution as grounds for recall, which charge shall state the act or acts complained of in concise language, giving a detailed description including the approximate date, location, and nature of each act complained of, and shall be signed by the person or persons making the same, give their respective post office addresses, and be verified under oath that he or they believe the charge or charges to be true.[27]

The attorney general, within 15 days of the filing of a petition for the recall of a statewide elected officer, must determine whether the reasons cited in the petition constitute malfeasance, misfeasance, or a violation of the oath of office.[28] The Washington statute also requires the sponsor(s) of the recall petition to file a financial disclosure statement—contributors and expenditures—when the petitions are filed.[29]

The New Jersey Supreme Court in 1964 affirmed a superior court ruling that the recall can be employed to remove a municipal officer only for a cause connected with office holding and not for conduct anterior to the date the officer assumed office.[30]

Ohio, Virginia, and Mississippi have unique removal provisions that are similar to a standard recall provision in that the removal process is initiated by voter petitions, but no recall election is held.

The Ohio Constitution directs the state legislature to enact laws "providing for the prompt removal from office, upon complaint and hearing, of all officers, including state officers, judges, and members of the General Assembly, for any misconduct involving moral turpitude or for other cause provided by law; . . . "[31] State law authorizes citizens to file charges against an officer in the court of common pleas in the county where the officer resides, and removal proceedings will be commenced if the petition containing the charges is signed by at least 15 percent of the electorate who voted in the last gubernatorial election in the concerned jurisdiction. The removal proceedings are tried by a judge unless the officer subject to removal demands a jury trial which must involve a 12-member jury; removal requires the approval of 9 members of the jury.[32]

Virginia voters, by means of petitions with signatures equal to 10 percent of the votes cast for the office in the last election, may initiate removal proceedings in the circuit court; the named officer may demand a trial by jury.[33]

Mississippi voters may petition the governor to remove a county officer from office for malfeasance, but the governor is not required to honor the request.[34]

The self-executing Wisconsin constitutional recall provision prevents legislative tampering with the recall by stipulating "no law shall be enacted to hamper, restrict, or impair the right of recall."[35]

Restrictions on Use

Constitutional, statutory, and local charter provisions typically place restrictions on the exercise of the recall. The constitutions of Alaska, Idaho, Louisiana, Michigan, and Washington exclude judicial officers from the recall. Writing in 1914, Albert M. Kales emphasized:

> A judge is one of the most helpless of all elective officers. He can run on no platform; he can have no political program. He can not point dramatically to any achievements on behalf of the people. Whether he is a good judge or not is a matter of expert opinion that only a comparatively few persons are competent to pass upon. His reputation can be easily blasted by the circulation of false statements. He may even be hurt by the performance of his duty in a particular case.[36]

The Montana recall law is the only one providing for the recall of appointed as well as elected state officers.[37] In addition, a number of local charters authorize the recall of appointed as well as elected officers. The City of Greeley, Colorado, has an unusual charter provision authorizing voters at an election held every six years to terminate the employment of the city manager.[38] However, the section of the charter of Long Beach, California, authorizing the recall of the city manager was repealed in 1972.

Although the Ohio Supreme Court in 1922 held that the constitutional removal section provides for the removal of a public officer "only 'upon complaint and hearing,'"[39] the court in 1948 made an exception for charter cities by holding that such a city may provide for the recall in its charter without violating the constitutional removal provision because "it is not for the court to question the wisdom or desirability of provisions of such charters in respect to purely local affairs."[40] However, the Court of Common Pleas held in 1916 the recall is not applicable to members of a board of education because a school district is not a municipal corporation and the statutory provision applies only to elected municipal officers.[41] In Oregon during the period 1965–76, 65 (41 percent) of the 159 recall petitions involved school board members.[42]

The charters of local governments typically exempt certain elected officers from the recall. In Massachusetts, elected town meeting members, described in Chapter 2, are exempted from the recall by the town charter in Billerica, Natick, and Saugus, and the Avon Charter exempts public library trustees. In Minnesota, state law allows certain municipalities to employ the recall, but the charges against an officer must be malfeasance and/or nonfeasance.

Constitutional and statutory provisions authorizing employment of the recall often prohibit its use during the first two months (Montana) or year of an elected officer's term of office and a second recall during the same officer's term of office unless the petitioners pay for the cost of the preceding recall election. Louisiana law prohibits a second recall attempt within 18 months of the previous unsuccessful recall election.[43]

The Arizona Constitution stipulates:

> No recall petition shall be circulated against any officer until he shall have held his office for a period of six months, except that it may be filed against a member of the legislature at any time after five days from the beginning of the first session after his election. After one recall petition and election, no further recall petition shall be filed against the same officer during the term for which he was elected, unless petitioners signing such petition shall first pay into the public treasury which has paid such election expenses, all expenses of the preceding election.[44]

Colorado and Oregon have similar constitutional restrictions on the employment of the recall. In Wisconsin, an officer may not be removed during his first year in office.[45] North Dakota does not permit a recall election involving the same officer within three months of the previous election or more than two such elections within one year.[46]

The recall may not be employed against a local government officer in California during the first 90 days and the last six months of a term of office or if the incumbent won a recall election during the previous six months.[47] The San Francisco "home rule" charter does not allow a recall election during the first six months of an officer's term of office.[48]

There are no restrictions on the use of the recall, other than time period or frequency, in California, North Dakota, Ohio, South Dakota, and Wyoming. Kansas law enumerates the grounds for recall—"conviction of a felony, misconduct in office, incompetence, or failure to per-

form duties prescribed by law."[49] In Florida, the reason for the recall
of a local officer must be one or more of the following: malfeasance,
misfeasance, neglect of duty, drunkenness, incompetence, inability, or
commision of a felony. In New Mexico, a school board member may be
removed from office for malfeasance, or misfeasance, or violation of oath
of office. The grounds for the recall of all elected officers, except judges
of courts of records who are exempt, are the same in Washington as the
grounds for the recall of New Mexico school board members.

Petition Requirements

The recall is similar to the petition referendum and the initiative in that
action originates with the voters. The first step in initiating voter removal of a state officer in eight states—Alaska, Arizona, California,
Georgia, Idaho, Kansas, Oregon, and Washington—is the filing and
publishing or posting of a notice of intent to circulate a recall provision.[50] A filing fee of $100 is required in Alaska, but the fee is refunded
if verified signatures equal to 25 percent of the votes cast for the office
in question at the last election are filed by the deadline for petition.[51]
Kansas also levies a $100 filing fee.[52]

In California, the notice must be served in person or by registered
mail, and an affidavit of the manner and time of service must be filed
with the secretary of state. The California notice of intention must include the name and title of the officer to be recalled, a statement not
exceeding 200 words of the reasons for the proposed recall, and the name
and address of one to five recall proponents. The officer subject to the
recall within 7 days of receipt of the notice may file a response of up
to 200 words with the secretary of state and must serve a copy of the
response in person or by certified mail to one of the recall proponents
named in the notice. (See Figure 5-1.)

Although the statute implementing the Wisconsin constitutional
recall provision contains a requirement that a reason(s) for the recall
must be included in the petition, the attorney general issued an opinion
in 1948 that an implementing statute could not impose an obligation
on the voters that expressly had been omitted from the constitutional
provision.[53]

Each recall petition must contain a declaration by the circulator
that each signature is a genuine one.[54] Petitions must be filed within
a stated number of days—ranging from 60 days in Wisconsin to 270
days for state officers in Washington—after the certifying officer noti-
fies proponents that the form and wording of the filed proposed petition are correct.[55]

Successful collection of the required number of certified signatures on petitions results in a special election to determine whether the named officer(s) shall remain in office until the expiration of the regular term of office. In California, filing of the requisite number of signatures directs the governor to call a special recall election for a state officer within 60 days of certification of the sufficiency of the signatures.[56] Within 14 days of receiving a certificate of signature sufficiency, a local governing body in California must issue an order that an election be held within 80 to 125 days after the governing body has issued the order for the election.[57] The San Francisco "home rule" charter, however, specifies that the recall election must be held within 60 to 75 days.[58]

The most common petition requirement is signatures equal to 25 percent of the votes cast for all candidates in the last general election for governor in the involved unit or the officer whose recall is sought.[59] In Oregon, the number is one-quarter of the votes cast in the last election for supreme court justice and in North Dakota the requirement is 30 percent of the votes cast for governor. Kansas has the highest signature requirement; that is, 40 percent of the votes cast for the officer subject to recall at the last general election. The California requirement is the lowest; that is, 20 percent for members of the board of equalization, judges, and state legislators, but only 12 percent of the votes cast for the other state officers in the last general election for the officer subject to recall. The "home rule" charter of the city and county of San Francisco specifies that a recall election will be held if signatures equal to 10 percent of the registered voters are obtained on recall petitions.[60]

In some states, there is a geographical requirement relative to the minimum number of petition signatures for the recall of an officer elected on a statewide basis. The California Constitution stipulates that the required 12 percent of the last vote for a state office must include signatures equal to at least 1 percent of the last vote cast for the office in each of five counties.[61]

Signatures on recall petitions are subject to challenge and the required number refers to certified petition signatures. In North Dakota, the secretary of state is directed to "conduct a representative random sampling of the signatures contained in such petitions by use of questionnaires, post cards, telephone calls, personal interviews, or other accepted information techniques, or any combination thereof, to determine the validity of the signatures."[62] Oregon law provides that petitions requiring more than 15,000 signatures may be verified through statistical sampling.[63]

In 1980, Barrow County (Georgia) Probate Judge Laurie Bramlette rejected recall petitions presented to her because signatures matching voting records did not total 30 percent of the registered voters. Although her decision was upheld by the Georgia Superior Court, the

Georgia Supreme Court reversed the lower courts' decision on the basis of the voters "intent" to sign the petitions in spite of the fact the recall statutes stipulates "the elector shall sign his name as it appears on the registration books."[64]

The recall provision in Arizona requires completion of verification of signatures on recall petitions within ten days of their submission.[65] In Wisconsin, the verification of signatures on a petition for the recall of state officers must be completed within three days and for the recall of local officers within ten days.[66]

Figure 5–1.

PETITION FOR RECALL

TO THE HONORABLE _____ *(Secretary of State, Clerk of* _____ *County,*
Board of Supervisors, etc.) _____ :

    Pursuant to the California Constitution and California election laws, we the undersigned registered and qualified electors of the ____ *(County/City/District)* ____ of _____,
California, respectfully state that we seek the recall and removal of *(Name of Recallee),*
holding the office of ____ *(Name of Office)* ____, in ____ *(Name of County/City/District)* ____,
California.

    We demand an election of a successor to that office.[1]

    The following Notice of Intention to Circulate Recall Petition was served on _____
(Name of Recallee) _____ :

(Insert complete text of Notice of Intention)

(Name and address of proponents)

    The answer of the officer sought to be recalled is as follows:

(Insert Statement – 200 words or less)
(If no answer, so state.)

    Each of the undersigned states for himself/herself that he or she is a registered and qualified elector of the ____ *(County/City/District)* ____ of _____, California.[2]

		THIS COLUMN FOR OFFICIAL USE ONLY	
Petition must be set in at least 6-point type	YOUR SIGNATURE AS REGISTERED TO VOTE · PRINT YOUR FULL NAME AT LENGTH		Space should be at least 1" wide.
	RESIDENCE ADDRESS · CITY · ZIP		
	YOUR SIGNATURE AS REGISTERED TO VOTE · PRINT YOUR FULL NAME AT LENGTH		
	RESIDENCE ADDRESS · CITY · ZIP		

(continued)

The Recall Election

The typical recall constitutional, statutory, and/or local charter provision stipulates the recall process is terminated should the public officer against whom the petitions are directed resign from the office. Should the officer resign, the vacancy is filled in the manner provided by law.

The Arizona Constitution stipulates that the failure of the public officer to resign within five days of the filing of a recall petition requires the issuance of an order for a special election to be held within 20 to 30 days after the issuance of the order.[67] Under provisions of the New Jersey optional municipal charters law, a municipal officer subject to recall must be notified by the municipal clerk of the sufficiency of the recall petitions within two days of verification of the signatures, and the clerk must order the holding of a recall election within 60 to 90 days of the filing of the petitions if the officer does not tender his or her resignation within 5 days after the service of the notice.[68] A similar

Figure 5–1. Continued

DECLARATION OF PERSON CIRCULATING SECTION OF RECALL PETITION

I,   *(Name)*   declare:

1. My place of residence and residence voting address at the time of execution of this declaration is _____, in _____ County, California, and I am a registered qualified elector in   *(County/City/District)*   ;

2. I personally circulated the attached petition for signing;

3. I saw each of the appended signatures on the attached petition being signed, and to the best of my knowledge and belief, each signature is the genuine signature of the person whose name it purports to be; and

4. The appended signatures were obtained between the date of _____ and _____ inclusive.

I declare under penalty of perjury under the laws of the State of California that the foregoing is true and correct.

_____   _____ [3]
         (Date)   *Signature of Circulator*
                                              Printed Name of Circulator

[1] In case of city officer, the phrase "demand an election of a successor" should be omitted. A city recall ballot must contain a question on how a successor is to be chosen if the recall prevails e.g., "We demand an election to determine whether *(Name of Recallee)* shall be removed from office and whether the vacancy, if it occurs, shall be filled by appointment or by special election.

[2] It is suggested that petitions be printed on 8½"×14" paper in order to maximize number of signature spaces you can print on a sheet of paper.

[3] If signature spaces are printed on both sides of a sheet of paper, the above information, except for the declaration of circulator, must appear on *each* side of the paper.

Source: Office of the secretary of state, Sacramento, California.

provision is contained in the charter of the town of Billerica, Massachusetts.[69]

The reasons advanced in support of the recall of a public officer are printed on the recall ballot, but the number of words is limited; 200 is the most common limit.[70] Reasons advanced in support of the recall in Oregon "could best be described as subjective and emotional."[71] Similarly, the officer whose recall is sought may submit a statement of justification of conduct in office. San Francisco publishes a voter information pamphlet containing a sample ballot, the proponents' statement of reasons for the proposed recall, the officer's reply to the reasons, and paid advertisements. The 24-page pamphlet issued for the special recall election of Mayor Dianne Feinstein in 1983 contained 49 paid advertisements – 37 in favor of the mayor and 12 in favor of recall.[72]

In nine state, voters in a recall election simply vote on the question of whether the officer should be recalled. A majority affirmative vote *ipso facto* removes the officer from office in most jurisdictions. However, the charter of the town of Oxford, Massachusetts, stipulates that "a majority vote of the voters to recall such elective officer shall not be effective unless a total of at least fifty percent of the electors entitled to vote on the question shall have voted, and unless the number of votes cast in favor of recall shall exceed the number of votes he received on the last occasion he was elected to office."[73]

The vacancy resulting from an affirmative removal vote is filled according to law and may involve a second special election to select a successor. If an officer is recalled, Montana law directs that "the vacancy shall be filled as provided by law, provided that the officer recalled may in no event be appointed to fill the vacancy."[74] The charter of the city and county of San Francisco provides that the mayor appoint a successor to the recalled officer for the unexpired term.[75]

A separate election on the question of recalling an officer has the advantage of allowing voters to concentrate on the question of the removal of the incumbent without having their attention diverted by the claims of other candidates, but suffers from the disadvantage of increasing governmental costs if a special election is held to fill the vacancy should the officer be recalled.

In Colorado and Wisconsin, two questions appear on the recall ballot: the question of recalling the named officer and the question of selecting a successor in the event the incumbent is removed from office. This type of recall election has resulted in the removal of the incumbent by a majority vote and his simultaneous reelection by a plurality vote as the other candidates split the vote opposed to the incumbent.

In Arizona and Nevada, the ballot pits the incumbent against challengers. The California Constitution provides "a state officer who is not recalled shall be reimbursed by the state for the officer's recall election expenses legally and personally incurred."[76]

Proponents of the recall typically recruit and endorse a replacement candidate, and campaign for his or her election. In the only judicial recall election in Wisconsin, recall proponents in 1977 did not endorse a replacement candidate for fear of dividing voters favoring the recall of judge Archie Simonson of Dane County.[77]

Absentee voting is permitted in recall elections as in other elections and may play an important role in determining the outcome of the recall effort (Figure 5-2). California law facilitates absentee voting and this fact was reflected in the 1983 recall election of San Francisco Mayor Dianne Feinstein – absentee ballots accounted for in excess of 36 percent of the total number of ballots cast.[78]

Restrictions on Appointive Office

To prevent an officer subject to the recall from resigning from office and being reappointed to the same office, state laws and local charters typically prohibit the appointment of the officer to the same or similar office for a period of years, most commonly two. Federal and state case law make clear that such a provision does not violate the equal protection of the laws clause of the Fourteenth Amendment to the U.S. Constitution.

Michigan law not only forbids a recall officer to be a candidate to fill the vacancy caused by the employment of the recall, but also prohibits a recalled officer from being "appointed to fill a vacancy in an elective office in the electoral district or governmental unit from which the recall was made during the term of office from which the officer was recalled."[79] Similarly, an officer resigning after a recall petition has been filed against him is ineligible for appointment to a public office "during the term of office from which the officer was recalled."[80]

Campaign Finance

A recall election can be expensive for the public officer subject to the recall and to the government involved. Mayor Dianne Feinstein of San Francisco raised in excess of $344,000 in a campaign to defeat a 1983 attempt to recall her from office, and the cost to the city and county of San Francisco to hold the recall election was approximately $450,000.[81] The California Corrupt Practices Act does not apply to the recall.[82]

Figure 5–2.

ABSENT VOTER

OFFICIAL BALLOT

CITY OF ROY
PIERCE COUNTY, WASHINGTON

SPECIAL ELECTION—MAY 25, 1976

INSTRUCTIONS: To vote for or against a proposition place "X" in appropriate ☐ following the proposition

PROPOSITION NO. 1

RECALL—MAYOR GARY ROUSH

Shall Gary Roush, the elected Mayor of the City of Roy, be recalled on the following charge which alleges malfeasance, misfeasance or violation of his oath of office: He utilized Pierce County Manpower Program employees (Ralph D. Craddock, Jeffery B. Craddock, Michael W. Cooper) to perform manual yard work services at the Mayor's personal property during summer 1975?

FOR the Recall of
Gary Roush, Mayor
of the City of Roy .... ☐

AGAINST the Recall
of Gary Roush, Mayor
of the City of Roy .... ☐

Source: Pierce County Board of Elections.

The Oregon recall law requires the sponsors of a recall petition to file with it "a sworn statement by one of them giving the name and address of all contributors and members of their recall organization" prior to circulation of the petition to the public for signatures.[83] The Washington recall statute prohibits corrupt practice acts defined, among other things, as "any consideration, compensation, gratuity, reward, or thing of value or promise thereof" designed "to induce a voter to sign or refuse to sign a recall petition."[84]

The Georgia code stipulates that the Campaign and Finance Disclosure Act applies to a recall campaign in the same manner as the act applies to candidates.[85] Washington law requires the organizers of a recall to submit a report on their expenses when filing recall petitions and makes a recall campaign subject to the state's corrupt practices act.[86]

As pointed out in an earlier section, the California Constitution mandates the reimbursement of the election expenses of a state officer who survives a recall attempt.

Legal Issues

A number of legal issues relating to the referendum and the initiative, examined in Chapters 3 and 4, apply to the recall. In particular, legal challenges of the sufficiency of recall petition signatures have been common. Writing in 1930, Bird and Ryan concluded:

> The courts have proved so dependable a haven of refuge for several officials whose recall has been sought, that some authorities have been led to declare that any public official, by retaining the services of a clever attorney, can almost completely immunize himself from the process.[87]

A Political or a Judicial Process?

Courts in general have held the recall is a political rather than a judicial process.[88] In other words, judicial guarantees protecting the rights of defendants do not apply when the recall is employed and there is no requirement that an officer subject to the recall be charged with cause — malfeasance, misfeasance, or nonfeasance — unless the state constitution or statute mandates the charging of cause as in Florida and Washington.

Interesting, George M. Mecham of the Legal Services Subcommittee of the Utah state legislature in 1976 reversed his earlier opinion that a recall act would be constitutional, but noted "impeachment is a judicial process; recall a political process."[89]

The U.S. District Court ruled on several occasions that no person has a federal constitutional right to hold a state or local elective office.[90] And the highest court in several states, commencing as early as 1913, issued rulings containing a broad interpretation of the statutes authorizing the employment of the recall.[91]

Locally Drafted Charters

The state constitution and/or statutes in 47 states authorize voters in all or specified types of political subdivisions to draft, adopt, and amend a charter.[92]

In reporting that 33 cities and towns in Massachusetts have charters authorizing the employment of the recall, the Massachusetts Legislative Research Council in 1979 raised the question whether such charter provisions violate a provision of the "home rule" constitutional amendment forbidding "regulating elections by local charter."[93] The report noted:

> There are no cases interpreting this provision although it was the basis for one of the arguments recently used to strike down an ordinance of the City of Boston limiting campaign expenditures. . . . However, the Elections Division of the Secretary of State's office has interpreted section 7 (1) in the past to forbid only the regulation of voting rights and the details of election administration, in other words, matters which are regulated by statutes, . . . It is therefore assumed that recall provisions established by a home rule charter subject to certain standards established by the legislature are valid, although the matter will not be completely free from doubt until some authoritative judicial determination is made.[94]

A similar question has been raised relative to recall provisions in Connecticut municipal charters. Some ambiguity surrounded aspects of the constitutional grant of discretionary authority to cities and towns in this state. Twenty municipal charters provide for the recall of local officers. Five recall provisions were authorized by special act charters approved by the general assembly or other special acts, and consequently the legal status of these provisions is clear. Fifteen locally drafted and adopted charters, however, contain recall provisions and their validity has been questioned by local government experts because the enabling statute implementing the constitutional grant of local discretionary authority stipulates that "no provision of this chapter shall be deemed to empower any town, city, or borough to draft, adopt, or amend a charter which shall affect matters concerning qualifications and admission of electors . . . ; conduct of and procedures at elections; election contest; . . . "[95]

In 1985, the Connecticut Supreme Court unanimously invalidated the recall provision in the locally drafted and adopted charter of Watertown by noting the general assembly had delegated specific powers to municipalities and "a fortiori, if the legislature had intended to confer the recall power on municipalities it would have done so explicitly."[96]

In 1971, Judge Robert J. Testo of the Connecticut Superior Court ruled that the section of the Westport Charter governing recall elections does not apply to school board members because they are agents of the state and not municipal officers.[97] Four years later, the Georgia Supreme Court ruled the language in the state constitution mandating removal of an officer under specified circumstances was not preemptive and did not preclude the employment of the recall.[98]

The most major court decision involving the constitutionality of the "home rule" recall charter provision was issued by the Pennsylvania Supreme Court in 1976 and invalidated the provisions of the Philadelphia Charter that had been employed by opponents of Mayor Frank L. Rizzo.[99] The court's majority based its decision on varying interpretations of a section of the Commonwealth's 1874 Constitution specifying how public officers can be removed.[100]

Jefferson B. Fordham, former dean of the University of Pennsylvania Law School, has been highly critical of the court's decision. In 1977, he wrote:

> Since the 1922 home rule amendment is amendatory of the constitution, it must, as an elementary rational matter, be regarded as controlling over the provisions of the Constitution of 1874 with which it is inconsistent. . . . The opinion of the court and the concurring opinions do not even cite the 1968 amendment, let alone refer to its text and consider the meaning and effect of its language with specific reference to the nature and scope of home rule powers directly granted by this constitutional amendment.[101]

Loss of a Quorum

The successful employment of the recall can result in the inability of a legislative body to take action should a quorum be lacking because of the removal of public officers. The problem, of course, will not occur if state law or the local charter provides for the simultaneous election of replacements for officers recalled or the appointment of sufficient replacements to achieve a quorum. State law and local charters commonly authorize a local council to coopt members to fill vacancies on the council. However, cooptation typically is not possible unless a quorum exists on the council.

In Washington, the recall of all three Yakima County commissioners in 1916 created a most unusual situation. The action of the governor in appointing three replacements was challenged, but the Washington Supreme Court upheld the validity of the appointments by referring to an 1890 statute providing the governor was empowered "to see that all offices are filled, and the duties thereof performed."[102]

Arcadia, California, in 1939 was faced with a lack of a quorum on its five-member council as two members had been recalled and one member resigned subsequent to the recall election. Existing California law authorized the voters at the recall election either to authorize the council to fill the vacancies or call a special election. Since the voters did not call a special election, the court ruled the two remaining members of the council constituted a quorum for the purpose of filling the vacancies regardless of the fact that state law stipulated a majority of the council constitutes a quorum.[103] Earlier, the Kentucky Supreme Court ruled that a statute stipulating vacancies on a school board shall be filled by the remaining members was valid even in the absence of a quorum, absent contrary statutory provisions.[104]

In 1970, voters in Tacoma, Washington, recalled five of the nine members of the city council who had been charged with conspiracy to hire an unqualified city manager and to award a cable television franchise to the Tacoma Cable Company without seeking expert advice.[105] Since the four remaining council members did not constitute a quorum, they were unable to employ the city charter provision allowing the council to fill a vacancy in its membership by cooptation.

In deciding how to fill the vacancies, the assistant city attorney advised the city manager that the state constitution authorizes the governor to fill vacancies in state offices if no other provision for filling vacancies exists and state law directs the governor to "see that all offices are filled. . . . "[106] Per consequens, the city petitioned Governor Daniel J. Evans to appoint a member to the council to bring its members up to a quorum; Governor Evans appointed Allan R. Billett to fill a vacancy.[107]

An Evaluation

The question of adopting the recall has been the subject of controversy in many states and local jurisdictions, but the recall generally has not been a major source of controversy in most jurisdictions that adopted it when measured in terms of voluntary abandonment. Because the device appears to be an attempt to apply a modified form of direct democracy to a representative democracy, philosophical arguments have abounded in support of and in opposition to citizen-initiated action to remove a public representative from office prior to the end of his or her term of office. Per contra, state laws providing for the automatic vacating of a public office by an incumbent convicted of a felony have not generated controversy.

Arguments in Favor

Six major arguments are advanced in support of the recall by its proponents.

1. *The recall is supported on the same ground as electoral democracy; that is, the recall strengthens popular control of government by allowing voters to remove public officers who are corrupt or incompetent, or who fail to reflect accurately the views of the electorate on major issues.* In other words, voters should possess the power to replace officers who are "misrepresentatives" instead of "representatives" of the electorate. Referring to the recall, William Allen White wrote in 1910, "this tightening grip of the people upon their state government . . . has been intelligent, gradual, well-directed growth of popular power."[108]

2. *The electoral system fails to produce accountable and responsive public officers.* Albert M. Kales in 1914 explained:

> The movement for the recall began just as soon as it was generally perceived that our system of frequent elections to fill a large number of offices did not prevent the extra-legal government from placing in office men loyal to it. The movement for the recall is the frankest admission that this system of elections has been a failure. The real cause for this failure was the fact that too much voting had overloaded the voter and his resulting political ignorance had delivered him into the hands of an organization which in effect cast his ballot for him.[109]

Bird and Ryan advanced a similar argument in 1930: "When the electorate realizes more fully that it is frequently preyed upon, through its government, by certain classes of corporations, it will find even more effective use for the recall."[110]

3. *The recall—in common with the sword of Damocles—reminds public officers that corruption and/or inefficiency will not be tolerated.* Charles A. Beard reported in 1938, "the people of California apparently are convinced that it is an agency of security against official betrayal of public trust and an excellent weapon of defense."[111] In 1961, the Massachusetts Supreme Judicial Court wrote the recall is "a device to make elected officers responsive to the opinions of the voters on particular issues. The implications of a recall under the statute is not

of misconduct, but only that the voters prefer not to have the recalled official continue to act."[112]

4. *The availability of the recall increases citizen interest in public affairs and reduces alienation since citizens possess a device for removing public officers in whom they have lost confidence.*

5. *The recall increases the willingness of voters to remove restrictions from state constitutions and local charters that hamper the operation of and increase the cost of government, and lead to officers devoting time to finding ingenious ways of evading the restrictions.* Voters, it is contended, do not need to rely upon constitutional and local charter restrictions and prohibitions to protect their interests since they possess the authority to remove any officer abusing the public trust. Furthermore, citizen understanding of government will be promoted by less complicated state constitutions and local charters that are confined to fundamentals.

6. *The recall encourages the electorate to approve proposed constitutional and local charter amendments increasing the term of office for elected officials which in many jurisdictions are too short and necessitate continuous campaigning for reelection.* Whereas Jacksonian democracy advocated frequent elections as a means of holding public officers accountable, the recall helps to persuade citizens to agree to longer terms for elected officers since the former have a mechanism to maintain continuous responsibility on the part of the latter. Advocates maintain that the recall is an admonitory device and its existence alone is sufficient to ensure office holders act responsibly.

Arguments in Opposition

Twelve major arguments are advanced in opposition to the recall.

1. *The primary antipodal reason advanced against the recall is the existence of other and more effective means of removing a public officer from office that do not suffer the disadvantages of the recall.* Other methods of removing public officers include (1) employment of the impeachment process with charges preferred by one house of a bicameral state legislature and the trial by the other house or a special impeachment court except in Oregon;[113] (2) legislative address (a joint resolution of the state legislature or a resolution of one house directing the governor in 28 states to remove a named officer);[114] (3) statutory or constitutional authorization for the governor to remove officers; and (4) constitutional or statutory provisions automatically removing an officer convicted of a felony. In addition, interpellation of officers may be conducted by a legislative body to uncover evidence that may lead to the employment of one of the above removal methods.[115] These methods of removal, however, cannot be employed simply because an officer does not follow the views of his or her constituents.

2. *Voters should not be allowed to make additional electoral mistakes during the interim between general elections.* In 1912, Ellis P. Oberholtzer wrote:

> The independent makers, administrators, interpreters, and enforcers
> of the law are to become the puppets of the people, to obey their

changing whims or else to surrender their places to those who shall be more willing to follow popular direction. And why is this done? Because, it is said, of the corruption of legislators, governors, and judges, because of the inability of the people to choose from among their number honest and intelligent men to represent them in the halls of government. The people have failed once; they are to be given the opportunity to fail again in a larger sphere in a more menacing way.[116]

The above argument, of course, is an undemocratic one premised upon the belief that voters are incapable of exercising perspicacious judgment in voting for candidates for public office.

3. *The use of the recall for ideological reasons is undesirable.* Oregon Secretary of State Norma Paulus in 1979 advanced a third argument against the recall. She objected to its employment "for philosophical reasons instead of the traditional reasons of malfeasance or corruption."[117] To cite one example from another state illustrating her point, petitions to recall the chairperson of the Westport (Connecticut) Board of Education appeared immediately after she cast the deciding vote to authorize the enrollment of "slum" children from Bridgeport in an elementary school.[118]

4. *The recall will restrain unduly innovative and energetic public officers.* Because the recall is similar to the "Sword of Damocles," fear has been expressed that the recall will encourage timorousness on the part of elected officers.

Association County Commissioners of Georgia objects to the recall because "it enfeebles the whole process of representative government . . . " and "in Hall County it became a tool for swift punishment of a whole board who made an unpopular, although economical decision."[119] The association added: "No one 'bats a thousand' every day. Barring evidence of gross incompetence, office holders should not be harassed by constant threats of recall. . . . Recall should be reserved for extreme circumstances."[120]

President Gil Barrett of the association, who had been subject to an unsuccessful attempt to secure the required number of recall petition signatures, pointed out in 1981 all recall attempts "have centered on some unpopular decision a county commissioner or a whole board made. In some cases, they haven't had to be unpopular with more than a handful of people for a petition to start circulating and threatening the office holder."[121]

5. *A number of highly qualified men and women will not seek elective office if the recall exists for fear it will be employed against them if they take a stand on a controversial issue that is unpopular with a group of voters.* Even if the public officer could win a recall election, he or she would be faced with the harassment of a recall campaign, and the added costs of being a public officer in terms of the time and funds that must be devoted to a defense against the charges.

6. *The recall may be employed for partisan purposes.* A candidate who lost the general election may promote a recall election in anticipation of a smaller turnout of voters and the possibility of recalling and replacing the public officer. The recall also may be employed to change the political party control of a legislative body. In 1983, two Democratic state senators were recalled by

Michigan voters and their replacements were Republicans which gave the Republican party control of the senate. The former Democratic majority floor leader complained that the affirmative vote to remove the two senators from office was smaller than the opposition vote in the 1982 general election.[122] He added the recall stifles "visionary planning" and represents a "signal to the public that the best way to get something done is to begin a recall procedure."[123]

7. *Governmental costs are increased by the need in most instances to call and hold a special recall election, and, in some jurisdictions, a second election to select a replacement for a recall officer.*

8. *By holding a simultaneous election for a successor in the event the public officer is removed, the recall may result in the election campaign overshadowing the reasons advanced for the recall, thereby encouraging the electorate to devote inadequate attention and analysis to the question of whether the officer should be recalled.*

9. *Frivolous recall petitions can be circulated to harass conscientious public officers and possibly discourage them from seeking reelection to office.* The White Panthers, a group of approximately 20 radicals, successfully collected the required number of signatures on petitions to force a recall election on April 26, 1983, on the question of whether Mayor Dianne Feinstein should be removed from office. Thomas W. Stevens, a spokesman for the organization, declared "we're on the Marxists, Leninists, Maoists, Castroist side of most questions" and sought the recall of the mayor because she signed a city ordinance banning the possession of pistols.[124] He added the ban would penalize poor persons unable to secure adequate police protection.

10. *The recall may be abused by well-organized and well-financed organizations to achieve their special interests.* A 1979 editorial in *The Sunday Oregonian* commented:

> A diagnosis of southern Oregon's recall epidemic suggests but does not conclude, that a right-wing conspiracy is one source of recall fever. Conservative elements have been driving forces in many of the recall drives.[125]

11. *The reason(s) prompting a recall in fact may not be of such magnitude as to warrant removal of a public officer.* All members of the Easton (Massachusetts) School Committee, for example, were recalled from office because the members appointed a person from another state, instead of the assistant principal, as the new high school principal.[126]

12. Finally, *opponents object to the recall of judges on the ground they should not be subject to partisan political intrigues and forced to write opinions that will court favorable public reactions.* In 1911, the American Bar Association approved a resolution denouncing the recall of judges.[127]

Conclusions

Voters employing the recall act de facto as the jury trying a public officer on charges contained on petitions initiated by a recall group. In contrast to criminal charges, the grand jury process is bypassed although the officer subject to a recall petition and election also may be subject to criminal action if a wrong has been committed. The officer, of course, can seek judicial review of alleged procedural errors in the petition process and alleged invalid signatures on petitions.

Where authorized, the recall most often has been utilized on the local level and seldom has been employed on the state level. Lynn J. Frazier of North Dakota is the only governor to have been removed from office by a recall election (1921). The following year, he was elected U.S. senator.

Similarly, the recall of judges is unusual. Only one judge has been recalled in Wisconsin. Judge Archie Simonson was recalled on September 7, 1977, because of his remark that a fifteen-year-old defendant charged with sexually assaulting a girl was reacting to a wide-open society with commercial sex services, nude entertainment bars, and provocative women's clothing.[128] Until 1983, no state legislator had been recalled in California since 1919 when a senator was recalled.

The recall has not produced a new era of public official responsibility, yet it has not caused extensive disruption of state and local governments as had been feared by some of the early recall opponents. Where used, public officers have been removed from office for malfeasance, misfeasance, public unhappiness with the appointment or removal of a public officer, and citizen displeasure with a policy decision(s). Bird and Ryan concluded in 1930:

> Twenty-five years of the operation of the recall in the state of its first adoption have realized neither the highest hopes of its sanguine originators nor the darkest prophecies of its cynical opponents. . . . It has been used most effectively, at times, to drive from office unfaithful, incompetent, and arbitrary officials; but it also has been employed, on occasion, without justification or beneficial result.[129]

Charles A. Beard in 1935 reported, "no one expected the recall to give intelligence to any constituency or to escape the perils of popular prejudices and tumult, and experience with it confirms the correctness of such anticipations."[130]

Admittedly, there are other methods of removing a public officer, but these methods are difficult to employ and often are time consuming. The impeachment process can be utilized to charge, try, and remove a public officer, but state legislatures with a few exceptions do not meet on a year-round basis. Furthermore, impeachment requires charges of malfeasance, misfeasance, and/or nonfeasance, which may not be the reason(s) for voter dissatisfaction with a public officer. If an officer's position on a major issue does not reflect the will of the electorate, the petition referendum and/or the recall should be available to the elector-

ate. Voters should have the means available to rectify their philosophical differences with a public officer as well as to remove an officer
for malfeasance, misfeasance, and nonfeasance.

Although the United States is organized on the national, state, and
local levels (with the exceptions of many New England towns) as repub-
lics or representative governments, voters are the fountainhead of sovereign political power and simply have delegated their authority to public
representatives. Consequently, voters clearly possess the authority to
reserve to themselves the right to reverse decisions of their representatives and/or remove representatives failing to follow majority opinion.
While this principle is an obvious one, not all state and local governments have adopted the petition referendum and the recall. Voters in
some jurisdictions have been convinced by opponents of the recall that
on balance it weakens representative government.

The recall can serve as a valuable adjunct to representative government and as an inducement to voters to agree to longer terms of office
for elected officers in jurisdictions with short terms necessitating nearly
continuous campaigning for reelection. Although the recall has the
potential for encouraging "single issue" politics, this undesirable type
of politics generally has not been a product of the recall. If voters are
dissatisfied with a policy decision made by a legislative body, use of the
petition referendum is the proper approach to resolving an issue rather
than employment of the recall.

Where possible, a recall election should be held in conjunction with
a general election because ad hoc elections tend to have relatively low
voter participation and a higher cost per ballot cast. Consideration can
be given to suspending the officer until a recall election is held in conjunction with a general election. On the other hand, serious charges
against a public officer should be tried by the citizen jury expeditious-
ly to facilitate fairness to the public officer subject to the recall. We
agree with a 1965 Louisiana court decision that

> the jurisprudence by which this court is bound holds that a recall
> petition is deemed abandoned by laches when the recall petitioners
> do not actively pursue their remedy so as to require substantial com-
> pliance with the mandatory statutory requirements that recall elec-
> tions be held expeditiously within a limited period after the recall peti-
> tion is first presented for processing to government authorities.[131]

In sum, citizens in a representative political system should have
the authority to initiate the removal of public officers and the process
of removal should be expeditious in instances of grossly undesirable
behavior by a public officer. Nevertheless, it also should be axiomatic

that the initiation of recall proceedings should not be too easy or the proceedings will be instituted for frivolous reasons. To the extent possible, a recall election should be held in conjunction with a general election to ensure maximum voter participation in the decision on whether to recall a public officer. To date, the electorate has been perspicacious in judging the charges against an officer in a recall election.

Whereas the recall generally has been employed against a single public officer, the neighborhood government movement seeks to replace all city officers, appointed and elected, with neighborhood government officers appointed or elected by residents of each neighborhood. Chapter 6 examines the views of the proponents of neighborhood governments, and assesses the community school boards and community boards in New York City, and administrative reforms instituted in large cities.

Notes

1. *Constitution of Michigan*, Art. 2, § 8.
2. Frederick L. Bird and Frances M. Ryan, *The Recall of Public Officers: A Study of the Operation of the Recall in California* (New York: Macmillan, 1930), p. 22.
3. 47 *Congressional Record*, 2964 (August 15, 1911).
4. Ibid.
5. *Ervien v. United States*, 251 U.S. 41 (1919).
6. Walter E. Weyl, *The New Democracy: An Essay on Certain Political and Economic Tendencies in the United States* (New York: Macmillan, 1912), p. 298.
7. Ibid., pp. 304–5.
8. Ellen Torelle, comp., *The Political Philosophy of Robert M. LaFollette* (Madison, Wis.: The Robert M. LaFollette Company, 1920), p. 174.
9. Alaska, Arizona, California, Colorado, Georgia, Idaho, Kansas, Louisiana, Michigan, Nevada, North Dakota, Oregon, Washington, and Wisconsin.
10. *Constitution of Arizona*, Art. 8, § 1.
11. *Constitution of Alaska*, Art. 11, § 8.
12. Arkansas, Florida, Georgia, Hawaii, Massachusetts, Minnesota, Mississippi, Missouri, Nebraska, New Jersey, New Mexico, Ohio, Pennsylvania, South Dakota, Tennessee, West Virginia, and Wyoming.
13. *Constitution of California*, Art. 2, § 19.
14. *New Jersey Laws of 1950*, chap. 210 and *New Jersey Statutes Annotated*, § 40:69A–210 (1976).
15. *Town of Billerica (Massachusetts) Charter*, Art. 6, § 6–4.
16. *Town of Oxford (Massachusetts) Charter*, Chap. 7, § 6.
17. *Constitution of Wisconsin*, Art. 13, § 12.
18. 68 *OAG (Wisconsin)*, 148 (1979).

19. Ibid., at 146. See also *State ex rel. Martin v. Zimmerman*, 233 Wis. 16, 288 N.W. 454 (1939).

20. *Michigan Public Acts of 1954*, Number 116 and *Michigan Compiled Laws Annotated*, §§ 168.121 and 168.149 (1967).

21. *Constitution of the United States*, Art. 1, §§ 5-6 and Fourteenth Amendment, § 3. See also *Keogh v. Horner*, 8 F. Supp. 933 (D. Ill., 1934); *Burchell v. State Board of Election Commissioners*, 252 Ky. 823, 68 S.W. 427 (1934); and *State ex rel. 25 Voters v. Selvig*, 170 Minn. 406, 212 N.W. 604 (1927).

22. *Arizona Laws of 1973*, Chap. 159 and *Arizona Revised Statutes*, §§ 19-221 and 19-222 (1967 and 1984 Supp.).

23. *The Town Manager Plan in Massachusetts* (Boston: Massachusetts Federation of Taxpayers Associations, Inc., 1949), p. 10.

24. Joan Vennochi, "Mansfield Split After Recall Election," *The Boston Globe*, December 15, 1982, pp. 29-30.

25. *ICMA Newsletter*, June 21, 1976, p. 3.

26. *Constitution of Washington*, Art. 1, § 33. Malfeasance is "bad" performance of duties and misfeasance is "incompetent" performance of official duties.

27. *Revised Code of Washington*, § 29.82.010 (1981).

28. Ibid., § 29.82.020.

29. Ibid., § 29.82.070.

30. *Westpy v. Burnett*, 82 N.J. Super. 239, 197 A.2d 400 (1964); affirmed 41 N.J. 554, 197 A.2d 857 (1964).

31. *Constitution of Ohio*, Art. 2, § 38.

32. *Ohio Revised Code*, § 3.08 (1976).

33. *Virginia Laws of 1975*, Chap. 515 and 595, and *Code of Virginia*, §§ 24.1-79.5 and 24.1-79.7 (1980).

34. *Constitution of Mississippi*, § 139 and *Mississippi Code Annotated*, § 25-5-7 (1972).

35. *Constitution of Wisconsin*, Art. 13, § 12.

36. Albert M. Kales, *Unpopular Government in the United States* (Chicago: University of Chicago Press, 1914), p. 125.

37. *Montana Laws of 1977*, Chap. 364 and *Revised Code of Montana*, § 2-16-603 (1983).

38. *Greeley (Colorado) City Charter*, § 4.3.

39. *State ex rel. Hoel v. Brown*, 105 Ohio St. 479 at 487 (1922).

40. *State ex rel. Hackley v. Edmonds*, 150 Ohio St. 203 at 218 (1948).

41. *Dayton v. Thomas*, 28 Ohio Dec. 261, 20 Ohio N.P. (n.s.), 539 (1916).

42. *The Historical Development and Use of the Recall in Oregon* (Salem: Legislative Research, 1976), p. 13.

43. *Louisiana Acts of 1921*, extra session, No. 121, § 9 and *Louisiana Revised Statutes*, § 1300.13 (1956).

44. *Constitution of Arizona*, Art. 8, § 5.

45. *Constitution of Wisconsin*, Art. 13, § 12.

46. *North Dakota Laws of 1979*, Chap. 271, § 1 and *North Dakota Century Code*, § 16.1-01-11 (1981).

47. *California Laws of 1976*, Chap. 1437 and *California Elections Code*,

§§ 27007–7008 (1977 and 1984 supp.). For details on the recall procedure in California, see *Procedure for Recalling State and Local Officials* (Sacramento: California Secretary of State, 1982).

48. *Charter of the City and County of San Francisco*, § 9.108.

49. *Kansas Statutes Annotated*, § 25–4302 (1981).

50. For an example of a statutory requirement, see *California Elections Code*, §§ 27007 and 27030.5 (1977 and 1984 supp.).

51. *Alaska Laws of 1960*, Chap. 83 and *Alaska Statutes*, § 15.45.480 (1982 supp.).

52. *Kansas Laws of 1976*, Chap. 178 and *Kansas Statutes Annotated*, § 25–4306 (1981).

53. 37 *OAG* (Wisconsin) 91 (1948). See also *Constitution of Wisconsin*, Art. 13, § 12; *Wisconsin Laws of 1933*, Chap. 44; *Wisconsin Laws of 1965*, Chap. 666; *Wisconsin Laws of 1977*, Chap. 403; and *Wisconsin Statutes*, § 9.10(2)(a) (1967 and 1984 Supp.).

54. For an example, see the *Constitution of Arizona*, Art. 8, § 2.

55. See *Revised Code of Washington*, § 29.82.025 (1965 and 1984 Supp.).

56. *Constitution of California*, Art. 2, § 15.

57. *California Laws of 1976*, Chap. 1437 and *California Elections Code*, §§ 27230–7231 (1977 and 1984 supp.).

58. *Charter of the City and County of San Francisco*, § 9.111.

59. For details, see *The Book of the States, 1980–81* (Lexington, Ken.: The Council of State Governments, 1980), p. 198.

60. *Charter of the City and County of San Francisco*, § 9.111. Prior to voter approval of Proposition A in November 1983, the signature requirement was 10 percent of the vote cast for the office in the last election.

61. *Constitution of California*, Art. 2, § 14(b) and *California Elections Code*, § 27211(b) (1977 and 1984 supp.).

62. *North Dakota Laws of 1981*, chap. 241, § 1 and *North Dakota Century Code*, § 16.1-01-10 (1981).

63. *Oregon Laws of 1957*, chap. 608 and *Oregon Revised Statutes*, § 249.008 (1983 supp.).

64. *Segars v. Bramlett*, 245 Ga. 386, 265 S.E.2d 279 (1980). See also *Georgia Code Annotated*, § 89–1901 *et seq.* (1980).

65. *Arizona Laws of 1973*, Chap. 159, § 17 and *Arizona Revised Statutes Annotated*, § 19–208.011A (1975).

66. *Wisconsin Laws of 1965*, Chap. 666; *Wisconsin Laws of 1977*, Chap. 403; and *Wisconsin Statutes*, §§ 9.10(3)(b) and 9.10(4)(a) (1967 and 1984 supp.).

67. *Constitution of Arizona*, Art. 8, § 3.

68. *New Jersey Laws of 1950*, Chap. 210 and *New Jersey Statutes Annotated*, § 40.69A–171 (1976).

69. *Town of Billerica (Massachusetts) Charter*, § 6–4.

70. For an example, see *Michigan Public Acts of 1978*, Public Act 533, § 1 and *Michigan Compiled Laws Annotated*, § 168.966 (1984 supp.).

71. *The Historical Development and Use of the Recall in Oregon* (Salem: Legislative Research, 1976), p. 11.

72. *San Francisco Voter Information Pamphlet: Special Recall Election, April 26, 1983* (San Francisco: Registrar of Voters, 1983).

73. *Town of Oxford (Massachusetts) Charter*, § 7-6-3.

74. *Montana Laws of 1977*, Chap. 364 and *Revised Code of Montana*, § 2-16-635 (1983).

75. *Charter of the City and County of San Francisco*, § 9.113.

76. *Constitution of California*, Art. 2, § 18.

77. "Winner in War Over Judge's Words," *The New York Times*, September 9, 1977, p. B1.

78. *California Elections Code*, § 1006 (1977). See also "Absentee Ballots Over 36% in San Francisco Recall," *Election Administration Reports* (May 2, 1983):5 and 7.

79. *Michigan Public Acts of 1978*, Act 533 and *Michigan Compiled Laws Annotated*, § 169.974 (1) (1984 Supp.).

80. Ibid., § 169.974 (2) (1984 Supp.).

81. Wallace Turner, "Bid to Oust San Francisco Mayor Polarizes Splinter Groups," *The New York Times*, March 26, 1983, p. 6, and "Absentee Ballots Over 36% in San Francisco Recall," pp. 5 and 7.

82. *California Government Code*, §§ 83100-122 (1976).

83. *Oregon Laws of 1979*, Chap. 190, § 136 and *Oregon Revised Statutes*, § 249.865 (1983).

84. *Washington Laws of 1965*, Chap. 9 and *Revised Code of Washington*, § 29.82.220 (1965).

85. *Official Code of Georgia Annotated*, § 89-1916 (1982).

86. *Washington Statutes*, §§ 29.82.070 and 29.82.220 (1981).

87. Bird and Ryan, *The Recall of Public Officers*, p. 193.

88. For examples, see *Dunham v. Ardery* , 43 Okla. 619, 143 P. 381 (1914); *Topping v. Houston*, 94 Neb. 445, 153 N.W. 796 (1913); and *In re Bower*, 41 Ill.2d 277, 242 N.E.2d 252 (1968).

89. *Recall: At Issue in Utah* (Salt Lake City: Office of Legislative Research, 1976), p. 83.

90. For an example, see *Roche v. Foulger*, 404 F.Supp. 705 (1975).

91. *Topping v. Houston*, 94 Neb. 445, 153 N.W. 796 (1913); *Dunham v. Ardery*, 43 Okla. 619, 143 P. 381 (1914); and *In Re Rice*, 35 Ill.App.2d 79 at 94, 181 N.E.2d 742 at 749 (1962).

92. Joseph F. Zimmerman, *State-Local Relations: A Partnership Approach* (New York: Praeger, 1983), p. 26.

93. *Report Relative to Recall of Local Officials* (Boston: Massachusetts Legislative Research Council, 1979), pp. 8 and 32. Thirty-one municipalities have drafted and adopted "home rule" charters; 15 other municipalities operate under provisions of special laws authorizing the recall; and 6 municipalities have special charters providing for the recall. See *Recall of Elected Officials in Massachusetts Municipalities* (Boston: Massachusetts Executive Office of Communities and Development, 1982).

94. *Report Relative to Recall of Local Officials*, p. 32.

95. *Connecticut General Statutes*, Chap. 99, § 192a (1969).

96. *Simons v. Canty*, 195 Conn. 524 at 532 (1985). See also *Statutory*

Authority Under Home Rule for Recall (Hartford: Connecticut Office of Legislative Research, February 28, 1974), pp. 2–3.

97. *Sherman v. Kemish*, 29 Conn. Sup. 198, 279 A.2d 571 (1971).

98. *Smith v. Abercrombie*, 235 Ga. 741, 221 S.E.2d 802 (1985).

99. *Citizens Committee to Recall Rizzo v. The Board of Elections*, 470 Pa. 1, 367 A.2d 232 (1976). See also the *Philadelphia Home Rule Charter*, §§ 9–100 and 9–101.

100. *Constitution of the Commonwealth of Pennsylvania*, Art. 6, § 7. The original section 4 was renumbered by a 1966 constitutional amendment as section 7.

101. Jefferson B. Fordham, "Judicial Nullification of a Democratic Political Process – The Rizzo Recall Case," *University of Pennsylvania Law Review* 126 (November 1977):14 and 17.

102. *Gilbert v. Dimmick*, 89 Wash. 182, 154 P. 163 (1916).

103. *Nesbitt v. Bolz*, 13 Cal. 677, 91 P.2d 879 (1939).

104. *Douglas et al. v. Pittman et al.*, 239 Ky. 548, 39 S.W.2d 979 (1931).

105. "Tacoma, in Recall Election, Votes Five Councilmen Out of Office," *The New York Times*, September 17, 1970, p. 30.

106. "City of Tacoma Interdepartmental Communication" from Assistant City Attorney Geoffrey C. Cross to City Manager Marshall McCormick dated August 25, 1970. See also *Constitution of Washington*, Art. 3, § 13 and *Revised Code of Washington*, § 43.06.010 (2) (1981).

107. "Minutes of Special Meeting of the Tacoma City Council," September 29, 1970, p. 1.

108. William Allen White, *The Older Order Changeth: A View of American Democracy* (New York: Macmillan, 1910), p. 60.

109. Kales, *Unpopular Government in the United States*, p. 122.

110. Bird and Ryan, *The Recall of Public Officers*, p. 350.

111. Charles A. Beard, *American Government and Politics*, 7th ed. (New York: Macmillan, 1935), pp. 532–33.

112. *Donahue v. Selectmen of Saugus*, 343 Mass. 93 at 96, 176 N.E.2d 34 at 36 (1961).

113. The unicameral Nebraska legislature possesses the impeachment power and impeached officials are tried by the Supreme Court. The New York Constitution provides for a Court for the Trial of Impeachments composed of the Senate and the Court of Appeals. *Constitution of New York*, Art. 6, § 24. An initiated constitutional amendment approved by Oregon voters in 1910 stipulates "public officers shall not be impeached." *Constitution of Oregon*, Art. 7, § 6.

114. For a provision providing for address by the Senate, see the *Constitution of Pennsylvania*, Art. 6, § 4.

115. Interpellation refers to the requirement that an appointive officer appear before either house of the state legislature "to answer written and oral interrogatories relative to any matter, function, or work" of the officer. *Wisconsin Laws of 1915*, Chap. 406 and *Wisconsin Statutes*, §§ 13.28–13.30 (1972).

116. Ellis P. Oberholtzer, *The Referendum in America Together with*

Some Chapters on the Initiative and the Recall (New York: Charles Scribner's Sons, 1912), p. 455.

117. Benny Willis, "State Officer Says Recalls are Misused," *Eugene Register-Guard*, December 14, 1979, pp. 1B–2B.

118. "Westport Split Over Busing Vote," *The New York Times*, December 10, 1970, p. 56.

119. "Abuse of Recall Power Substitutes Popularity for Leadership," *Georgia County Government Magazine* 31 (May 1979):50.

120. Ibid.

121. Gil Barrett, "Recall Act is Being Used to Punish Local Leaders for Differences of Opinion," *Georgia County Government Magazine* 33 (October 1981):2.

122. Candace Romig, "Two Michigan Legislators Recalled," *State Legislatures* 10 (January 1984):5.

123. Ibid.

124. Wallace Turner, "Fringe Group Forces Ouster Vote on Coast Mayor," *The New York Times*, February 9, 1983, p. A24.

125. "Recall Fever Infects Oregon," *The Sunday Oregonian*, August 12, 1979, p. C2.

126. *Report Relative to Recall of Local Officers*, p. 44.

127. *Reports of the American Bar Association*, Vol. 36, 1911, pp. 231–32.

128. "Winner in War Over Judge's Words," *The New York Times*, September 9, 1977, p. B1.

129. Bird and Ryan, *The Recall of Public Officers*, p. 342.

130. Beard, *American Government and Politics*, p. 532.

131. *Cloud v. Dyess*, 172 So.2d 528 at 530 (La.App., 1965).

Chapter 6

NEIGHBORHOOD POLITY

The neighborhood government movement, originating in the 1960s, sought to establish a system of micropolitan governments within large cities in order to make the governance system subject to greater control by and more responsive to the electorate. This development in large measure is attributable to the growing centralization of political power in these cities over the previous 60 years.

The closing decade of the nineteenth century and the opening decade of the twentieth century properly may be termed a reform era. References were made in Chapters 3 to 5 to the progressives and populists who supported the petition referendum, the initiative, and the recall. A closely related movement – the municipal reform movement – developed as a reaction to machine control of large cities and associated corruption.[1]

In addition to cleaning up corruption, reformers sought to improve the economy and efficiency of municipal service delivery and the quality of representation of the citizenry through the use of limited voting, cumulative voting, and proportional representation (P.R.).[2] The scientific management movement, originating in the 1890s, had a major impact upon many municipal governments as reformers pressed for the employment of the scientific method to determine the most economical and efficient way of providing services to citizens.[3]

Heavy emphasis was placed by reformers upon functional consolidation and creation of a strong municipal executive in whom responsibility for administration could be centralized. They specifically desired to abolish all elected boards and commissions with administrative responsibilities and transfer their functions to the mayor whose administrative and veto powers would be increased substantially. In other

words, administrative authority would be integrated in a hierarchy with
the mayor at the apex. The reformers also sought to reduce the power
of political parties and councilmen with bases in wards by replacing the
partisan ward systems of electing the large bicameral city council with
a small unicameral council elected at large by nonpartisan ballots.

Proponents of a strong executive stressed that the integration of
authority would result in the achievement of economies of scale, mobilization of the city's resources to meet critical needs in the most effective manner, and uniform service provision throughout the city. By
1950, the reformers achieved their goal of executive integration in many
cities.

Relatively little criticism was directed at the reform model of municipal government until the early 1950s when academics began to
criticize the model as one incorporating middle class values.[4] In the
1960s, two new groups advocating political decentralization emerged.
The first group developed the public choice theory which innately supports the existing fractionated system of local government.[5] These
theorists favor a large number of small units of local government on the
grounds such units maximize citizen participation, governmental responsiveness to citizens, and choice of residential location on the basis
of services offered and taxes levied. The theory, of course, is predicated
largely on the existence of a broad grant of discretionary authority by
the state to its general purpose political subdivisions, a subject examined in Chapter 7, and citizens possessing sufficient financial resources to have a choice of residential location.

The second group of reformers urged the breaking up of large cities
into neighborhood governments or conversion of the cities into two-tier
governmental systems. This chapter focuses upon the neighborhood
government movement in large cities and the response to the movement
in the form of the community school system and community boards in
New York City.

Neighborhood Government

Most supporters of neighborhood government advocated the redistribution of political power by the establishment of a federated city. The present city government would be retained to handle functions most suitable
for performance on a broad areal basis (such as refuse disposal, sewerage
treatment, and water supply) and newly established neighborhood governments would perform functions closest to the citizens such as day-
care programs, health services, libraries, neighborhood parks, and schools.

Agitation for the creation of a system of neighborhood governments was concentrated in black ghettos where the failure of city governments to provide needed facilities and quality services had been most notable. The growth of citizen interest in neighborhood governments gained impetus following the civil disorders of the mid-1960s which dramatized the multitudinous problems of severely disadvantaged groups and the inability of local governments to respond to the needs of these groups. Milton Kotler, a leading advocate of neighborhood governments, contended:

> The absolute rule of Negro communities by outside forces has reached the highest degree possible without precipitating rebellion. At the point when practically all decisions affecting public life are made on the outside, a politically confident and conscious people, aspiring to be free, must insist upon a share in local rule.[6]

Regardless of whether one agrees with Kotler's assessment, it is apparent that government by consent of the governed did not exist in many neighborhoods in large cities in the 1960s.

Local government has been highly praised as grass-roots government close to the people. Nevertheless, the growth of a ponderous bureaucracy slowed down administrative decision making and traditional municipal institutions did not appear to be able to cope with the varying problems found in different neighborhoods. As a result, many citizens in the 1960s became alienated from their local government and felt it was unrepresentative and unresponsive, and the average person was powerless to influence the policy-making processes in a significant way.[7]

The concept of neighborhood government is in accordance with American political traditions favoring citizen participation and training, decentralization of political authority, and small units of local government. The interest in subcity or microgovernments reflected a desire for access to government by reducing the geographical scale of local government and for a return to participatory democracy as epitomized by the New England town meeting, a subject examined in Chapter 2. Kotler asked: "Can't the residents and mothers of the neighborhood determine the kind of day-care program that best fits the community? The same can also be said of recreation, libraries, schools, health, welfare, and so forth. What does a community gain in the unitary centralized control of these programs by a central structure of some millions of people?"[8]

Neighborhood government means "control" or "control-sharing" and must be contrasted with officially sponsored citizen participation programs on the neighborhood level that are advisory in nature and often little more than symbolic. Citizen participation, whether it be in the form of information or consultation, does not satisfy proponents of neighborhood government who insist that a fundamental change in the decision-making process within cities is essential. The most alienated citizens view officially sponsored citizen participation programs as cooptation; that is, a process to secure the commitment and support of citizens for programs developed by the bureaucracy. Power is not shared and citizen participation is designed merely to give legitimacy to a program.

Although multi-purpose neighborhood governments have not been established to date, the 1969 New York State legislature established a community school district system in New York City effective on July 1, 1970.

The New York City Community School Districts

Until the middle of the twentieth century, the New York City public school system generally was considered to be one of the best large city school systems. The system, however, commenced to undergo a major change in the composition of its student body as middle-class white families moved to suburban municipalities in large numbers and were replaced by poor black and Puerto Rican families. By the late 1960s, the student population was approximately 32 percent black and 22 percent Puerto Rican, and the proportion of fifth grade students reading at or above their grade level in ten predominately black schools ranged from 14 to 44 percent compared to a range of 31 to 73 percent for fifth grade students in chiefly white schools.

Reacting to the problems of the city's school system, the 1961 state legislature enacted a law abolishing the city's board of education and replacing it with a new one.[9] The beginning of the school decentralization movement can be dated to this law since the new board of education was directed to appoint local school boards possessing advisory powers. Community control advocates were dissatisfied with the 25 advisory boards as they lacked policy-making powers and were considered to be ineffective in influencing the policies of the central board of education. Although the number of boards was increased to 31 in 1965, they continued to fail to make effective inputs into the educational policy-making process.

The overwhelming majority of black leaders until 1967 supported the unitary citywide school system as they viewed it as the best mechanism for improving education for black students through school integration. The board of education in 1967 assured black leaders that Intermediate School 201, under construction, would be an integrated school, but the school upon its opening was attended primarily by black and Puerto Rican pupils. Convinced they had been betrayed by the board of education, a number of black leaders concluded only black control of schools would ensure quality education for black students and began to argue for community control of schools by pointing out that whites control their school districts in suburban areas. A factor contributing to the demand for neighborhood-controlled schools was the growing belief that the exodus of white families to the suburbs made racial integration in the public schools an impossibility.

Preceding and contributing to the development of community control of schools in New York City were three Ford Foundation-funded demonstration school districts – Ocean Hill–Brownsville, Intermediate School 201 Complex, and Two Bridges. Considerable controversy erupted as the boards of the demonstration districts sought to control their own budgets, hire and fire teachers, and establish the curriculum. The Council of Supervisors and Administrators and the United Federation of Teachers (UFT) vigorously opposed the three demonstration school boards, and animosities intensified in 1967 as the three districts kept their schools open during the UFT's citywide strike. When the Ocean Hill–Brownsville district board attempted, without preferring formal charges, to remove one principal, five assistant principals, and thirteen teachers, UFT removed its members from the district. Racial animosities came out into the open as the black and Puerto Rican district contended it was fighting a repressive white organization – the UFT.

Community School Districts

Extensive political maneuvering and debate in the state legislature in 1968 and 1969 led to enactment of a law establishing a federated school system as of July 1, 1970.[10] The product of legislative compromise, the decentralization law was criticized by advocates and opponents of community control with the former contending not enough power is granted to the community school boards and with the latter maintaining too much power is given to the boards. Fearing that militants might secure control of districts if each had a relatively small population and desiring to make the new districts conform as closely as possible to the existing advisory districts, the legislature directed an interim City Board of Education to establish 30 to 33 districts. Thirty-one districts were formed in 1970 and a thirty-second district was established in 1973. The 1970 population of districts ranged from 109,357 (District 23) to 576,000 (District 2). To date, the district lines have not been changed with the exception of the division of District 16 in 1973 to form an additional district.

Each nine-member community school board has jurisdiction over

public schools through junior high school. Each board hires and establishes the salary of a district superintendent of schools, determines cur-
ricula subject to city and state standards, recommends sites for new
schools, appoints teacher aides, operates recreational programs and
social centers, enters into contracts for maintenance and repair of school
facilities up to an annual maximum of $250,000, and submits an an-
nual budget to the chancellor of the citywide school system who possesses powers similar to the powers of a superintendent of schools.

The City Board of Education retains control over all other public
schools, and may suspend, supersede, or remove a community school
board or any member of a community school board. The board of education also possesses extensive financial and personnel powers.[11]

To ensure adequate representation for minority groups – ethnic,
ideological, racial, and religious – the legislature included in the decentralization law a provision mandating the use of P.R., a type of preferential voting providing representation to groups in accordance with their
voting strength. Although blacks exceeded 20 percent of the city's
population in 1970, there were only two blacks on the 37-member city
council. Twenty-seven council members were elected from single-mem-
ber districts and 10 were elected boroughwide by limited voting in 1969.
Each political party was restricted to nominating one candidate in each
of the five boroughs for the position of councilman-at-large and each
voter was allowed to vote for only one such candidate in his borough.

Seventy-seven (28 percent) of the 279 community school board
members elected in 1970 were blacks and Puerto Ricans – 44 were elected in 6 of the districts and the remainder in 15 of the other 25 districts.
The P.R. election results reflected accurately the voting strength of the
two groups. While the 14 percent turnout of eligible voters was average
for local school board elections not held in conjunction with general
municipal elections in New York State, the black and Puerto Rican turnout was lower. Participation at the polls by voters at or near the bot-
tom of the socioeconomic scale is typically lower than participation by
groups higher on the scale, and there was a boycott of the election by
militants advocating complete community control of schools.

The May 1, 1973 election witnessed 841 candidates seeking the 288
seats on the 32 boards. Thirty-eight percent, or 110, of those elected
were black, Chinese, or Puerto Rican; these groups made up approximately 36 percent of the city's population. Seven districts elected only
white candidates and four districts (two in Brooklyn and two in Manhattan) elected only blacks and Puerto Ricans. Blacks were elected to
membership on 23 (72 percent) of the boards and Puerto Ricans were
elected to membership on 18 (56 percent) of the boards.[12]

Evaluated by the criterion of voter participation, the 1973 community school board election was a clear disappointment as only 370,204

(10.38 percent) of the eligible voters cast ballots. Nevertheless, the election resulted in increased minority representation on the boards. Voter turnout in the 1975 community school board election declined to 9.8 percent of the eligible voters, and candidates backed by the United Federation of Teachers won control of 21 of the 32 boards, a not surprising development when voter participation is low. Turnout of voters in the 1977, 1980, and 1983 elections averaged between 8 and 9 percent of the eligible voters.

The school decentralization law unfortunately contains several ambiguous provisions relative to the powers of the community school boards. To cite one example, a board is empowered to "appoint, define the duties, assign, promote, and discharge all its employees and fix their compensation and terms of employment." The City Board of Education, however, is designated by the same statute as "the government or public employer of all persons appointed or assigned by the city board or the community boards."

Even if there were no ambiguities in the assignment of powers to the city board and the community boards, one would anticipate interlevel friction since the former board is appointive and takes a citywide viewpoint in contrast to the elective community boards whose views naturally tend to be more parochial. On many occasions, the chancellor suspended local school boards for failing to obey his directives to reduce pupil instruction time, conduct bilingual programs for Spanish-speaking students, collect ethnic data, or for attempting to establish their own school calendars. A major controversy involved the refusal of the District 26 board to supply data on the ethnic and racial background of its students and teachers.

The dispute was a bitter one during which the charge of racism freely was hurled at the five-member board majority. District 26 is basically a white middle-class neighborhood in northeastern Queens; approximately 4,000 of the 16,000 pupils were bused into the district from other sections of the city to promote integration. The chancellor initially superseded the board and designated a special trustee to collect the ethnic and racial data, but was frustrated by the refusal of the 27 principals in the district to turn over the requested data. In response to this roadblock, the chancellor suspended the board.

The board's refusal to supply the ethnic and racial data was based upon the fear that the data would lead to a system of hiring quotas or the dismissal of white teachers to promote integration of the faculty.[13] A special telephone poll of 573 households in the district by *The New York Times* revealed that 70 percent of the residents supported the board's position. Following the collection of the ethnic and racial data, the chancellor reinstated the board.[14]

In 1983, District Boards 25, 26, and 29 were suspended by Chancellor Frank J. Macchiarola for canceling or threatening to cancel classes because of a snowstorm. President Joseph Albergo of Board 29 maintained "it didn't make sense to insist that every school be open. He should have let the school boards use their brains and decide what was best for the children in each district."[15]

Evaluation

The State Charter Revision Commission for New York City in 1974 reported "that parents were intensely interested in boundaries – so interested that even the possibility of slight changes could provoke a severe reaction. Parents evidenced a latent fear that *district* changes might be followed by *school* changes. . . . Accordingly, they tended to favor the *status quo*. Thus any attempt at even minor changes in school district lines in the interests of coterminality with other services should be approached with caution."[16]

The commission also reported that the community school boards used public funds as well as "central authorities might have under a centralized system"; there has been an increase in the number of black and Spanish-speaking principals, assistant principals, and teachers; anxiety among teachers has been increased as they fear "being replaced" and having "their authority in the classroom undermined by 'unprofessional' standards"; accountability of school personnel to the public has been increased; there is little "evidence that there has been more or less educational change under decentralization than there would have been in a centralized system"; citizen participation while not increasing greatly became "more intense" with parent and community groups gaining "power and confidence in their dealings with professional staff – particularly with the principals"; decentralization "achieved its major objective of 'reconnecting' the schools to the communities, especially in low-income areas"; and whether decentralization has increased the achievement of pupils cannot be determined.[17]

In the same year, Professor Diane Ravitch of Columbia University Teachers College wrote that the system "on the whole is functioning," reading scores increased slightly during the past year, and black and Puerto Ricans had been promoted to supervisory positions, but that attendance and crime continued to be problems.[18] She also reported that "the tendency of some local boards, especially in racially changing districts, has been to retard integration, either by fighting to keep their children in their own districts or to keep another district's children out. There have also been integration disputes within districts."[19]

In 1975, the Council of Supervisors and Administrators issued a position paper reporting that decentralization had achieved its objective of increasing "the sense of identification of parents and children with their schools" and school district boundaries "have become meaningful to the parents and to the staff," but pointing out that the central board of education remains remote, the community school boards and superintendents "have become engulfed in a deluge of paperwork and administrative matters," the role of the community superintendent relative to that of the community school board is unclear, there has been a large turnover of community superintendents and "a startling trend . . . towards the choice of supervisors for the schools based upon their membership in the particular ethnic makeup of the district," and "great fiscal confusion, mismanagement, and even evidence of malfeasance have appeared in some districts."[20]

Available evidence reveals that the early proponents of political decentralization of schools were overly optimistic regarding its positive educational impact. Reading scores of the city's pupils, as measured by the California Achievement Test, fell sharply during the late 1960s and early 1970s, but commenced to rise as the school decentralization system became more firmly established. In 1985, reading test scores rose from 55.5 percent of the national average to 56.8 percent.[21] The aggregate reading score masks sharp differences between the scores of pupils in the various community school districts. The highest score—84.0 percent—was achieved by students of the generally middle-class District 26 in Queens. The lowest score—36.0 percent—was recorded in low-income, minority District 6 in Manhattan.

Scores on the national standardized mathematics test in 1984 revealed the same pattern with the highest scores—84.4 and 79.0 percent—achieved in middle-class districts in Queens and Staten Island—and the lowest scores—46.6 and 47.6 percent—recorded in low-income minority districts in Manhattan and the Bronx.[22] All but three of the community school districts scored higher on the test in comparison with scores on the 1983 test.

Experts studying reading scores are unable to determine the impact of school decentralization because of the presence of other factors, including the city's fiscal crisis and near bankruptcy in 1975 that limited the amount of discretionary funds for schools, the back to basics movement that commenced in the 1970s, and the California Achievement Test being given in only two versions since 1978.

Dr. Kenneth B. Clark, a psychologist and a member of the State Board of Regents, maintained in 1980 "decentralization did not make a damn bit of difference."[23] In the same year, Professor Michael A. Krasner of Queens College concluded "decentralization has failed both politically and educationally," but provided no supporting evidence.[24]

An interesting development has been the growth of black-operated private schools in New York City. While the demand for the political decentralization of the city's school system came primarily from the black community, an increasing number of black parents have taken their children out of the public school system and placed them in private schools.[25] A number of these schools originated as nursery schools and grew into elementary and junior high schools as confidence in the public school system declined among black parents.

The New York Times in 1980 editorially viewed decentralization in more positive terms by referring to experience in the city with a unitary school system.

> Yet the shortcomings of decentralization should not obscure its benefits. The centralized Board of Education's long failure to respond to local needs should not now be forgotten. A succession of teacher strikes, civil rights boycotts, and parent protests had brought the system to the brink of collapse and civil disorder. Decentralization helped defuse the anger and enabled crippled schools to function again. In some districts today, the desire of middle-class parents to tighten academic standards has been heeded. In others, like East Harlem, locally created "magnet" schools have raised the chance that talented children will succeed. And throughout the City, the proportion of minority teachers has been doubled.[26]

Assessed politically, the decentralized school system has been a disappointment in terms of voter participation in school board elections. In part, the blame for the relatively low voter turnout can be placed upon the decision of the state legislature to separate community school board elections from municipal and state elections. Statewide, voter participation in school district special elections tends to be low although slightly higher than the participation rate in New York City. The voting rate is related directly to the socioeconomic status of the population with low status groups having the lowest voter turnout. If held in conjunction with municipal elections where the turnout is approximately 40 percent of the eligible voters, community school board elections undoubtedly would attract a significantly larger number of voters although the number would be lower than those casting ballots in the municipal elections.

Low voter turnout allows an organized group to obtain over-representation. To date, the principal beneficiary of such a turnout has been the United Federation of Teachers. A number of observers have expressed unhappiness with the Federation's dominance of many community school board elections. Diane M. Morales, a District 3 community school board member, described UFT as "an organization whose primary interest is the welfare and protection of its membership—many times in direct opposition to the safety, well-being, and educational achievement of children."[27]

Holding community school board elections in conjunction with municipal elections will increase the role of political parties; a role that has been growing as the parties increasingly recognize the political importance of the boards. In 1983, Assemblyman Melvin H. Miller stated "school boards have a lot of power, that in essence they are hidden governments."[28]

No survey of public opinion relative to the community school system has been undertaken, but a survey of principals in elementary and junior high schools in 1980 revealed that 52 percent favored recentralizing the system under the City Board of Education and an additional 7 percent would recentralize the community school districts into five borough systems.[29] Nevertheless, there has been no public agitation for recentralization of the community school districts, and the state legislature in 1983 and 1984 failed to act upon a bill—A. 891 and S. 780 —providing for the creation of a temporary state commission to study and make recommendations relative to the effectiveness of the community school system.

New York City Community Boards

Community control activists in the 1960s also demanded the establishment of general purpose neighborhood governments throughout the City of New York. The city's response took the form of a new system of administrative decentralization which was reinforced by a city charter amendment and ratified by the voters in 1975, reorganizing and strengthening the powers of the 59 community boards whose members are appointed by the presidents of the five boroughs. According to the Fainsteins, "the association of community control with racial militancy, especially with black power, was one of the factors which helped to defeat the movement, at least in its more radical form."[30]

Administrative Decentralization

The amalgamation of all local governments within a five-county area by the state legislature in 1898 to form New York City did not prove to be a panacean solution for service delivery problems, and administrative decentralization was relied upon to coordinate the delivery of services on a subcity basis. Although this type of decentralization al-

lows many decisions to be made on a less than citywide basis in unifunctional or multifunctional districts, control remains in the hands of the
regular city government.

Decentralized service delivery has a long history in American
cities, but initially was restricted to the establishment on a neighborhood basis of fire stations, police precincts, certain recreational facilities,
and schools. Subsequently, various departments began to establish administrative districts to expedite the provision of services, and in 1968
the National Commission on Urban Problems (Douglas Commission) advised that the following services could be provided on a district basis:
building and housing code inspection, job recruitment, certain job training programs, several recreational programs, police-community relations programs, collection of certain fees, distribution of food stamps,
public health clinics, Head Start programs, and complaint bureau.[31]

While designed to solve certain problems, the proliferation of districts created another problem. The boundaries of the districts established by the various departments seldom were coterminous and interagency coordination typically was lacking completely or was poor.
Writing with reference to service districts lacking coterminous boundaries, the Task Force on Jurisdiction and Structure of the State Study
Commission for New York City pointed out "the separate agencies
are, in effect, separate single-purpose governments, each going its own
way."[32]

Although the optimal area for service performance varies from
function to function and from subfunction to subfunction, it is highly
desirable to establish coterminous boundaries for the service districts
of all city agencies. Any loss in efficiency and economy resulting from
coterminous boundaries probably would be more than offset by the
benefits flowing from improved communications and coordination of the
activities of the agencies.

Administrative decentralization by regular city departments in
New York City by 1970 resulted in the creation of 23 health districts,
75 police precincts, 58 sanitation districts, 31 school districts, 44 social
service centers, and a large number of recreation areas. The proliferation of districts with noncoterminous boundaries impeded interagency
coordination and confused residents attempting to register complaints
or obtain information.[33] The organizational morass involving a hodge-
podge of district lines was compounded by the creation in the 1960s of
what were viewed as innovative organizations and programs designed
to improve service delivery and citizen communications with the government – antipoverty boards, community health centers, community
corporations, "little city halls," "model cities" advisory boards, multiser-
vice centers, neighborhood conservation bureaus, urban action task

forces, and a community advisory board for each hospital under the jurisdiction of the New York City Health and Hospitals Corporation.

The State Charter Revision Commission for New York City carefully studied the existing system of administrative decentralization and the impact the establishment of coterminal districts would have on the delivery of services. In transmitting its preliminary recommendations the commission wrote:

> The individual New Yorker lives within a jurisdictional maze. Almost none of the political or administrative districts originally designed to serve him covers the same area. The lines delineating the territories served by these districts were drawn long ago, have been revised in piecemeal fashion, and have the net effect of making it more awkward and difficult than it should be for the ordinary citizen to get things done.[34]

The six amendments to the city charter, proposed unanimously by the commission, received the sanction of the electorate in 1975 and became effective in 1977. One of the new sections of the charter provides for the development of coterminous service districts with the exceptions of community school districts and fire department districts, and the linking of these coterminous service districts to reconstituted community boards. The fire department is required to organize its districts to coincide as closely as possible with the community districts.

City agencies were given until January 1, 1980, to reorganize their delivery systems to provide the following services within the community districts: police patrol services, street cleaning and refuse collection services, local parks and recreation areas, and "social services, including community services, community development, and special services for children."[35] The following services are provided either on a community district or multicommunity districts basis depending upon whether each district is large enough for the achievement of economy and efficiency in service provision: housing code enforcement, neighborhood preservation and related housing rehabilitation services, street maintenance and repair, sewer maintenance and repair, and health services other than municipal hospitals.

The city charter stipulates that

> the head of each designated agency shall assign to each such district at least one official with managerial responsibilities involving the exercise of independent judgment in the scheduling, allocation and assignment of personnel and equipment, and the evaluation of the performance or the management and planning of programs. Each such official shall have operating or line authority over agency programs, personnel, and facilities within the local service district.[36]

In addition, each agency is required to prepare annually a list of prior-ities, projected activities, and programs within each community district; report its direct operating expenses within each district to the communi-ty board; and provide each board with current information on agency operations and programs within the district.

Although proposals for the creation of community councils or boards date from 1947, no action was taken on these proposals until 1951 when Manhattan Borough President Robert F. Wagner, Jr. ap-pointed 12 community planning councils with 15 to 20 members. Re-named community planning boards, their original role was to serve as advisory mechanisms to improve citizen input into the city's decision-making process. The 1963 city charter provided for the appointment of community planning boards by each of the five borough presidents and a total of 62 were appointed.[37] In 1969, the charter was amended to change the names of the boards to community boards and enlarge their membership.[38] The amendment also stipulated that all city de-partments and agencies required to hold public hearings must refer mat-ters to the concerned community board.

Each board has up to 50 members appointed by the borough presi-dent for overlapping two-year terms with half of the members appointed from nomination lists submitted by members of the city council repre-senting any part of the district and the two at-large council members representing the borough. City councilmen in each community board district are nonvoting members of the board. In 1975, voters rejected a proposed amendment to the city charter providing for the election of community board members which is responsible for

(a) Preparation of plans for the growth, improvement, and develop-ment of the community district.

(b) Submission of capital and revenue expense budget priorities.

(c) Participation in the planning of individual capital projects fund-ed in the capital budget and review of scopes and designs for projects.

(d) Initial review of all applications of public and private agencies and developers for use of land in the community district.

(e) Assistance to agencies in the preparation of service statements for the community district.

(f) Dissemination of information about city services and programs and the processing of complaints and inquiries of district resi-dents.[39]

Relative to the budget process, each city agency delivering ser-vices annually must transmit to each board a district resource state-ment containing in detail budget and service information, including priorities. The boards are required by the city charter to hold public hearings during the budget process and annually make a formal budget submission to the city. City agencies inform the boards of the reasons why their priority recommendations, if any, have been rejected.

Each community board is authorized by the city charter to appoint a district manager to serve at the pleasure of the board.[40] The manager, in cooperation with 11 city agencies providing services, establishes a district service cabinet to coordinate the delivery of services.[41] A representative of the department of city planning also serves on the cabinet.[42] Since the community school districts were established by the state education law, the city charter could not require these districts to have boundaries coterminous with those of the community boards or that the school districts be represented on the district service cabinets.

The chairman of the community board is an ex officio member and the district manager is the chairman of the cabinet. According to a report issued by the State Charter Revision Commission for New York City:

> The manager will have no authority to give orders to his fellow cabinet members, since most of them will be appointees of the Mayor or the Mayor's commissioners. If he is the sort of person who commands their respect and offers them help and leadership based on his knowledge and understanding of the community and the job they are appointed to do, he should have little difficulty in getting the wishes of the community representatives of the boards considered and the local services unified and improved.[43]

To strengthen relationships between the city government and neighborhoods, Mayor Edward I. Koch on February 8, 1978, issued an executive order creating a community board assistance unit to work with the 59 boards, provide professional assistance to the boards and district managers, and coordinate implementation of the revised city charter.[44] The executive order also established a community liaison unit to maintain contact with community groups – including civic, block, neighborhood, and tenant associations – to ensure that the complaints and problems of these groups receive attention by high-level city officials. The unit also arranges the mayor's monthly "constituent hours" and "town hall" meetings in neighborhoods.

Evaluation

Citizens Committee for New York City, Incorporated recommended that residents evaluate the performance of their community board by asking the following questions:

- Is the board representative of the community?
- Is any ethnic, political, economic, or geographical group substantially over or under represented relative to its numbers in the community?
- Are the times and locations of board meetings and committee meetings well publicized at least a week in advance?
- Is the meeting room large enough to accommodate the public?
- Are there adequate opportunities for the public to be heard by the board in a public session or other forum?
- Do members listen to the speakers during public session or talk among themselves?
- Are members of the public encouraged to serve on board committees and are they permitted to do meaningful work?
- Are meetings orderly and purposeful – or chaotic and unduly prolonged?
- Are all members given an equal opportunity to speak?
- Are the by-laws adhered to in the conduct of the meeting?
- Do members with a conflict of interest (financial or otherwise) declare that conflict?
- Are issues followed up on, or are votes taken and then forgotten?[45]

With the exceptions of the representation questions, the focus of the above series of inquiries is on the internal operations of individual boards rather than upon the operation of the community board system.

The Representation Issue

Referring to citizen participation organizations in federally sponsored programs, Robert K. Yin et al. wrote in 1973:

> The data suggest that appointment of citizens is the weakest method. The reasons are probably varied.
> Because those appointing tend to choose citizens already known as prominent or outspoken figures, this process seems less likely to help develop skills for participants not previously involved in community activities. The dangers of cooptation are quite great, as individuals friendly to the wishes of management of services are frequently chosen. In either event, less than one-half of the cases using appointment procedures were successful in influencing the program, compared to 60 per cent of those relying on election and self-election.[46]

A 1980 study of six community boards revealed that more than three-fifths of the interviewees did not feel the boards represented their communities and 90 percent of the respondents in the two middle-class areas pointed out there was a lack of minority representations.[47] The poverty area boards in particular were unrepresentative since they tended to be composed of persons who worked in the community.

The public's perceptions that the boards are not fully representative may be responsible for the poor attendance by citizens at board
meetings. A related problem is the poor attendance of certain board
members at board meetings. David Lebenstein, founder and past president of the citywide Coalition of Community Boards, reported that "too
often board members are uninformed and take very narrow local parochial viewpoints."[48] On the positive side, representatives of the boards
constitute the majority of speakers at the public hearings held on the
mayor's executive budget.

The experience of community school board elections suggests that
the use of P.R. would make the community boards more representative
of their respective communities. Election of board members, however,
might aggravate the amount of resentment existing on the part of city
councilmen toward the boards which might produce rivals to the councilmen. Currently, the boards perform some of the roles performed by
councilmen and have replaced to a considerable extent political clubs
as major actors in the governance system. The appointive system has
proved to be a valuable mechanism for the borough presidents to influence local politics and they undoubtedly would resist strongly any
attempt to change the selection system to an elective one.

Regardless of their representativeness, the boards provide citizens
in a neighborhood with problems an additional access point to the city
government.

Complaint Handling

Prior to the establishment of community boards, there was no central
point in a neighborhood where a citizen could register complaints about
city services with the exception of the period in the late 1960s and early
1970s when Mayor John V. Lindsay's "little city halls" were operating.

Only one major study of complaint handling by community boards
has been undertaken. A Columbia University research team conducted
such a study for the mayor's community assistance unit and the city
council president's office by visiting the offices of 16 boards and survey-
ing 33 additional boards by telephone.[49] Major findings included:

- Nearly 50 percent of the boards received between 500–1,500 complaints
  per year. The average is 1,252;
- The more complaints received, the greater the percentage of complaints
  that get recorded;
- 80 percent keep a log book to record complaints;
- 30 percent use a formal system to track the status of a complaint in an
  agency;
- 50 percent contact the complainants to tell them what is happening;

- The most common problems, and emergencies are *less* likely than other situations to be recorded;
- Boards *estimated* that an average of 73 percent of all complaints get resolved;
- DGS, Buildings, and Traffic were rated the least responsive agencies by board staff;
- Queens, Brooklyn, and Staten Island received the most complaints;
- Resolution time for complaints did not vary by borough, except for potholes . . . ;
- Boards are most satisfied with agency action when response is quickest, when a greater proportion of complaints get resolved, and when the staff has less interaction with the agency;
- District managers are fairly satisfied, on the whole, with agency responses to complaints.[50]

The above findings lead to the conclusion that boards in general lack proper complaint handling procedures which undoubtedly contributes to less effective and efficient resolution of complaints.

Monitoring of Services and Budgeting

The city charter assigns community boards a role in the city's expense and capital budgeting processes.

To make meaningful inputs into the budgeting processes, the boards must monitor effectively the performance of city agencies delivering services. Limited evidence on service monitoring suggests that the boards' performance has been mixed. According to David Lebenstein, "at least a third of the community boards fail because they don't know how to fulfill even their most basic responsibilities."[51]

A 1980 study reported that the city approved approximately 57 percent of the capital budget and community development program requests submitted by the boards.[52] Boards were most successful in having their park and playground project requests approved; nearly four-fifths of the requests were funded.

Land Use

One of the potentially most important functions assigned to boards by the city charter is preparation of plans for the development and improvement of their respective districts.

The charter established the uniform land use review procedure (ULURP) which assigns community boards a role in zoning changes, special permits, franchises, and sale or transfer of city-owned property. Upon filing of an application with the requisite city agency for a land use change, the application is transmitted to the concerned community board(s) which has 60 days to conduct a public hearing, obtain community comments by other means, and develop a recommendation for transmittal to the city planning commission or the board of standards and appeals. If the former rejects a recommendation, a written reason for the rejection must be sent to the community board and the board of estimate. The latter has 60 days to make a final decision on the application.

If the board of standards and appeals rejects the recommendation of a community board, the latter has the option within 30 days of appealing to the board of estimate, which is granted 30 days to make a decision on the appeal and an additional 30 days to evaluate the application.

The city planning commission generally has accepted the recommendations of the community boards, and most reversals by the board of estimate of decisions of the board of standards and appeals have been based upon recommendations of the community boards.[53]

The effectiveness of the community boards' performance of their land use role is reflected in the frequent complaints of real estate developers that the boards possess too much power and either delay or scare off development.[54] A 1984 editorial in *The New York Times* reported land use review by community boards "has worked well to insure neighborhood participation in big development projects like Lincoln West, or the sale of air rights over city property. Lately, however, the city has found the procedure can result in dangerous delays when applied to projects like interim emergency shelters and leased jail space."[55]

The District Cabinet and District Manager

While some city councilmen have expressed resentment toward community boards, city agencies delivering services generally have become supportive of the boards.

City departments initially tended to view the boards as threats, but have come to the conclusion that boards can be of assistance to the departments. Commissioners are supportive of neighborhood cabinets in part because they reduce the number of complaints and other matters being referred to the commissioner's offices. The parks department has been very successful in mobilizing the support of community boards for its budget request and, as a result, has received additional city funding. Commissioner of Sanitation Norman Steisel stated, "the boards' request help me to get equipment I might not otherwise get. A lot of district superintendents understand now how they can use the boards to help solve their problems."[56]

As one would anticipate, the various commissioners do not delegate the same amount of discretionary authority to their district superintendents. According to David Lebenstein, the governmental system still is a highly centralized one headed by a strong mayor.[57]

The district cabinets function successfully in their roles as service-coordinating bodies and mechanisms for communications with neighborhood residents. The community boards, through the district manager who serves as chairman of the cabinet, have a direct line for transmitting complaints and inquiries about services to the responsible district superintendents who, in turn, are able to provide answers to citizen complaints and inquiries via central points; that is, the community boards.

The first district managers principally were products of Mayor Lindsay's "little city halls" and had direct ties to the administration. The newer managers tend to be former executive assistants who lack the ties of the first managers. The success of the community boards in monitoring service delivery depends in large measure upon the quality of the district managers and their ability to work cooperatively with personnel of agencies delivering services.

District managers become visible personalities in their communities and are afforded the opportunity of becoming candidates for public office. To date, district managers have been elected members of the city council and the state legislature.

Summary and Conclusions

Our review of the movement for the establishment of a series of neighborhood governments in New York City reveals that the new reformers have been partially successful in achieving their goals. Community school districts, community boards, and administrative decentralization systems have been established. The community school districts may be classified as a type of quasi-neighborhood government in that voters elect neighborhood school boards that have limited control over schools through the junior high level. The decentralized school system has been successful in reducing racial tensions and eliminating civil disorders.

The community boards are not genuine neighborhood governments because board members are not elected by the voters and the powers of the boards are purely advisory. The boards should be viewed as an innovative part of a decentralized system of service delivery and as mechanisms for improving the accountability of service providers to the citizenry.

There clearly is a need in New York City for greater coordination of the activities of community school boards, community boards, and nonprofit service agencies. Community boards in particular appear to be unaware of all the other neighborhood resources that could be mobilized in an attack upon local problems.

The centralization paradigm still holds sway in New York City and is under no threat from the neighborhood government movement. Nevertheless, opportunities for citizen participation have been created by the establishment of the community school boards with their 288 elected members and community boards with their approximately 2,700 appointed citizen members.

Chapter 7 focuses upon the citizen participation institutions and devices examined in Chapters 2 to 6 and offers suggestions to make them more effective while minimizing their potential disruptive effects. The chapter also stresses the importance of open government, ethical behavior by public officers, and a broad state grant of discretionary authority to local governments in terms of increasing the opportunities for meaningful citizen participation.

Notes

1. Lincoln Steffans, *The Shame of the Cities* (New York: McClure-Phillips, 1904); Lincoln Steffans, *Autobiography of Lincoln Steffans* (New York: Harcourt, 1931); and Martin J. Schiesl, *The Politics of Efficiency: Municipal Administration and Reform in America, 1880–1920* (Berkeley: University of California Press, 1977). The oldest and leading municipal reform organization is the National Municipal League established in 1894 and currently known as the Citizens Forum on Self-Government.

2. For details on alternative electoral systems, see Joseph F. Zimmerman, "The Federal Voting Rights Act and Alternative Election Systems," *William & Mary Law Review* 19 (Summer 1978): 621–60. See also *The Short Ballot: A Movement to Simplify Politics* (New York: The National Short Ballot Organization, 1916).

3. Frederick W. Taylor, "Governmental Efficiency," *Bulletin of the Taylor Society* (December 1916): 7–13. See also Dwight Waldo, *The Administrative State* (New York: Ronald Press, 1948), pp. 159–61.

4. One of the strongest attacks upon the municipal reform movement is Edward C. Banfield and James Q. Wilson, *City Politics* (Cambridge: Harvard University Press and the M.I.T. Press, 1963). Nonpartisan elections, an important reform plank, have been criticized by many academics, including Eugene C. Lee in *The Politics of Non-partisanship* (Berkeley: University of California Press, 1960).

5. See Charles M. Tiebout, "A Pure Theory of Local Expenditures," *Journal of Political Economy* 64 (October 1956): 412–24; and Robert L. Bish and Vin-

cent Ostrom, *Understanding Urban Government: Metropolitan Reform Reconsidered* (Washington, D.C.: American Enterprise Institute for Public Policy Research, 1973).

6. Milton Kotler, "Two Essays on the Neighborhood Corporation" in Joint Economic Committee's *Urban America: Goals and Problems* (Washington, D.C.: United States Government Printing Office, 1967), p. 176.

7. Central to the concept of alienation are feelings of political impotence and distrust of public officers.

8. Kotler, "Two Essays on the Neighborhood Corporation," p. 180. Political theorist Benjamin R. Barber in 1984 advanced a similar argument. See his *Strong Democracy: Participatory Politics for a New Age* (Berkeley: University of California Press, 1984), p. 211.

9. *New York Laws of 1961*, Chap. 971.

10. *New York Laws of 1969*, Chap. 330, and *New York Education Law*, Art. 52-A, §§ 2590–2590-n (1981 and 1985 Supp.).

11. Kenneth R. McGrail, "New York City School Decentralization: The Respective Powers of the City Board of Education and the Community School Boards," *Fordham Urban Law Journal* 5 (Winter 1977): 239–78.

12. For further information on the 1973 election, see Joseph F. Zimmerman, "A Proportional Representation System and New York City School Boards," *National Civic Review* 63 (October 1974): 472–74 and 493.

13. Ari L. Goldman, "Poll Finds 70% of Residents Back Ousted Queens Board," *The New York Times*, March 20, 1978, pp. 1 and D8.

14. Ari L. Goldman, "Anker Reinstates the Queens Board He Suspended in the Dispute Over Collection of School Racial Data," *The New York Times*, April 6, 1978, p. 35.

15. William G. Blair, "3 School Boards Seeking an End to Suspensions," *The New York Times*, February 17, 1983, p. B5.

16. *Impact of School Decentralization in New York City on Municipal Decentralization* (New York: State Charter Commission for New York City, June 1974), p. 58.

17. Ibid., pp. 133, 151, 154, 162, 175, 177, and 181.

18. Diane Ravitch, "School Decentralization, and What It has Come To," *The New York Times*, June 30, 1974, sec. 4, p. E5.

19. Ibid.

20. *Toward Action and Change: Decentralization* (New York: Council of Supervisors and Administrators, 1975), pp. 1–5. Charges of malfeasance continue to be made occasionally against community board officials. For an example, see Glenn Fowler, "Facing Charges, District 3 Chief Quits School Job," *The New York Times*, March 13, 1982, p. 27.

21. Larry Rohter, "Reading Scores in City's Schools Hit Their Highest Levels in Years," *The New York Times*, May 14, 1985, pp. 1 and B4.

22. Joyce Purnick, "Math Scores Rise in City's Schools," *The New York Times*, June 4, 1984, p. D18.

23. Edward B. Fiske, "Community-Run Schools Leave Hopes Unfulfilled," *The New York Times*, June 24, 1980, p. 1.

24. Michael A. Krasner, "Two Districts: Another Look at School Decentralization," *New York Affairs* 6 (1980): 68.

25. Thomas A. Johnson, "Black-Run Private Schools Lure Growing Numbers in New York," *The New York Times*, April 5, 1980, pp. 1 and 23.

26. "Decentralized Schools 'Next Decade,'" *The New York Times*, July 1, 1980, p. A18.

27. Diane M. Morales, "A Scapegoat Called School Decentralization," *The New York Times*, July 14, 1980, p. A18. See also Marcia Chambers, "Political Sway of Teachers Union Now Pervasive in Most Districts," *The New York Times*, June 26, 1980, pp. 1 and B6.

28. Frank Lynn, "Political Charges Traded in School Election Fight," *The New York Times*, April 27, 1983, p. B4.

29. Gene I. Maeroff, "Achievement Lagging in Community-Run Schools," *The New York Times*, June 25, 1980, p. B4.

30. Susan S. Fainstein and Norman I. Fainstein, "Local Control as Social Reform: Planning for Big Cities in the Seventies," *Journal of the American Institute of Planners* 42 (July 1976): 277.

31. National Commission on Urban Problems, *Building the American City* (Washington, D.C.: United States Government Printing Office, 1968), p. 351.

32. Task Force on Jurisdiction and Structure, *Re-Structuring the Government of New York City* (New York: State Study Commission for New York City, 1972), p. 26.

33. For a study of complaint handling, see John A. Kaiser, *Citizen Feedback* (New York: Office of the Mayor, April 1971).

34. *Preliminary Recommendations of the State Charter Revision Commission for New York City* (New York: The Commission, June 1975), p. 205.

35. *New York City Charter*, § 2704.

36. Ibid., § 2704 (d). Mayor John V. Lindsay during his second term (1970–74) implemented an experimental program for the decentralized delivery of services by eight departments, established an office of neighborhood government, and created a neighborhood cabinet with representatives from eight departments in each of five community board districts.

37. *New York City Charter*, § 84 (1963).

38. *New York City Local Law 39 of 1969.*

39. *Final Report of the State Charter Revision Commission for New York City* (New York: The Commission, August 21, 1975), p. 13. See also the *Uniform Land Use Review Procedure* (New York: New York City Planning Commission, June 1, 1976).

40. *New York City Charter*, § 2800 (f).

41. Ibid., § 2705.

42. Ibid., § 191 (b) (5).

43. *A Charter Revision Guide for Community Board Members* (New York: State Charter Revision Commission for New York City, 1976), p. 22.

44. *New York City Executive Order No. 6* (February 8, 1978).

45. *Lend a Hand in Your Community Board* (New York: New York City Community Board Assistance Unit, 1980), pp. 6–7.

46. Robert K. Yin, William A. Lucas, Peter L. Szanton, and J. Andrew Spindler, *Citizen Organizations: Increasing Client Control Over Services* (Santa Monica, California: RAND, April 1973), p. 65.

47. INTERFACE, *Special Needs of Community Boards in Poverty Areas: Representing Middle Class, Lower Middle Class, and Poverty Areas* (New York: Community Service Society of New York, 1980), p. 22.

48. David Lebenstein, "A Report Card," *New York Affairs* 6 (1980): 13.

49. *Complaint Handling by New York City Community Boards* (New York: New York City Community Assistance Unit, 1982).

50. Ibid., pp. I–II.

51. Lebenstein, "A Report Card," p. 11.

52. Serre Murphy and Ira Wechter, "The Boards and the Budget Process," *New York Affairs* 6 (1980): 47.

53. Maurice Carroll, "Neighborhoods Gain New Power in Political Shift," *The New York Times*, February 19, 1979, p. B1, and Alan S. Oser, "Zoning Appeals Raise Issue of Jurisdiction of 2 Boards," *The New York Times*, December 22, 1978, p. A30.

54. Leslie Bennetts, "Local Boards Air the Voice of the People," *The New York Times*, May 16, 1983, p. 27.

55. "Ulurp Offers a Voice, Not a Vote," *The New York Times*, June 5, 1984, p. A26.

56. Bennetts, "Local Boards Air the Voice of the People," p. 27.

57. Lebenstein, "A Report Card," p. 10.

Chapter 7

POPULISM REVIVED

The conclusion is inescapable that adequate participatory instruments have been devised to ensure that state and local governments are responsive and accountable to the electorate. Not all of the mechanisms, however, are universally available. The open town meeting is restricted to New England states and Montana is the only other state that specifically authorizes the use of the town meeting. Furthermore, legal and other impediments often prevent the achievement of the full potential of the voter decision-making mechanisms and other participatory devices.

This chapter contains summary comments on the various decision-making instruments described and analyzed in the previous five chapters and offers prescriptions, based upon best practice and/or logic, for increasing the effectiveness of the instruments as we approach the twenty-first century.

Particular stress is placed upon the need for high ethical standards for public officers, open government, and a broad state grant of discretionary authority to local governments as prerequisites for widespread and effective citizen participation.

Regardless of whether the prescriptions are adopted and implemented by state and local governments, a book focusing upon participatory democracy must address and answer the question whether the initiative and its associated referendum are threats to representative government. This question, of course, is not applicable to direct democracy in the form of the open town meeting.

Direct Popular Control

One of the most controversial governance issues is the degree to which the electorate should participate directly in decision making. Political scientists in general have not been strong advocates of citizen law making. Political theorist Benjamin R. Barber in 1984 pointed out:

> The distrust of democracy is in fact as old as political thought itself. Philosophers have always approached popular rule with suspicion, preferring to link justice to reason and harmony in the abstract. The Greeks paid democracy no compliment when they associated it with the disorder of the rabble (ochlocracy).
>
> This bias persisted into the modern political era when, with the rise of actual democratic regimes, it found its way into the doctrines of separation of powers, checks and balances, and limited government.[1]

Proponents of the leadership-feedback model of citizen participation, described in Chapter 1, are adamant in their opposition to direct or pure democracy in the form of the open town meeting, the initiative, and the referendum. To them, citizen participation to a large extent should be symbolic in nature. Jeffersonians, Jacksonians, and populists, on the other hand, argue sovereignty resides in the citizenry who wisely reserve to themselves the authority to make laws directly without intervening institutions and to remove public officers in whom the voters have lost confidence.

The open town meeting, the petition referendum, and the initiative can be employed to enact or repeal laws. The recall, of course, is a special election held for the purpose of removing an officer from office prior to the expiration of his or her term.

The Open Town Meeting

Chapter 2 contains our conclusions that the open town meeting is functioning well in the smaller New England towns and no evidence has been developed suggesting that an elected body of representatives would exercise more sagacity in reaching decisions on issues.

The open town meeting in small towns has met the challenges as a more complex society developed over a period of two and one-half centuries by making refinements in procedures. Abandonments of the open town meeting have been relatively few and have involved towns with large populations adopting charters providing for a city council, representative town meeting, or town council. The logic of the open town meeting accounts for its tenacious hold in numerous towns.

As issues became more complicated and pervasive, it was apparent to townspeople there was a need for preliminary study of issues prior to decision making by voters. In effect, the town meeting developed a legislative committee system performing the research and reference functions typically performed by committees of a legislative body composed of elected representatives. As with the typical legislative assembly, a number of members of the greater assembly – the town meeting – serve on various committees.

The most important role performed by a committee in any legislative system is the provision of guidance. Members become subject-matter experts and through the committee mechanism provide advice to the ultimate decision-making body. A major advantage of the open town meeting is that any citizen may serve on a committee. In contrast, the role played typically in the law-making process by voters elsewhere is limited to voting to help elect one or more representatives. Citizens who do not seek election in a representative local government system generally do not have an opportunity for "officially" making input into the legislative body. Of course, they may supply information to their representatives. The governor or a local chief executive may appoint an advisory committee to provide input, as described in Chapter 1, but opportunities to serve on such committees typically are limited. In the open town meeting, any citizen can volunteer to serve on one or more committees.

The two most important town meeting committees are the finance and planning committees. The former has performed most effectively as a budget preparation unit and its guidance is widely sought by citizens. Similarly, the planning committee plays a crucial role, especially in towns undergoing relatively rapid development.

If the open town meeting lacked an effective system of citizen advisory committees, one would have to conclude the meeting could function successfully only in the very small towns not facing complex issues.

The existence of citizen government in the form of the open town meeting also encourages citizen participation in program execution. New England town government qualifies as citizen government in that numerous town positions are held on a part-time basis by citizens. With the exceptions of towns with a town manager, citizens serving as selectmen are the chief executive of the town and most commonly serve on a part-time basis. However, a number of rapidly growing towns in Connecticut have provided that the "first" selectman's position will be full time because of the volume of business conducted by the town. In effect, the "first" selectman becomes a de facto town manager in contrast to a de jure town manager who is appointed by the board of selectmen and derives his most important powers from the town charter.

We reject Madison's view relative to "the infirmities incident to collective meetings of the people. Ignorance will be the dupe of cunning, and passion the slave of sophistry and declamation."[2] Madison, of course, did not foresee the development of citizen advisory committees – particularly the finance and planning committees – which assist voters in making intelligent decisions at town meetings and help to offset the influence of interest groups.

Voter turnout at town meetings is low compared to the turnout at the early town meetings. As a result, citizens attending the meeting constitute a de facto representative town meeting. Fears have been expressed that such a meeting, while appearing to be democratic, may be masking special interest government. The latent power of the open town meeting should not be underestimated. Citizen apathy in terms of attendance is overcome whenever the de facto meeting makes an unpopular decision. By means of an initiative petition, voters displeased with town meeting decisions may call a special town meeting for the purpose of reconsidering and possibly reversing earlier decisions.

We agree with Barber that "democracy is neither government by the majority nor representative rule: it is citizen self-government."[3] Town meeting decision making is possessed of inherent and maximum legitimacy. Of the various types of direct citizen law making, the New England open town meeting is the principum.

The Referendum

The referendum is based upon the beliefs the judgmental powers of the voters are superior to those of elected representatives on major controversial issues and there are fundamental issues that should be decided only by the electorate. While disagreement exists relative to the quality of decisions made by the electorate as compared to decisions made by elected representatives, there is general agreement that fundamental documents should be adopted or amended only with the consent of the voters. There is no disputing the conclusion of Professor Eugene C. Lee of the University of California, Berkeley, relative to the referendum:

> The belief in the referendum, of course, arises from imperfections of representative institutions. It must be evaluated not against some theoretical model of democracy, but in the declining electoral participation, weakened political parties, television-dominated election

campaigns funded by massive contributions, legislatures dominated by pressure groups – all set in the context of an economic, social, and political environment of frightening complexity.[4]

Nevertheless, mandatory constitutional requirements for referenda on questions of borrowing funds and levying or increasing taxes are undesirable as they have led state and local government officers to develop ingenious ways of circumventing the requirements by issuance of "moral obligation" bonds at higher rates of interest which are exempt from the referendum requirement under the special fund legal doctrine, entrance into lease-purchase agreements for facilities and equipment, creation of exempt special districts which further fractionate the local government system, and reckless borrowing to avoid a mandatory tax referendum.[5] Lease-purchase agreements, of course, have the potential for the incorporation of terms favorable to a state or municipal government, but typically are a more expensive mechanism for financing needed facilities and equipment when employed to avoid a referendum requirement.

Constitutional extra-majority approval requirements for borrowing funds, levying taxes, annexing territory, and other actions are relatively common. If the required approval vote is two-thirds of those casting ballots, a negative vote is equal to two positive votes. Although such requirements do not violate the equal protection of the laws clause of the Fourteenth Amendment to the U.S. Constitution, one can argue the requirements violate the spirit of the "one-person, one-vote" concept by allowing a minority of the voters in a referendum to veto proposed changes in the governance system.[6] This minority may not represent the views of a majority of registered voters.

On the other hand, these requirements help to ensure that affirmative decisions are made by a larger percentage of the registered voters in view of the fact that failure to vote on referenda questions is common. Furthermore, extra-majority approval requirements help to prevent frivolous changes in fundamental documents.

A key question in a representative governmental system is whether all laws enacted by legislative bodies should be conditional ones subject to validation or invalidation by the electorate. The petition or protest referendum originally was designed to reduce the influence of political bosses and interest groups in the state legislature, thereby making the law-enacting body more representative of the public interest. Today, special interest groups play major roles in petition referendum campaigns, in part because the U.S. Supreme Court has gutted the states' corrupt practices statutes relative to the application of expenditure limits to corporations, a subject examined in greater detail in Chapter

3. Only an amendment to the U.S. Constitution, an improbable development, would allow states to limit individual or corporate expeditures in referendum campaigns.

The increased corporate involvement in referendum campaigns notwithstanding, we reject the dogma that laws enacted by a legislative body should be immutable unless amended by the body or declared unconstitutional by a court. We are convinced the petition referendum is a desirable device for allowing the electorate to reverse decisions of their elected representatives and will not be employed frequently. In other words, the sovereign corrective must be available as a reserve weapon of the electorate. We recommend, however, adoption of a new type of protest referendum that would allow voters to collect signatures on petitions to suspend a law and afford the legislative body a stated period of time to repeal or amend the law; failure to repeal or amend the law would lead automatically to a referendum on the question of the repeal of the law. A companion section is needed in the constitutional authorization provision to prevent abusive employment of "emergency" preambles to make impossible the employment of the petition referendum. Since it would be extremely difficult to develop noncontroversial criteria for the determination of whether a genuine emergency exists in any given circumstance, it would be preferable to stipulate in the constitutional provision that an "emergency" preamble could be added to a bill only upon receipt of a written recommendation from the governor and approval by a two-thirds vote of all members elected to each house of the state legislature.

Petition fraud apparently has not been a serious problem, but the cost of collecting petition signatures on a statewide basis presents serious problems for small citizen organizations. The larger and/or wealthy interest groups, of course, have a major advantage in terms of signature collection in a large geographical jurisdiction. There is no ready solution to this problem because geographical distribution requirements for signatures on statewide petitions perform an important function in demonstrating that there is general interest in the subject of the petitions throughout the state, and guarantee the expense of a referendum will be avoided if such interest is lacking.

To ensure the fairness of referenda, all proposition questions to be placed upon the ballot should be worded by a nonpartisan or bipartisan panel. Experience has demonstrated that regular election officers have been tempted to frame a referendum question in such a manner as to draw a desired response from the voters. In addition, it is essential to place a limit on the number of referendum questions that may be placed upon a single ballot. Richard S. Childs and Woodrow Wilson in 1909 based the National Short Ballot Organization on the premise that citizens are overburdened and confused by a requirement that all or most offices be filled by election.[7] They argued that most executive branch officers should be appointed by the chief executive who can be held accountable by the voters. Similarly, the electorate will be able to hold a small municipal council elected at-large accountable and act intelligently upon a small number of referenda questions.

While Illinois's limit of three questions may be too restrictive, failure to impose a reasonable limit can lead to a dozen or more issues being decided by a very small minority of the voters. The average voter easily can be overburdened in terms of the number of referred matters and may ignore all but the questions that are most important to him or her, thereby leaving the decisions on the bulk of the questions to be made principally by interest groups and their supporters.

Limited available evidence is inconclusive with respect to the value of voter information pamphlets distributed by state and local governments holding referenda. One study, referred to in Chapter 3, indicated voters relied heavily upon such pamphlets, but a second study in a different state indicated the contrary. It appears that the value of the pamphlets depends in part upon how carefully they are worded, the technical complexity of the issue, and the manner in which the information is presented. If one supports referenda, one also should favor the preparation and distribution of voter information pamphlets as a device for helping the electorate to make informed decisions.

We cannot agree with the conclusion of David Butler and Austin Ranney that referenda "divide the populace into victors and vanquished. They force decisions often before the discussion process has had a chance to work itself out fully. Surely this is a great deficiency."[8] The language employed by Butler and Ranney is too strong and many of the issues referred to the voters are old ones that have been subject to a large amount of discussion. Their point relative to discussion, however, reinforces our conclusion that voter education campaigns are essential for the best working of the referendum device.

Frequent use of the petition referendum would weaken representative government by discouraging innovative individuals from seeking legislative office and encouraging legislative bodies to refer issues to the voters. Fortunately, the petition referendum to date has not had these undesirable effects. Referenda, however, will become more common in the future because of the renewed popularity of the direct initiative in state and local governments where its use is authorized. Furthermore the advisory referendum allows a representative body at any time to benefit from citizen feedback which improves legislative proposals and can produce a double rapport in which each party – the legislative body and the voters – has faith in the other.

The Initiative

The dilatoriness of legislative bodies on certain issues is well known. A voter remedy is the initiative. The indirect form, described in Chapter 4, in essence is a petition for the redress of grievances and possesses the potential for allowing voters to determine issues to be placed upon the legislative agenda while the direct initiative enables the electorate to decide which proposed laws will be placed directly upon the referendum ballot. If a legislative body fails to act upon a proposal, the indirect initiative permits voters to substitute their collective wisdom on the proposal for that of the elected representatives.

In common with the petition referendum, the initiative originally was designed to break the power of special interests, especially private corporations such as railroad companies, in state legislatures. The focal points of the agitation for employment of these two participatory democracy devices were the Midwest and California. Even today, these devices are found principally in the Midwest and western states.

Many of the issues involving the initiative are the same as the ones involving the referendum. We specifically reject the "Pandora Box" argument that authorization of the initiative will produce flagitious results. Nevertheless, care must be exercised to prevent petition fraud and improperly worded questions being placed on the ballot, and to ensure voters are provided with sufficient information to allow them to make sound decisions. Preparation and distribution of complete and impartial information by the concerned government are essential to informed voter decision making. A statewide signature distribution requirement on initiative petitions is desirable to guarantee that a proposal is of interest to voters in more than one geographical area of a state.

During earlier periods when state legislatures met biennially for short sessions, there obviously was a great need for the direct initiative. Today, 47 states hold annual legislative sessions and in many states the legislature meets for a significantly longer period of time. As a consequence, the indirect statutory initiative is preferable to the direct initiative which offers the voters only a binary choice on the resulting referendum ballot. The former type takes advantage of the legislative process that allows for the incorporation, modification, and deletion of language to improve a legislative proposal prior to its enactment as law. Frequent successful employment of the direct statutory initiative, on the other hand, probably would result in a number of technically defective laws being approved. The indirect initiative preserves the role of the legislative body and enhances prospects for perfection of a legislative proposal.

Currently, only the Massachusetts Constitution authorizes the employment of a type of indirect constitutional initiative. If the General Court fails to approve a constitutional amendment proposed by initiative petitions, the proposition will appear on the referendum ballot only if the proposal received the affirmative votes of one-quarter of the members in each of two joint sessions. While the direct constitutional initiative has not been employed frequently, the Massachusetts approach is the preferable one.

Where the indirect and direct statutory and constitutional initiatives are authorized, there should be no restrictions imposed upon the ability of the concerned legislative body to place alternative propositions on the referendum ballot. The voters should be accorded the opportunity of selecting what they perceive to be the superior proposal.

To overcome the objection the initiative does not permit compromises and restricts the voter to cast an affirmative or a negative ballot, the state constitution could be amended to require the state legislature to place a minimum of three alternative propositions on the ballot and authorize the use of preferential voting to determine the proposition approved.

The total number of referred matters placed on the ballot – whether by the legislative body, the petition referendum, or the initiative – should be restricted to prevent voter fatigue and decision making on individual propositions by a minority of the total number of citizens participating in the balloting. If an initiated proposition is defeated by the voters, the proposition should not be eligible for placement on the referendum ballot by the initiative for two years.

Initiated measures generally cannot be repealed or amended by the concerned legislative body or are subject to such action by the legislative body only upon the expiration of a stated period of time. The reason for these restrictions is clear; that is, hostile legislative bodies otherwise could frustrate the public will. Nevertheless, constitutional, statutory, and local charter authorizations for the employment of the initiative by voters should permit amendment of an initiated law by a two-thirds vote of the legislative body or by a majority vote on receipt of an emergency message from the governor or local chief executive outlining the need for amendment(s) to correct technical deficiencies or alleviate unexpected major adverse consequences flowing from an initiated law.

Fortunately, voter-initiated measures generally have not caused serious problems for governments and in some instances have forced legislative bodies to address issues they deliberately had been avoiding. The general property tax is recognized by citizens and officials as an inequitable tax, yet state legislatures typically have not enacted a law providing for a comprehensive reform of the tax and its administration. The availability of the initiative in California and Massachusetts allowed disgruntled voters to enact Propositions 13 and 2½, respectively, limiting the property tax as described in Chapter 4. The initial reaction of many local government officers to the propositions suggested that they would have disastrous consequences for local governments. The worst fears have not materialized, and the state legislatures in these two states have been forced to reexamine the total system of state–local finance and to make necessary adjustments to prevent the most undesirable consequences that could flow from the propositions.

The "pain" of taxation stimulates taxpayers' interest in governmental affairs. The "tax revolt," where the direct initiative is authorized, will continue as the majority of citizens apparently believe they are overtaxed. The withholding income tax is a "silent" type of tax for many workers concerned only with their take-home pay and reduces citizen participation in contrast to the property tax which is a very "visible" tax to most property owners who therefore exhibit greater interest in governmental affairs.

The most disturbing factor associated with the statewide employment of the initiative is the large campaign expenditures of certain interest groups. Unfortunately, there is no effective mechanism for offsetting such expenditures other than the preparation and distribution, by governments and public interest groups, of impartial voter information in the form of pamphlets.

Professor David H. Everson of Sangamon State University concluded that ballot propositions generally do not increase the participation of registered voters, but "that intense and salient issues on the ballot may produce surges in voter involvement and turnout."[9] Professor David B. Magleby of Brigham Young University in 1984 recommended that initiative propositions be decided upon at general elections to promote greater participation by the electorate.[10] While it is reasonable to assume that adoption of his recommendation would increase voter participation relative to initiative propositions, the question must be raised whether there will be an increase in intelligent voting on the proposals if the larger voter participation is the result of partisan contests for office. Voters may devote their attention primarily to electoral competition and devote less time to study the pros and cons of propositions on the ballot.

We recommend that a model constitutional article for the indirect initiative should contain the following provisions: (a) The attorney general and/or community affairs department should be directed to provide petition drafting services to sponsors of initiatives. (b) Upon submission of a certified petition, a conference should be held at which the attorney general or community affairs department explains initiative wording problems, if any, to sponsors and suggests amendments if needed. (c) If a defeated proposition is resubmitted to the voters within two years, sponsors should be required to obtain additional signatures on petitions equal to 2 percent of the votes cast for governor in the last general election in the affected jurisdiction. (d) The state constitution should authorize employment of the initiative for the purpose of placing the question of calling a constitutional convention on the ballot.

The Recall

In a representative system of government the recall should be a last-resort weapon employed by disgruntled voters only when other avenues for removal of voter dissatisfaction have proved to be of no avail. If a public officer is accused of malfeasance, misfeasance, or nonfeasance of duties, or is convicted of a felony, the preferable approach is the removal of the officer through standard procedures authorized by law. If a state executive or judicial officer, for example, has been accused of violating the public's trust, the appropriate body of the state legislature should conduct an investigation and decide whether the officer should be impeached. An alternative would be constitutional or legislative authorization for the governor to investigate charges against a state officer and remove the officer if the charges are substantiated.

The recall possesses the potential for abuse unless the authorizing provision restricts its employment to cases involving malfeasance, misfeasance, or nonfeasance. A restriction of this nature, of course, is not self-administering and the courts would be called upon to determine whether the evidence supports the authorized grounds for employment of the recall. If there are no restrictions upon the use of the recall, it may be employed by the losing candidate in the previous election in a second attempt to gain office or the charges may be the result of a grudge or philosophical differences of opinion on issues. Experience reveals that the dangers of the unrestricted recall are small and are outweighed by its associated advantages.

When employed, one election should be held to determine if an officer should be removed from office and to select a replacement if the officer is removed. Under no circumstance should an officer subject to the recall be allowed to be a candidate to succeed himself in the event of removal. In addition, the vote on the question of recalling an officer should be held in conjunction with a general election if possible to maximize voter turnout and no recall election should be allowed until an officer has served for a minimum of six months.

The recall seldom has been employed on the state level and its frequency of use on the local level has not been great. To a certain extent, the infrequency of its use may be due to its restraining effect upon officers who recognize its existence is a threat to their continuance in office if they step out of line with majority opinion.

A Threat to Representative Government?

Available evidence suggests that voters increasingly will bypass the legislative process in jurisdictions where the direct initiative exists on issues generating intense feelings. Many "liberals" are opposed to the initiative, the petition referendum, and the recall today because these weapons of direct democracy have been employed by "fiscally conservative" groups. The weapons, of course, are available to all groups and successful use of the weapons by one group is an inadequate ground for their abolition. Interestingly, these devices originally were advocated and employed by "liberal" reformers.

While many members of a number of legislative bodies believe they are under attack by voters employing the direct initiative, the petition referendum, and the recall, the distrust of legislative bodies reflected by these popular participatory devices flows in large measure from legislative actions and inaction on important questions. The major issues dealt with by state legislatures and councils of large local governments affect the vital interests of groups which expend huge sums of money to secure election or defeat of individual legislators and their challengers, and the enactment or defeat of bills.

The vastly greater cost of campaigning for public office since the advent of radio and especially television, and the nearly full-time nature of a growing number of state legislatures have increased the dependence of the average legislator upon interest groups for campaign funds in an era when political parties have grown weaker and provide less funding for candidates. The estimated average campaign cost for a seat in the California legislature is approximately $400,000.

If a legislator's campaign is financed to a significant extent by interest groups and the legislator in voting is responsive to the concerns of these groups, investigative reporting will discover the relationship and the media will publicize these developments, thereby engendering public distrust of the legislative process. Compounding the problem for legislative bodies is the occasional case involving the conviction of a legislator for violating the public's trust and accepting graft in various forms.

The current distrust of most legislative bodies by many citizens appears to be similar to the diffidence generated in the mid-nineteenth century by corrupt financing of canals and railroads in several states which led to the adoption of numerous constitutional restrictions being placed upon these bodies with many of the restrictions currently in effect.[11]

Interest group involvement in the state legislative process today differs in significant ways from mid-nineteenth century involvement and most of the resulting constitutional restrictions no longer are fully effective because legislatures have discovered ways of totally or partially circumventing the restrictions.

In part, agitation for employment of the direct initiative, the petition referendum, and the recall stemmed from the same legislative behavior motivating the adoption of constitutional provisions restricting legislative procedures and powers; that is, the appearance of undue corporate influence in state legislatures, especially in the Midwest and California. John E. Murphy, Jr., majority leader of the Massachusetts House of Representatives, in 1984 stated the General Court disregarded demands for reductions in spending and taxation, and added, "we treated them [citizen leaders] very rudely, and we were proud."[12]

Conditions at many state capitols today, compared to the nineteenth century, are different in several respects because of the growth of professional legislative staff, public interest groups, and single interest groups; adoption of more stringent ethical standards and "sunshine" laws (financial disclosure, open meetings, access to public records laws); decline of the major political parties; greater candidate and special interest financing of election campaigns; disappearance of the canal and railroad companies as major lobbying groups; investigative reporting; consumer advocacy by executive branch officers; and other developments.

At the local level, the role performed by municipal research bureaus has been replaced largely by public interest groups that conduct research, publicize their findings, and lobby for approval of their proposals by chief executives and governing bodies.

The uneasiness generated in the minds of many legislators by growing citizen activism has led some legislators and observers of the legislative process to conclude that public decision making by representative bodies is in danger of being replaced by popular decision making. This view is an alarmist one as the use of the direct initiative and the petition referendum has involved only a minute fraction of 1 percent of the decisions made by legislative bodies.

A similar fear has been expressed by Magleby who concluded, after a comprehensive study of the initiative, that "government by initiative could well lead to an immobilized and ineffectual government, two shortcomings the process was designed to correct."[13] Magleby, however, fails to supply evidence to support this view.

Whereas Proposition 13 in California and Proposition 2½ in Massachusetts each had a major impact on the state–local finance system, the impact has not been as disastrous as feared by many opponents and has forced the state legislature to address the entire governmental finance system in a comprehensive manner.

The reader should be aware that initiative drives can be led by legislators, especially by minority party members unable to achieve their goals – including a weakening of the majority party – through the legislative process. In California, Republican members of the Assembly played major roles in the campaign for voter approval of Proposition 24 imposing new rules upon the state legislature, reducing its budget, and restricting the powers of the leader of each house. In Colorado, similar roles were played by Democratic members of the state legislature.

The greatest danger associated with the joint use of the direct initiative and the referendum is their potential employment by numerous single-interest groups concerned only with their individual proposals and failing to understand the need for integrating the proposals into logical and consistent policies for the governmental jurisdiction. In a complex society, compromises (trade-offs) are essential on many issues in order to develop a public policy on each issue which will not contribute to the aggravation of other public problems.

An effective governmental system develops a broad consensus on the solution of major public problems. Popular decison making in the form of the direct initiative and the referendum is incapable of developing such a consensus. This fact leads to the conclusion that the indirect initiative is preferable to the direct initiative. The former in effect can warn a legislative body that there is widespread citizen dissatisfaction with the governing body and voters will make the public policy decisions directly if the elected representatives fail to take satisfactory action on each issue of major concern to the electorate.

In effect, the indirect initiative represents a compromise between advocates of the direct initiative and legislators opposed to the initiative in any form. The indirect initiative also allows the legislative body to examine carefully the citizen-sponsored proposition and to confer with the sponsors in an attempt to reach a satisfactory compromise if legislative leaders are convinced the proposition is in need of modification. Specifically, we reject the supposition that the initiative undermines representative government.

Large City Governance

The dramatic developments in many large cities in the 1960s demonstrated the inability of these cities to be responsive in an effective manner to the needs and desires of certain minority groups. What is needed are city charter provisions attuned to the special environment within which large city governments operate. In particular, the charter should be capable of activating differentiated responses to the problems of cohesive segments of the electorate and the community. The city government, however, must be more than a reactor. The government must reach out to the people, and be accessible to all segments of the community. Furthermore, provisions should be incorporated in the charter to ensure that citizen participation in all forms, including voting, is promoted and public officials are guided by the highest ethical standards in exercising their assigned duties.

A Two-Tier System

A unitary government in a large city will experience great difficulty in ensuring that citizens have ample opportunity to participate in the decision-making process. In fact, the discontent, which emerged in large cities in the 1960s, appears to be attributable in part to the development of a ponderous municipal bureaucracy that slowed down the administrative decision-making process, the unrepresentativeness of city councils and school boards, and the inability of traditional municipal institutions in general to solve the multitudinous problems of citizens, especially poor ones. Residents of disadvantaged neighborhoods often are alienated from the city government that they perceive as being unable and perhaps unwilling to meet their needs. And many minority group members have become convinced they are being short-changed by a closed decision-making process.

Although all editions of the *Model City Charter*, including the current one, provide for concentration of political power in city hall, this prescription has not cured the ills of large cities. Serious consideration should be given to the incorporation in the charter of each large city of provisions for neighborhood government and administrative decentralization.

Neighborhood Government

One can argue that political realities in the closing years of the twentieth century necessitate a new organizational accommodation and a major redistribution of political power and resources to produce new institutions sensitive to subcity issues, restore a sense of community, and meet the needs of neighborhoods by ensuring policies are determined and implemented with neighborhood inputs.

Milton Kotler, a leading advocate of neighborhood government in large cities, suggested that the private, nonprofit neighborhood corporation, chartered by the state and governed by a town meeting, is the most desirable mechanism for forming a new government and increasing public alertness and popular participation in decision making.[14] The neighborhood corporation, Kotler suggested, will develop realistic local programs and achieve genuine accomplishments since residents know their own needs and the corporation will be able to respond quickly to these needs. Kotler cautioned the transfer of authority would require a period of time during which the corporation would solidify its position in the neighborhood and be converted into a public corporation.

Law making by an assemblage of citizens in various neighborhoods of a large city, according to Barber, also will increase opportunities for citizen implementation of policies. He noted in 1984:

> In urban neighborhoods the possibilities are endless: common action could transform trash lots into pocket parks or urban farms; rehabilitate unused store-fronts as community education centers.[15]

A second approach would be to base a two-tier governmental system for large cities upon the metropolitan Toronto model where the upper-tier unit is responsible for areawide functions such as water supply, major roads, and sewage treatment, and lower-tier units are responsible for functions closest to the people such as health and social services.[16] Certain functions—roads are an example—would be the shared responsibility of the two levels. A number of functions could be performed on a wholesale–retail basis. Solid waste could be collected by the lower-tier units and disposed of by the upper-tier unit. Similarly, the upper-tier unit could develop water supplies, but the lower-tier units could distribute the water.

Evidence from metropolitan areas in several nations demonstrates the effectiveness of a two-tier system of local government. We also have evidence of the success of such a two-tier system within a city in the United States. Political decentralization of the New York City school system, mandated by the New York State legislature in 1969 and analyzed in Chapter 6, has defused what had been an explosive situation. Currently, a two-tier system exists with 32 community school boards, elected by proportional representation (P.R.), exercising jurisdiction over public schools from pre-kindergarten through junior high school. Each board hires and establishes the salary of a district superintendent of schools, contracts for repairs and maintenance, determines the curriculum in conformance with city and state standards, recommends school sites, operates social centers and recreational programs, and appoints teacher aides. Each school board consists of nine unsalaried members elected at-large for a two-year term.

The upper-tier unit—New York City Board of Education—is in charge of high schools and special schools not under the jurisdiction of community boards, and is authorized to suspend, remove, or supercede a community school board or remove any of its members. The board also retains extensive financial and personnel powers, including the preparation of the capital budget and the disciplining and licensing of teachers.

Administrative Decentralization

An alternative or supplement to political decentralization is administrative decentralization—division of the city into unifunctional or multifunctional service delivery districts. This type of decentralization long has been employed in cities and is reflected in the location of certain public facilities—fire stations, police precincts, many parks, and schools—on the neighborhood level. In contrast to a neighborhood government, the director of each administrative district reports to a superior in city hall.

Not all administrative decisions can be made on a decentralized basis, but decisions rendered at the neighborhood level reduce the scale of city government in the eyes of citizens and promotes coordination of services on the subcity level.

Our review in Chapter 6 of the formation of coterminous service delivery districts, with the exceptions of community school and fire department districts, in New York City and the linkage of the districts with community boards through the mechanism of neighborhood cabinets indicates that service delivery in general has improved and citizen input into the citywide decision-making system has been facilitated. In time, the boards may be converted from appointed into elected bodies and function as the legislative bodies of genuine neighborhood governments.

Experience in New York City reveals clearly the various problems flowing from a proliferation of service district lacking coterminous boundaries. The lack of coterminology not only impeded interagency coordination, but perhaps more importantly frustrated citizens attempting to obtain information on service delivery or to register complaints. With few exceptions, large cities should require administrative agencies delivering services to have coterminous boundaries.

Whereas the New York City Charter mandates the appointment of community boards by the borough presidents, it would appear to be preferable to allow citizens, by means of petitions or referenda, to determine whether they want such a board in their neighborhood, and the manner of selection and number of board members. The charter should enumerate the major responsibilities of the boards and ensure their inputs into the city's policy-making process by mandating that various city departments and the city council consult the boards prior to taking action directly affecting their neighborhoods. In addition to developing plans for the future growth and improvement of the neighborhood for incorporation in the city's long-range development plan, each board could be directed to submit to the chief executive and the city council priority recommendations for the city's capital and expense budgets, conduct an initial review of all land use applications, contribute to the formulation of neighborhood service delivery plans by city agencies, publicize the availability of city services, receive and investigate complaints relative to city service provision, and monitor the efficiency and the effectiveness of service delivery. In other words, a community board can serve as a two-way communication vehicle between city hall and neighborhood residents by disseminating information from city officials and providing citizen feedback to city proposals and service provision.

While possessing only the right to provide advice to administrative agencies, a board may be able to establish complete rapport with district administrators and its advice may become "informal" citizen control.

Open and Ethical Government

Aristotle stressed the importance of an educated citizenry in the following terms:

> But if the citizens of a state are to judge and to distribute offices according to merit, then they must know each other's characters; where they do not possess this knowledge, both the election to offices and the decisions of lawsuits will go wrong.[17]

Similarly, open government is essential for the full and effective functioning of participatory democracy because of the limited resources possessed by citizens in comparison to the resources of elected and appointed government officers. The purposeful withholding or hiding of most information on governmental operations clearly is unethical and also makes informed citizen participation in government an impossibility. Similarly, citizens may be harmed by other unethical actions of public officers.

Ethical Behavior

Ethical problems are as old as organized society, but often assume a more subtle form in advanced industrial societies. The early laws designed to promote ethical standards in the public service were restricted to the prohibition of conflicts of interest such as a municipal officer entering into a contract with the municipality.

To deal with situations involving the "gray" area between the "black" and "white" areas of conduct, the state constitution and local government charter should mandate the adoption of a code of ethics, including provisions for open meetings and public access to city records, and the establishment of a board of ethics. The latter preferably should include the attorney general or municipal attorney as an ex officio member.

A code of ethics provides a reference framework for municipal personnel, facilitates self-regulation of behavior by providing guidelines relative to acceptable conduct, and increases public confidence in the integrity of public officials and employees. While the function of providing advice to municipal personnel can be performed by either a single official or a board, the latter appears to be preferable in terms of citizen involvement and is the most common form. The major function of the board is to provide advice in response to requests from municipal personnel inquiring whether a proposed action would be ethical. Publication of advisory opinions, with appropriate deletions to preserve the privacy of those making the requests, will in time build up a common law of ethics on a case-by-case basis and provide guidance to other personnel contemplating similar actions.

Whereas conflict-of-interest laws make illegal specified actions by government officers, "sunshine laws" are designed to bring into the open the personal interests of officers, the decision-making process, and official records in the belief that public knowledge of a potential conflict of interest will deter unethical behavior, and information on government officers and operations will help citizens to make intelligent judgments on candidates and issues on election day. Included in "sunshine laws" are requirements pertaining to financial disclosure by government officers, open meetings of governing bodies, and freedom of information.[18]

Financial Disclosure

Financial disclosure laws are related closely to conflict-of-interest laws and codes of ethics for public officers. A mandated disclosure requirement preferably should be restricted to a listing of sources of income and should not include the amounts received from each source. The requirement also might be limited to specified sources of income exceeding a stipulated amount. The required disclosure statement should contain the name and address of each creditor to whom a specified amount is owed, due date of the debt, interest rate, date and original amount of the debt, existing special conditions, and a statement indicating whether the debt is secured or unsecured. Retail installment debt and mortgage debt on a personally occupied home might be exempted from the disclosure requirement.

The disclosure requirement should not apply to most part-time citizen officials in small municipalities who serve without compensation or receive only minor stipends. Service on a nonpaid board or commission represents a sacrifice of time and money. A disclosure requirement might make the sacrifice too great for a number of competent citizens.

Many public officers view a financial disclosure requirement as an invasion of personal privacy and may resign their positions if required to make a detailed financial disclosure. Furthermore, recruitment of officers may be hindered if potential candidates for appointment or election conclude the requirement would necessitate making public information they desire to keep confidential.

To be effective, the financial disclosure statements must be audited periodically to ensure their accuracy. The nature of the audit, obviously, will be influenced by the specific disclosures made in each statement. Should the number of statements be large, a random audit should suffice as a determinant of the accuracy of the filed statements.

Open Meetings

In camera decision making has been common and hinders informed citizen participation in the governance process. To throw light ("sunshine") on the decision-making process and to allow citizens to monitor it, many governments in recent years have enacted open meeting laws mandating that decisions be made at public meetings with specified exceptions where the public interest would be injured by an open decision.

These laws help to ensure that high ethical standards will apply to the decision-making process and *in camera* sessions will be limited to a relatively small number of cases such as acquisition of property, disciplinary action, salary negotiations, or matters that could prejudice a government's position in a law suit.

In adopting an open meeting law, care must be exercised in defining the term "meeting." The Council of State Governments recommends that the term "be defined as the convening of a governing body for which a quorum is required in order to make a decision or to deliberate toward a decision on any matter."[19] In addition, it is essential to define the term "governing body" precisely, require that adequate public notice be given to interested individuals and organizations of the place and time of meetings, and specify the exceptions to the open meeting requirement. Furthermore, complete and accurate records of meetings should be made and maintained as such records allow citizens unable to attend a meeting to examine the proceedings.

Freedom of Information

To what extent should citizens have access to the official records of a
government? There is no simple answer to this question as all governments have a legitimate need to keep certain records confidential to protect individuals and the general public.

A precise dividing line between confidential and public information does not exist, and it is apparent that citizens cannot play a full
role in the governance system if important information is withheld from
them. Since confidentiality can be employed as a shield to hide unethical
actions and information from the citizenry, a mechanism is needed to
resolve disputes regarding the disclosure of official information marked
confidential. The 1977 New York State Legislature addressed this problem by creating a Committee on Public Access to Records charged with
developing guidelines for the release of official information by state
and local government agencies, and providing advice in the case of
disputes.[20]

Ethical problems also are involved in the purposeful delay in providing information in response to requests by citizens. And a conflict
can exist between a freedom of information law and a privacy law. For
example, the federal Privacy Act of 1974 requires executive agencies
to keep confidential personal information, yet the federal Freedom of
Information Act requires agencies to make executive branch records
available for inspection or copying except "to the extent required to prevent a clearly unwarranted invasion of personal privacy. . . . "[21]

Responsibilities of Public Servants

The ethos guiding the behavior of government officers and employees
ideally should be the Roman maxim *Salus Populi Suprema Lex Est*; that
is, "Let the welfare of the people be the supreme law." To implement this
maxim, officers and employees should be guided by the following canons
of equitable treatment of all citizens.

1. *Equal access*: All citizens — regardless of color, creed, economic status,
   ethnicity, or race — should have the same access to officers and services.
2. *Equal consideration*: Officers and employees should consider the requests of all citizens equally.
3. *Equal responsiveness*: Officers and employees should respond equally
   to all groups and citizens petitioning the government.
4. *Equal service provision*: Services should be provided in a nondiscrimi-
   natory manner to all citizens.
5. *Equal appeals treatment*: The administrative appeals system should
   treat all appellants in the same impartial manner.
6. *Equal taxation*: Tax administration must be certain and not arbitrary.
7. *Equal respect for the law*: Officers and employees must show the same

respect for the law that they expect citizens to show. In particular, officers and employees must not engage in *ultra vires* actions. Citizens
typically are not familiar with the laws granting authority to officers
and hence officers often can exceed their authority without challenge
by the citizenry. Such conduct is unethical.

Local Discretionary Authority

The greatest potential for citizen participation exists in local governments because they are responsible for the delivery of the bulk of the
public services and their smaller geographical scale facilitates citizen
involvement. Meaningful citizen participation depends in part upon local
governments possessing reasonably broad discretionary powers.[22]

All legal relationships between a state and its local governments
originally were based upon the *Ultra Vires Rule*, also known as Dillon's
Rule, which denies the existence of inherent powers of local self-gov-
ernance and emphasizes the plenary powers of the state legislature.
Several states in the early decades of the twentieth century commenced
to rely in part upon the *Imperium in Imperio* approach to the division
of legal authority between the two planes of government. This approach
involves the establishment of a federal relationship between a state and
its local governments by strictly dividing authority between the two
planes. In other words, an empire is established within an empire. In
practice, *Imperium in Imperio* has been relatively ineffective in broad-
ening and isolating local government powers from state legislative preemption because courts generally interpret municipal or local affairs
narrowly.

Dissatisfaction with the *Imperium in Imperio* approach induced
the American Municipal Association in 1952 to engage Dean Jefferson
B. Fordham of the University of Pennsylvania Law School to examine
the problems of the legal relationships of a state with its political subdivisions. Dean Fordham in his 1953 report included model constitutional provisions for a devolution of powers approach to granting local
discretionary authority designed to avoid narrow judicial interpretation
of local government powers.[23]

Fordham proposed that the state constitution delegate to each
municipal corporation adopting a charter all powers capable of delegation subject to preemption by general law with the exceptions of the
powers to enact "civil law governing civil relations" and to "define and
provide for the punishment of a felony."

Although the devolution of powers approach is a legislative supremacy approach, devolution of powers in several states has broadened

considerably the discretionary authority of local governments with the exception of Alaska where an unbelievable Alaska Supreme Court decision interpreted the constitutional devolution of powers provision as a type of *Imperium in Imperio.*[24]

In most states, a dual or tripartite system of legal relationships exists between the state and its political subdivisions for two reasons. First, the devolution of powers provisions in the state constitution does not apply to all types of political subdivisions in several states. Second, only the Alaska, Montana, and Pennsylvania constitutions devolve upon local governments all the powers recommended by Dean Fordham, and the Alaska Supreme Court reduced the scope of the constitutional delegation of discretionary authority to political subdivisions. New York State simultaneously employs the three approaches with the result that public officers and citizens generally are uncertain as to the extent of local discretionary authority in many areas of governmental activity.

The only national study of local discretionary authority revealed that most states retain very tight control over the finances and personnel of local governments, grant the broadest authority relative to government structure, and retain reasonably tight control over the exercise of authority in various functional areas by local governments.[25]

Retention of relatively broad powers over political subdivisions makes the state legislature a target for interest groups, seeking to obtain achievement of their goals, which have been frustrated in their quest at the local level. State legislatures have been responsive to many interest groups which bypass local governments and seek enactment of state laws mandating that political subdivisions take certain courses of action. The only national survey of state mandates revealed that most states imposed a substantial number of mandates upon their political subdivisions and New York had mandates in 60 of the surveyed 76 functional areas.[26] A mandate effectively takes a decision away from a local governing body which usually is accessible to citizens and the decision is made on a relatively permanent basis by the less accessible state legislature. In some instances, the decision is taken out of the hands of elected officials entirely. A number of states, for example, have enacted statutes providing for compulsory binding arbitration of impasses between municipal employers and unions representing firemen and policemen, thereby placing the determination of contract provisions beyond the influence of the citizenry.

Citizen participation obviously is more difficult in an era of centralization of political power. The trend to the upward transfer of functional responsibility, whether initiated voluntarily by local governments or mandated by the state legislature, generally has limited opportunities for effective participation by citizens and enlarged opportunities for the exercise of influence by well-funded special interest groups.[27]

Concluding Comments

The recent revival of populism, as evidenced by the more frequent employment of the direct initiative and resulting mandatory referendum, should not obscure the fact that most representative governments have been responsive to the citizenry in general. The number of voter-approved direct initiative propositions has been small and generally has not had a major adverse impact upon the system of law making by representative bodies.

Ideally, the process of establishing public policy should result in the integration of the views of citizens, elected representatives, and bureaucrats. The latter two groups have a special responsibility for promoting informed citizen involvement in the planning, decision making, and programming processes, but must avoid the temptation of engaging in cooptation.

No system of representation is perfect. Law making by elected representatives may foster the illusion that all proposals receive careful scrutiny prior to their approval, amendment, or rejection. While giving the appearance of relative simplicity as a political institution, representative government permits the manipulation of citizens. If elected officers are guided only by the highest ethical standards, citizens will have less need for corrective devices.

A quadrivium of correctives – voting in regular elections, the indirect initiative, the petition referendum, and the recall – should be available on a standby basis as circuit breakers and preferably should be triggered only by gross misrepresentation of the electorate. If triggered, full information in plain English must be made available to all voters. Media experts employed by proponents or opponents of a proposition may bombard the public with simple "jingles" and "slogans." This type of campaign cannot be legislated out of existence because of the guarantee of freedom of speech. Nevertheless, provision of full and accurate information to voters – a formidable task – combined with continuing public education programs can diminish the potential effectiveness of the 30-second media blitz, and permit the more effective enlistment of the vast reserves of talents and energies of citizens in the attack upon public problems.

In our judgment, there need not be an irreconcilable conflict between decision making by elected representatives and decision making directly by the voters. When such conflicts erupt as they periodically will, they can be resolved successfully and we will have conjoint decision making. As the fountain of authority, the electorate will have the instruments allowing it to decide when representative decision making should be replaced by direct democracy.

Notes

1. Benjamin R. Barber, *Strong Democracy: Participatory Politics for a New Age* (Berkeley: University of California Press, 1984), p. 94.

2. James Madison, *The Federalist Papers* (New York: New American Library, 1961), p. 360.

3. Barber, *Strong Democracy*, p. 211.

4. Eugene C. Lee, "The American Experience, 1778-1978." In *The Referendum Device*, ed. Austin Ranney (Washington, D.C.: American Enterprise Institute for Public Policy Research, 1981), pp. 60-61.

5. Jon A. Baer, "Municipal Debt and Tax Limits: Constraints on Home Rule," *National Civic Review* 70 (April 1981): 204-10.

6. *Lance v. Board of Education*, 170 S.E.2d 783 (1969), *Gordon v. Lance*, 91 S.Ct. 1889 (1971), and *Town of Lockport v. Citizens for Community Action at the Local Level*, 423 U.S. 808 (1977).

7. See *The Short Ballot: A Movement to Simplify Politics* (New York: The National Short Ballot Organization, 1916).

8. David Butler and Austin Ranney, eds., *Referendums: A Comparative Study of Practice and Theory* (Washington, D.C.: American Enterprise Institute for Public Policy Research, 1978), p. 226.

9. David H. Everson, "The Effects of Initiatives on Voter Turnout: A Comparative State Analysis," *The Western Political Quarterly* 34 (September 1981): 419.

10. David B. Magleby, *Direct Legislation: Voting on Ballot Propositions in the United States* (Baltimore: Johns Hopkins University Press, 1984), p. 195.

11. For details on New York State constitutional restrictions, see Joseph F. Zimmerman, *The Government and Politics of New York State* (New York: New York University Press, 1981), pp. 113-16.

12. Lucinda Simon, "Representative Democracy Challenged," *State Legislatures* 10 (August 1984): 13.

13. Magleby, *Direct Legislation*, p. 190.

14. Milton Kotler, *Neighborhood Government* (Indianapolis: Bobbs-Merrill, 1969), pp. 44-50 and 82-87.

15. Barber, *Strong Democracy*, p. 210.

16. Joseph F. Zimmerman, "Regional Governance Models: Greater Dublin and Greater London," *National Civic Review* 71 (February 1982): 84-90. Currently the conservative government in the United Kingdom is in the process of abolishing the Labour party-controlled Greater London Council, and a coalition government is restructuring the governance system in the greater Dublin area by dividing Dublin County into three new counties.

17. Benjamin Jowett, trans., *Aristotle's Politics* (New York: Carlton House, n.d.), p. 288.

18. For a more complete examination of these topics, see Joseph F. Zimmerman, "Ethics in Local Government," *Planning and Administration* 9 (Spring 1982): 33–45; and Joseph F. Zimmerman, "Ethics in the Public Service," *State and Local Government Review* 14 (September 1982): 98–106.

19. *Guidelines for State Legislation on Government Ethics and Campaign Financing* (Lexington, Ken.: The Council of State Governments, 1974), p. 4.

20. *New York Laws of 1977*, chap. 933 and *New York Public Officers Law*, §§ 84–90 (McKinney 1985 Supp.).

21. *Freedom of Information Act*, 88 Stat. 1896, 5 U.S.C. 552 (a)(2).

22. For details, see Joseph F. Zimmerman, *State-Local Relations: A Partnership Approach* (New York: Praeger, 1983).

23. Jefferson B. Fordham, *Model Constitutional Provisions for Municipal Home Rule* (Chicago: American Municipal Association, 1953). The Association has been renamed the National League of Cities and is headquartered in Washington, D.C.

24. *Jefferson v. State*, 527 P.2d 37 (1974).

25. Joseph F. Zimmerman, *Measuring Local Discretionary Authority* (Washington, D.C.: United States Advisory Commission on Intergovernmental Relations, 1981), pp. 52–59.

26. Joseph F. Zimmerman, *State Mandating of Local Expenditures* (Washington, D.C.: United States Advisory Commission on Intergovernmental Relations, 1978).

27. Joseph F. Zimmerman, *Pragmatic Federalism: The Reassignment of Functional Responsibility* (Washington, D.C.: United States Advisory Commission on Intergovernmental Relations, 1976).

BIBLIOGRAPHY

Books and Monographs

Achieving the Goals: Plans, Schedules, Priorities Developed by Dallas Area Citizens. Dallas: Goals for Dallas, 1970.

Adams, Herbert B. *The Germanic Origin of New England Towns*. Vol. 1, no. 2. Baltimore: Johns Hopkins University Studies in Historical and Political Science, 1882.

Almond, Gabriel A., and Sidney Verba. *The Civic Culture*. Princeton: Princeton University Press, 1963.

Alternatives for Washington: Pathways to Washington 1985, A Beginning. Citizens' Recommendations for the Future. Olympia, Wash.: Office of Program Planning and Fiscal Management, 1975.

Altshuler, Alan A. *Community Control: The Black Demand for Participation in Large American Cities*. New York: Pegasus, 1970.

Analysis of Elections for Community School Boards. New York: United Parents Association, 1970.

An Analysis of 1974 Ballot Proposals. Denver: Colorado Legislative Council, 1974.

Analysis of Special Voter Turnout Survey Shows Deep-Rooted Problems, Needed Reforms. New York: ABC News Political Unit, 1983.

Anderson, Dewey. *Government Directly by the People*. Stanford: Stanford University Press, 1942.

Austermann, Winnifred M., and Daniel E. Pilcher. *A Legislator's Guide to State Tax and Spending Limits*. Denver: National Conference of State Legislatures, 1979.

Axelrod, Regina S. *The District Manager and Decentralized Service Delivery in New York City*. Garden City, N.Y.: Institute of Suburban Studies, Adelphi University, n.d.

Bachrach, Peter. *The Theory of Democratic Elitism: A Critique*. Boston: Little, Brown, 1967.

Bacon, Edwin M., and Morrill Wyman. *Direct Elections and Law-Making by Popular Vote*. Boston: Houghton Mifflin, 1912.

Ball, Geoffrey H. *Research Needs in Citizen Involvement: Toward More Effective American Communities*. Menlo Park, Calif.: Stanford Research Institute, 1973.

Banfield, Edward C. *The Unheavenly City*. Boston: Little, Brown, 1970.

Banfield, Edward C., and James Q. Wilson. *City Politics*. Cambridge: Harvard University Press and M.I.T. Press, 1963.

Barber, Benjamin R. *Strong Democracy: Participatory Politics for a New Age*. Berkeley: University of California Press, 1984.

Barnett, James D. *The Operation of the Initiative, Referendum, and Recall in Oregon*. New York: Macmillan, 1915.

Barton, Allen H., et al. *Decentralizing City Government: An Evaluation of the New York City District Manager Experiment*. Lexington, Mass.: Lexington Books, 1977.

Bavas, Andrew L. *A National Survey of Citizens' Watchdog Organizations*. Chicago: Center for Urban Studies, University of Illinois, 1976.

Baylies, Francis. *Historical Memoir of the Colony of New Plymouth*. Vol. 1. Boston: Wiggin & Lunt, 1866.

Beard, Charles A. *American Government and Politics*, 7th ed. New York: Macmillan, 1935.

Bebout, John E. *Decentralization and the City Charter*. Lansing: Citizens Research Council of Michigan, August 1971.

Benson, Charles S., and Peter B. Lund. *Neighborhood Distribution of Local Public Services*. Berkeley: Institute of Governmental Studies, University of California, 1969.

Benson, Lee. *The Concept of Jacksonian Democracy*. New York: Atheneum, 1964.

Bentley, Arthur F. *The Process of Government: A Study of Social Pressures*. Chicago: University of Chicago Press, 1908.

Bezpaletz, Reuben D. *The Initiative and Referendum Process in South Dakota*. Pierre: South Dakota Legislative Research Council, 1978.

Bird, Frederick L., and Frances M. Ryan. *The Recall of Public Officers: A Study of the Operation of the Recall in California*. New York: Macmillan, 1930.

Bish, Robert L., and Vincent Ostrom. *Understanding Urban Government: Metropolitan Reform Reconsidered*. Washington, D.C.: American Enterprise Institute for Public Policy Research, 1973.

Blecher, Earl M. *Advocacy Planning for Urban Development*. New York: Praeger, 1971.

Boards of Finance, Chartered Municipalities: Terms of Office and Minority Representation. Hartford: Connecticut Public Expenditure Council, 1982.

Bolton, Geoffrey. *A Handbook for Town Moderators*. 2nd ed. Boston: Massachusetts Federation of Taxpayers Associations, 1954.

Bone, Hugh A. *The Initiative and the Referendum*. 2nd ed. New York: National Municipal League, 1975.

Booth, David A. *Metropolitics: The Nashville Consolidation*. East Lansing: Michigan State University Institute for Community Development and Service, 1963.

Bridenbaugh, Carl. *Cities in the Wilderness*. New York: Ronald Press, 1938.

Browning, Linda. *Citizen Involvement: A Report on Citizen Involvement in Small New England Communities*. Durham: New England Municipal Center, 1979.

Bryce, James. *The American Commonwealth*, 2nd ed. rev. Vol. 1. London: Macmillan, 1891.

Butler, David, and Austin Ranney, eds. *Referendums: A Comparative Study of Practice and Theory*. Washington, D.C.: American Enterprise Institute for Public Policy Research, 1978.

Caldwell, Lynton K., Lynton R. Hayes, and Isabel M. MacWherter. *Citizens and the Environment: Case Studies in Popular Action*. Bloomington: Indiana University Press, 1976.

Chamberlain, Mellen. *A Documentary History of Chelsea: 1624–1824*. Vol. 1. Boston: The Massachusetts Historical Society, 1908.

Chandler, Alfred D. *Local Self-Government*. Brookline, Mass.: Riverdale Press, 1908.

Channing, Edward. *Town and County Government in the English Colonies of North America*. Vol. 10, no. 10. Baltimore: Johns Hopkins University Studies in Historical and Political Science, 1884.

Chapman, Jeffrey I. *Rent Control in Los Angeles: A Response to Proposition 13*. Boston: Intercollegiate Case Clearing House, 1981.

Charter Removal Provisions. Hartford: Connecticut Public Expenditure Council, 1981.

Charter Requirements for Referenda on Bond Issues. Hartford: Connecticut Public Expenditure Council, 1982.

Citizen Action Guide to Energy Conservation. Washington, D.C.: Citizens' Advisory Committee on Environmental Quality, 1973.

Citizen Evaluation of Community Services in Oklahoma. Norman: Bureau of Government Research, University of Oklahoma, 1978.

Citizen Involvement in the Local Budget Process. Washington, D.C.: Center for Community Change, 1977.

Civello, Theresa R. *Funding Neighborhood Programs*. New York: Citizens Committee for New York City, and Community Service Society, n.d.

Clark, Terry N., ed. *Citizen Preferences and Urban Public Policy: Models, Measures, Uses*. Beverly Hills, Calif.: Sage Publications, 1976.

Clark, Terry N., and Lorna C. Ferguson. *City Money: Political Processes, Fiscal Strain, and Retrenchment*. New York: Columbia University Press, 1983.

Cobban, Alfred. *Rousseau and the Modern State*. 2nd ed. London: George Allen & Unwin, 1964.

Cohen, Rick. *Localism: Research Themes on Urban Smallness*. Rensselaerville, N.Y.: The Institute on Man and Science, 1979.

Community Activation in Rural Settings: A Replication Handbook. Boise, Id.: Mountain States Health Corporation, 1980.

Community Administration Within New York City: Home Town in the Big City. New York: Citizens Union Research Foundation, 1962.

Community Boards, Technical Assistance Needs and Special Projects. New York: New York INTERFACE Development Project, 1979.

Community Participation in Public Elementary Schools: A Survey Report. Washington, D.C.: Center for Governmental Studies, 1970.

Community Priorities & Evaluations: Results of the Eighth of a Series of a Continuing Citizen Consultations in Jefferson County, Kentucky. Louisville: Urban Studies Center, University of Louisville, 1977.

Composition of Boards of Education. Hartford: Connecticut Public Expenditure Council, 1982.

Congress Can Improve Our Economy and Preserve Our Nation by Authorizing the Voters at National Referenda to Approve or Reject Specific Bills

Enacted and Submitted by Congress. New York: National Initiative Referendum Association, 1978.

Connecticut's Home Rule Law: An Aid to Charter Commission Members. Hartford: Connecticut Public Expenditure Council, 1983.

The Connecticut Town Meeting. Storrs: Institute of Public Service, The University of Connecticut, 1964.

Connery, Robert H., ed. *Urban Riots: Violence and Social Change.* New York: The Academy of Political Science, 1968.

Cook, Nancy C. *Citizen Participation Issues.* Charlottesville: Mid-Atlantic Center for Community Education, The University of Virginia, 1979.

Cook, Terrence E., and Patrick M. Morgan, eds. *Participatory Democracy.* San Francisco: Canfield Press, 1971.

Cooley, Thomas M. *A Treatise on the Constitutional Limitations Which Rest Upon The Legislative Power of the States of the American Union.* 7th ed. Boston: Little, Brown, 1903.

Corporate Community Involvement. New York: Citizens Forum on Self-Government, n.d.

Crenson, Matthew. *Neighborhood Politics.* Cambridge: Harvard University Press, 1983.

Croly, Herbert. *Progressive Democracy.* New York: Macmillan, 1914.

Cummingham, James V., and Milton Kotler. *Building Neighborhood Organization.* Notre Dame, Ind.: University of Notre Dame Press, 1983.

Dahl, Robert A. *Polyarchy: Participation and Opposition.* New Haven: Yale University Press, 1971.

_____. *A Preface to Democratic Theory.* Chicago: University of Chicago Press, 1956.

_____. *Who Governs?* New Haven: Yale University Press, 1961.

Dahlberg, Jane S. *The New York Bureau of Municipal Research.* New York: New York University Press, 1966.

Decker, Larry E., and Virginia A. Decker, eds. *Administrators' and Policymakers' Views of Community Education.* Charlottesville: Mid-Atlantic Center for Community Education, The University of Virginia, 1977.

Demas, Boulton H. *The School Elections: A Critique of the 1969 New York City School Decentralization.* New York: Institute for Community Studies, Queens College, 1971.

de Tocqueville, Alexis. *Democracy in America.* 3rd American ed. New York: George Adlard, 1839.

De Wolf, Austin. *The Town Meeting: A Manual of Massachusetts Law.* Boston: George B. Reed, 1890.

A Discussion Draft for the Symposium on Decentralizing New York City Government. New York: The Association of the Bar of the City of New York, 1970.

The District Plan and Report: A Pilot Project in Improved Service Delivery for Communities in New York City. New York: The Nova Institute, 1979.

Drake, Francis S. *The Town of Roxbury.* Boston: Municipal Printing Office, 1905.

Drake, Samuel G. *The History and Antiquities of Boston, from Its Settlement in 1630 to the Year 1770.* Boston: Luther Stevens, 1856.

Dutchess County Court Monitors. Poughkeepsie, N.Y.: Dutchess County Court Monitors, 1983.

Easton, David. *A Systems Analysis of Political Life.* New York: John Wiley & Sons, 1965.

Eaton, Allen H. *The Oregon System: The Story of Direct Legislation in Oregon.* A. C. McClure, 1912.

Emerson, Patricia H. *Overview of Citizen Participation.* Seattle: League of Women Voters of Washington, 1976.

The End of the Road: A Citizen's Guide to Transportation Problem Solving. Washington, D.C.: National Wildlife Federation and Environmental Action Foundation, 1977.

Fainstein, Susan S., et al. *Community Leadership, the District Service Cabinets, and the Office of Neighborhood Government.* New York: Bureau of Applied Social Research, Columbia University, 1974.

Fairlie, John A. *Local Government in Counties, Towns, and Villages.* New York: Century, 1906.

Farr, Walter G., Jr., Lance Liebman, and Jeffrey S. Wood. *Decentralizing City Government.* New York: Praeger, 1972.

Fein, Leonard J. *The Ecology of the Public Schools: An Inquiry into Community Control.* Indianapolis: Bobbs-Merrill, 1972.

Fesler, James W. *Area and Administration.* University: University of Alabama Press, 1949.

Final Report: 1981-1982 Citizen Participation Project. New York: Fund for Modern Courts, 1982.

Financial Problems in the Detroit School District. Detroit: Citizens Research Council of Michigan, 1972.

Flanagan, Joan. *The Grass Roots Fund Raising Book: How to Raise Money in Your Community.* Chicago: Swallow Press, 1979.

Flynn, Edward J. *You're the Boss.* New York: Viking Press, 1947.

Ford, Paul L., ed. *The Writings of Thomas Jefferson.* Vol. 4. New York: G. P. Putnam's Sons, 1894.

Fordham, Jefferson B. *Model Constitutional Provisions for Municipal Home Rule.* Chicago: American Municipal Association, 1953.

Fox, Dixon Ryan. *The Decline of Aristocracy in the Politics of New York, 1801-1840.* New York: Harper Torch Book Edition, 1965.

Freeman, Kathleen. *Greek City-States.* New York: W. W. Norton, 1950.

Friedman, Nathalie, and Theresa F. Rogers. *Administrative Decentralization and the Public.* New York: Bureau of Applied Social Research, Columbia University, 1974.

Fuglesten, Harlan. *Voter Turnout in North Dakota: 1952-1982.* Grand Forks: Bureau of Governmental Affairs, The University of North Dakota, n.d.

Funding Needs of New York City's Community Boards. New York: The Nova Institute, 1981.

Gellhorn, Walter. *When Americans Complain: Governmental Grievance Procedures.* Cambridge: Harvard University Press, 1966.

Gittell, Marilyn. *Participants and Participation: A Study of School Policy in New York City.* New York: Center for Urban Education, 1967.

Gittell, Marilyn, et al. *Demonstration for Social Change: An Experiment in Local*

   Control. New York: Institute for Community Studies, Queens College,
      1971.
Gittell, Marilyn, and T. Edward Hollander. *Six Urban School Districts: A Com-
   parative Study of Institutional Response*. New York: Praeger, 1968.
Goals for Dallas: Submitted for Consideration by Dallas Citizens. Dallas: Goals
   for Dallas, 1966.
*Goals for Seattle: The Report of the Seattle 2000 Commission Prepared by the
   Citizens of Seattle and Adopted by the Mayor and the City Council*. Seat-
   tle, Wash.: Seattle 2000 Commission, 1973.
Gould, Lewis L., ed. *The Progressive Era*. Syracuse, N.Y.: Syracuse Universi-
   ty Press, 1974.
Green, F. C. *Jean Jacques Rousseau: A Critical Study of His Life and Writings*.
   London: Cambridge University Press, 1955.
Greenwald, Carol S. *Group Power: Lobbying and Public Policy*. New York:
   Praeger, 1977.
Greiner, John M., and Harry P. Hatry. *Coping with Cutbacks: Initial Agency-
   Level Responses to Massachusetts' Proposition 2½*. Washington, D.C.:
   The Urban Institute Press, 1983.
Guide to Community Board Participation in the Budget Process for Fiscal 1980.
   New York: The Nova Institute, 1980.
Guide for Establishing a Representative Town Meeting. Amherst: Bureau of
   Government Research, The University of Massachusetts, 1957.
*A Guide to Land-Use Decision Making for Community Boards in New York
   City*. New York: Community Service Society of New York, n.d.
Haddad, William F., and G. Douglas Pugh, eds. *Black Economic Development*.
   Englewood Cliffs, N.J.: Prentice-Hall, 1969.
Haller, William, Jr. *The Puritan Town-Planting in New England Colonial De-
   velopment 1630–1660*. New York: Columbia University Press, 1951.
Hallett, George H., Jr. *Proportional Representation: The Key to Democracy*.
   New York: National Municipal League, 1940.
Hallman, Howard W. *Community Control: A Study of Community Corporations
   and Neighborhood Boards*. Washington, D.C.: Washington Center for
   Metropolitan Studies, 1969.
———. *Community Corporations and Neighborhood Control*. Washington, D.C.:
   Center for Governmental Studies, 1970.
———. *Elements of a Local System for the Delivery of Manpower Services*.
   Washington, D.C.: Center for Governmental Studies, 1970.
———. *Neighborhood Control of Public Programs*. New York: Praeger, 1970.
———. *Neighborhoods: Their Place in Urban Life*. Beverly Hills, Calif.: Sage
   Publications, 1984.
———. *The Organization and Operation of Neighborhood Councils: A Practical
   Guide*. New York: Praeger, 1977.
Hamilton, Howard D., and Sylvan H. Cohen. *Policymaking by Plebiscite: School
   Referenda*. Lexington, Mass.: D. C. Heath, 1974.
Hanchey, James R. *Public Involvement in the Corps of Engineers Planning Pro-
   cess*. Fort Belvoir, Va.: United States Army Engineer Institute for Water
   Resources, October 1975.

Haskins, George L. *Law and Authority in Early Massachusetts*. New York: Macmillan, 1960.

Hatry, Harry P., et al. *How Effective are Your Community Services: Procedures for Monitoring the Effectiveness of Municipal Services*. Washington, D.C.: The Urban Institute and International City Management Association, 1977.

Haugen, Rolf N. B., ed. *Report of the Northern New England Assembly on the Ombudsmen: Citizen Protector*. Burlington: Governmental Research Center, The University of Vermont, 1969.

Haynes, George H. *Representation and Suffrage in Massachusetts, 1620–1691*. Baltimore: Johns Hopkins University Studies in Historical and Political Science, 1894.

Hazardous Waste Management: A Guide for Community Involvement in the San Francisco Bay Area. San Francisco: Association of Bay Area Governments, 1983.

Heginbotham, Stanley J. *The Evaluation of the District Manager Experiment*. New York: Bureau of Applied Social Research, Columbia University, 1974.

Hening, Jeffrey R. *Neighborhood Mobilization: Redevelopment and Response*. New Brunswick: Rutgers University Press, 1982.

Hicks, John D. *The Populist Revolt: A History of the Farmers' Alliance and the People's Party*. Lincoln: The University of Nebraska Press, 1961.

Hill, Dilys M. *The Planning and Management of Human Settlements with Special Emphasis on Participation*. The Hague: International Union of Local Authorities, 1975.

Hofstadter, Richard. *The Age of Reform: From Bryan to F.D.R.* New York: Alfred A. Knopf, 1955.

Homegrown Services: The Neighborhood Opportunity. Minneapolis: The Citizens League, 1983.

Hosmer, James K. *Samuel Adams: The Man of the Town Meeting*. Vol. 2, no. 4. Baltimore: Johns Hopkins University Studies in Historical and Political Science, 1884.

The Human Services Cabinet: An Assessment of the First Two Years of a Demonstration Project in Coordination of Service Delivery at the Community Level. New York: The Nova Institute, 1982.

Hunter, Floyd. *Community Power Structure: A Study of Decisionmakers*. Chapel Hill: The University of North Carolina Press, 1953.

Huntington, Samuel P. *American Politics: The Promise of Disharmony*. Cambridge: Harvard University Press, 1981.

Impact Evaluation Checklists for Land-Use Review. New York: The Trust for Public Land, n.d.

Initiative Legislation in California. Sacramento: State Chamber of Commerce, Agriculture, and Industry, 1950.

Initiatives for Community Self-Help: Efforts to Increase Recognition and Support. New York: The New World Foundation, 1980.

Initiative and Overrule Provisions in Connecticut Town and City Charters. Hartford: Connecticut Public Expenditure Council, 1981.

Initiative and Referendum . . . "NO" for Minnesota. Minneapolis: Citizens League, 1979.

INTERFACE. *Special Needs of Community Boards in Poverty Areas.* New York: Community Service Society of New York, 1980.

Johnson, Richard B., Benjamin A. Trustman, and Charles Y. Wadsworth. *Town Meeting Time.* Boston: Little, Brown, 1962.

Jowett, Benjamin, trans. *Aristotle's Politics.* New York: Carlton House, n.d.

Kales, Albert M. *Unpopular Government in the United States.* Chicago: The University of Chicago Press, 1914.

Kasperson, Roger E., and Breitbart, Myma. *Participation, Decentralization, and Advocacy Planning.* Washington, D.C.: Commission on College Geography, 1974.

Kincaid, John, John R. Todd, and James L. Danielson. *Migration and Public Attitudes in a New Sunbelt City: The Colony, Texas, 1982.* Denton: Department of Political Science, North Texas State University, 1983.

Koblentz, Joel, and Ronald Brumback. *Impact of the District Manager Experiment on Service Delivery.* New York: Bureau of Applied Social Research, Columbia University, 1974.

Kotler, Milton. *Neighborhood Government: The Local Foundations of Political Life.* Indianapolis: Bobbs-Merrill, 1969.

Kweit, Mary G., and Robert W. Kweit. *Implementing Citizen Participation in a Bureaucratic Society: A Contingency Approach.* New York: Praeger, 1981.

Ladd, Everett C., Jr. *Where Have all the Voters Gone? The Fracturing of America's Politial Parties.* New York: W. W. Norton, 1978.

La Noue, George R., and Bruce L. R. Smith. *The Politics of School Decentralization.* Lexington, Mass.: Lexington Books, 1973.

LaPalombara, Joseph G. *The Initiative and Referendum in Oregon: 1938–1948.* Corvallis: Oregon State College Press, 1950.

Latham, Earl. *The Group Basis of Politics.* Ithaca: Cornell University Press, 1952.

Lawmaking by Initiative. Springfield: Illinois Legislative Council, 1982.

The League of Women Voters of Massachusetts. *Massachusetts State Government.* Cambridge: Harvard University Press, 1956.

Lee, Euguene C., ed. *The California Governmental Process: Problems and Issues.* Boston: Little, Brown, 1966.

———. *The Politics of Non-Partisanship.* Berkeley: University of California Press, 1960.

Lee, Eugene C., and Larry L. Berg, eds. *The Challenge of California,* 2nd ed. Boston: Little, Brown, 1976.

Levin, Henry M., ed. *Community Control of Schools.* Washington, D.C.: The Brookings Institution, 1970.

Levin, Murray B. *The Alienated Voter.* New York: Holt, Rinehart and Winston, 1960.

Levine, Naomi. *Schools in Crisis.* New York: Popular Library, 1969.

Lipsky, Michael. *Protest in City Politics: Rent Strikes, Housing, and the Poor.* Chicago: Rand McNally, 1970.

Listening to the Metropolis. New York: Regional Plan Association, 1974.

Lobingier, Charles S. *The People's Law or Popular Participation in Law-Making.* New York: Macmillan, 1909.

Local Charter Provisions Re: Minority Representation on Legislative Body and Shared Legislative Authority. Hartford: Connecticut Public Expenditure Council, 1981.

The Local Initiatives Support Corporation. New York: The Ford Foundation, 1980.

Lopach, James J., and Lauren S. McKinsey. *Handbook of Montana Forms of Local Government.* Missoula: Bureau of Government Research, The University of Montana, 1975.

Lowi, Theodore. *The End of Liberalism.* New York: W. W. Norton, 1969.

Lydenberg, Steven D. *Bankrolling Ballots: The Role of Business in Financing State Ballot Question Campaigns.* New York: Council on Economic Priorities, 1979.

_____. *Bankrolling Ballots Update 1980.* New York: Council on Economic Priorities, 1981.

Lyons, W. E. *The Politics of City–County Merger: The Lexington-Fayette County Experience.* Lexington: The University Press of Kentucky, 1977.

MacLear, Anne Bush. *Early New England Towns: A Comparative Study of Their Development.* New York: Columbia University Press, 1908.

Magleby, David. B. *Direct Legislation: Voting on Ballot Propositions in the United States.* Baltimore: Johns Hopkins University Press, 1984.

Marshall, Patricia, ed. *Citizen Participation Certification for Community Development: A Reader on the Citizen Participation Process.* Washington, D.C.: National Association of Housing and Redevelopment Officials, 1977.

Mastro, Randy M., et al. *Taking the Initiative: Corporate Control of the Referendum Process through Media Spending and What to Do About It.* Washington, D.C.: Media Access Project, 1980.

Matthews, Harry G., and C. Wade Harrison. *Recall and Reform in Arizona, 1973.* Tucson: Institute of Government Research, The University of Arizona, 1973.

Merton, Robert K. *Social Theory and Social Structure.* Rev. ed. New York: Free Press, 1957.

Metcalf, Henry C., and L. Urwick, eds. *Dynamic Administration: The Collected Papers of Mary Parker Follett.* New York: Harper & Brothers, 1940.

Metz, Joseph G. *The Power of People-Power.* Woodbury, N.Y.: Barron's Educational Series, 1972.

Milbrath, Lester W. *Political Participation. How and Why Do People Get Involved in Politics?* Chicago: Rand McNally, 1965.

Model Cities: A Report on Progress. Washington, D.C.: National League of Cities and the United States Conference of Mayors, 1971.

Model City Charter. 6th ed. New York: National Municipal League, 1964.

Mowry, George E. *The California Progressives.* Berkeley: University of California Press, 1951.

Moynihan, Daniel P. *Maximum Feasible Misunderstanding.* New York: Free Press, 1969.

Mudd, John. *Neighborhood Services: Making Big Cities Work*. New Haven: Yale University Press, 1985.

Munro, William B. *The Government of the United States*. 4th ed. New York: Macmillan, 1937.

_____, ed. *The Initiative, Referendum, and Recall*. New York: D. Appleton, 1912.

A Nationwide Experiment to Strengthen and Improve Citizen Involvement in Community Decision-Making and Achievement. Washington, D.C.: Citizen Involvement Network, n.d.

Neighborhood Facilities and Municipal Decentralization: Volume II — Case Studies of Twelve Cities. Washington, D.C.: Center for Government Studies, 1971.

Neighborhood Governance. Columbus: Ohio Commission on Local Government Services, 1974.

Nye, Russel B. *Midwestern Progressive Politics*. East Lansing: Michigan State University Press, 1959.

Oberholtzer, Ellis P. *The Referendum in America*. New York: Charles Scribner's Sons, 1912.

Oliver, Leonard P. *The Art of Citizenship: Public Issue Forums*. Dayton, Ohio: Charles F. Kettering Foundation, 1983.

Padover, Saul. *The Complete Jefferson*. New York: Sloan and Pearch, 1943.

Paige, Lucius R. *History of Cambridge, Massachusetts: 1630–1877*. Boston: H. O. Houghton, 1877.

On Participation: A Casebook on Participation. Santa Monica, Calif.: Law in a Free Society, 1973.

Pateman, Carole. *Participation and Democratic Theory*. New York: Cambridge University Press, 1970.

Pelletier, Lawrence L. *The Initiative and Referendum in Maine*. Brunswick, ME.: Bowdoin College Bulletin, March 1951.

Planning and Zoning. Hartford: Connecticut Public Expenditure Council, 1981.

Pollock, James K. *The Initiative and Referendum in Michigan*. Ann Arbor: The University of Michigan Press, 1940.

Polsby, Nelson W. *Community Power and Political Theory*. New Haven: Yale University Press, 1963.

Powell, Lyman P., ed. *Historic Towns of New England*. New York: G. P. Putnam's Sons, 1889.

Powell, Sumner C. *Puritan Village*. Middletown, Conn.: Wesleyan University Press, 1963.

Proceedings of a Conference on Public Administration and Neighborhood Control. Washington, D.C.: Center for Governmental Studies, 1970.

A Program for Community Districts. New York: Citizens Union and Citizens Housing and Planning Council, 1964.

Proposals for Achieving the Goals: Prepared and Submitted for Consideration by Dallas Citizens. Dallas: Goals for Dallas, 1969.

Proposition 2½: Its Impact on Massachusetts. Cambridge, Mass.: Oelgeschlager, Gunn & Hain, 1983.

Public Administration and Neighborhood Control. Washington, D.C.: Center for Governmental Studies, 1971.

Public Participation in Regional Planning. New York: Regional Plan Association, 1967.

Public–Private Partnership: An Opportunity for Urban Communities. New York: Committee for Economic Development, 1982.

Rabushka, Alvin, and Pauline Ryan. *The Tax Revolt.* Stanford, Calif.: The Hoover Institution Press, 1982.

Ranney, Austin, ed. *The Referendum Device.* Washington, D.C.: American Enterprise Institute for Public Policy Research, 1981.

Roberts, Kenneth L. *Local Government in Maine.* Augusta: Maine Municipal Association, 1979.

Rogers, David, and Norman H. Chung. *110 Livingston Street Revisited: Decentralization in Action.* New York: New York University Press, 1983.

Rousseau, Jean Jacques. *The Social Contract and Discourses.* New York: E. P. Dutton, 1913.

Sabato, Larry. *Virginia Votes 1975–1978.* Charlottesville: Institute of Government, University of Virginia, 1979.

Sabine, George H. *A History of Political Theory.* 3rd ed. New York: Holt, Rinehart and Winston, 1961.

Schattschneider, E. E. *The Semisovereign People: A Realist's View of Democracy in America.* New York: Holt, Rinehart and Winston, 1960.

Schmidt, David D. *Ballot Initiatives: History, Research, and Analysis of Recent Initiative & Referendum Campaigns.* Washington, D.C.: Initiative News Service, 1983.

———. *Initiative Procedures: A Fifty-State Survey.* Washington, D.C.: Initiative News Service, 1983.

Schumpeter, Joseph A. *Capitalism, Socialism, and Democracy.* New York: Harper Brothers, 1942.

Schur, Robert, and Virginia Sherry. *The Neighborhood Housing Movement.* New York: Association of Neighborhood Housing Developers, 1977.

Scorecard Coterminality Project Final Report. New York: Fund for the City of New York, 1980.

Sears, David O., and Jack Citrin. *Tax Revolt: Something for Nothing in California.* Cambridge: Harvard University Press, 1982.

Selznick, Philip. *TVA and the Grass Roots.* Berkeley: The University of California Press, 1949.

Shalala, Donna E. *Neighborhood Governance: Issues and Proposals.* New York: The American Jewish Committee, 1971.

Sharpe, Theodore C. *Recall.* Grand Forks: The University of North Dakota, 1971.

Shipton, Clifford K. *Roger Conant.* Cambridge: Harvard University Press, 1944.

Shockely, John S. *The Initiative Process in Colorado Politics: An Assessment.* Boulder: Bureau of Governmental Research and Service, The University of Colorado, 1980.

Shore, William B. *Public Participation in Regional Planning.* New York: Regional Plan Association, 1967.

The Short Ballot: A Movement to Simplify Politics. New York: The National
    Short Ballot Organization, 1916.

Sly, John F. *Town Government in Massachusetts (1620–1930).* Cambridge: Harvard University Press, 1930.

Smith, Herbert H. *The Citizen's Guide to Zoning.* Chicago: APA Planners Press,
    1983.

Smith, T. V., and Eduard C. Lindeman. *The Democratic Way of Life: An American Interpretation.* New York: The New American Library, 1951.

Southern Community Resource Development Committee. *The People's Choice:
    An Approach for Involving Citizens in Community Decision Making.*
    Blacksburg: Virginia Polytechnic Institute and State University, 1973.

Spiegel, Hans B. C., ed. *Citizen Participation in Urban Development, Vol. I: Concepts and Issues.* Washington, D.C.: Center for Community Studies, NTL
    Institute for Applied Behavior Science, 1968.

Stanwick, Mary E. *Patterns of Participation: A Report of a National Survey
    of Citizen Participation in Educational Decision Making.* Boston: Institute
    for Responsive Education, 1975.

Steffans, Lincoln. *Autobiography of Lincoln Steffans.* New York: Harcourt,
    1931.

_____. *The Shame of the Cities.* New York: McClure-Phillips, 1904.

Stewart, William H., Jr. *Citizen Participation in Public Administration.* University: Bureau of Public Administration, The University of Alabama, 1976.

Stone, Margaret J. *Community Development Block Grants: A Strategy for
    Neighborhood Groups.* Berkeley, Calif.: National Economic Development
    and Law Center, 1978.

Sub-Urbs in the City. Minneapolis: The Citizens League, 1970.

Sundquist, James L., and David W. Davis. *Making Federalism Work.* Washington, D.C.: The Brookings Institution, 1969.

Syed, Anwar. *The Political Theory of American Local Government.* New York:
    Random House, 1966.

Tallian, Laura. *Direct Democracy: An Historical Analysis of the Initiative,
    Referendum, and Recall Process.* Los Angeles: People's Lobby Press, 1977.

Taxation and the Referendum in Michigan. Detroit: Citizens Research Council
    of Michigan, 1980.

Tercentenery of the Landing of the Popham Colony at the Mouth of the Kennebec River, August 29, 1907. Portland: Maine Historical Society, 1907.

Torelle, Ellen, comp. *The Political Philosophy of Robert M. LaFollette.* Madison,
    Wis.: The Robert M. LaFollette Company, 1920.

The Town Manager Plan in Massachusetts. Boston: Massachusetts Federation
    of Taxpayers Associations, 1949.

Tracking Community Services in New York City. New York: The Nova Institute,
    1978.

Truman, David B. *The Governmental Process: Political Interests and Public
    Opinion.* New York: Alfred A. Knopf, 1951.

*Two Hundred and One San Franciscans Express Their Views on the Problems
    Facing the City and What Needs to Be Done.* San Francisco: San Franciscans Seeking Consensus, 1984.

Usher, Roland G. *The Pilgrims and Their History*. New York: Macmillan, 1918.

Vote of the People: A Brief History and Compilation of All Measures Submitted to a Vote of the People of North Dakota from Statehood through 1974. Grand Forks: Bureau of Governmental Affairs, The University of North Dakota, 1975.

Waldo, Dwight. *The Administrative State*. New York: Ronald Press, 1948.

Warren, Donald I. *The Health of American Neighborhoods: A National Report*. Ann Arbor: Community Effectiveness Institute, 1982.

Webb, Kenneth, and Harry P. Hatry. *Obtaining Citizen Feedback: The Application of Citizen Surveys to Local Governments*. Washington, D.C.: The Urban Institute, 1973.

Webber, Edwin W. *Rhode Island Local Government and Administration*. Kingston: Bureau of Government Research, The University of Rhode Island, 1963.

Webster, Clarence M. *Town Meeting Country*. New York: Duell, Sloan, and Pearch, 1945.

Wertenbaker, Thomas Jefferson. *The Puritan Oligarchy: The Founding of American Civilization*. New York: Charles Scribner's Sons, 1947.

Weyl, Walter E. *The New Democracy: An Essay on Certain Political and Economic Tendencies in the United States*. New York: Macmillan, 1912.

White, William Allen. *The Old Order Changeth*. New York: Macmillan, 1910.

Whitmore, William H. *The Massachusetts Civil List for the Colonial and Provincial Periods: 1630-1774*. Albany: J. Munsell, 1870.

Wilbern, York, ed. *Democracy in Urban America*. Bloomington: Indiana University Press, 1969.

Williams, Thomas J. *Citizens' Evaluations of Local Government Services in a Southern Community: Determinants of Support*. Washington, D.C.: National Association of Schools of Public Affairs and Administration, 1977.

Winecup, Louise H. *Initiative and Referendum: An Informational Report*. Austin: Texas Advisory Commission on Intergovernmental Relations, 1979.

Winthrop, John. *The History of New England from 1630 to 1649*. Boston: Little, Brown, 1853.

Wood, Robert C. *Suburbia: Its People and Their Politics*. Boston: Houghton Mifflin, 1959.

Woods, William K. *Creative Local Initiative: All-America Cities 1981-1982*. New York: Citizens Forum on Self-Government, 1983.

Yin, Robert K., Robert W. Hearn, and Paul M. Shapiro. *Neighborhood Government in New York City: A Study of Administrative Decentralization and Service Integration*. Santa Monica, Calif.: RAND, 1973.

Yin, Robert K., William A. Lucas, Peter L. Szanton, and J. Andrew Spindler. *Citizen Organizations: Increasing Client Control over Services*. Santa Monica, Calif.: RAND, 1973.

Yin, Robert K., and Douglas Yates. *Street-Level Governments: Assessing Decentralization and Urban Services*. Lexington, Mass.: Lexington Books, 1975.

Young, James T. *The American Government and Its Work*. 3rd ed. New York: Macmillan, 1936.

You and Your Community Board. New York: League of Women Voters of the City of New York, 1978.

Zimmerman, Joseph F. *The Federated City: Community Control in Large Cities*. New York: St. Martin's Press, 1972.

_____. *The Government and Politics of New York State*. New York: New York University Press, 1981.

_____. *The Massachusetts Town Meeting: A Tenacious Institution*. Albany: Graduate School of Public Affairs, State University of New York at Albany, 1967.

_____. *State-Local Relations: A Partnership Approach*. New York: Praeger, 1983.

Government Reports and Documents

Abrams, Joan et al. *Complaint Handling by New York City Community Boards*. New York: New York City Community Assistance Unit, 1982.

Allocation Formulas: 1981–1982. Brooklyn: New York City Board of Education, 1981.

Arnstein, Sherry R., and Ellen I. Metcalf. *Effective Citizen Participation in Transportation Planning*. Vol. 2: *A Catalog of Techniques*. Washington, D.C.: Federal Highway Administration, 1976.

At Square One: Proceedings of the Conference on Citizen Participation in Government Decisionmaking. Washington, D.C.: Federal Interagency Council on Citizen Participation, 1977.

Building Partnerships. Washington, D.C.: The President's Task Force on Private Sector Initiatives, 1982.

A Charter Revision Guide for Community Board Members. New York: State Charter Revision Commission for New York City, 1976.

Citizen Participation in the American Federal System. Washington, D.C.: United States Advisory Commission on Intergovernmental Relations, 1980.

Citizen Participation in the Community Development Block Grant Program. Washington, D.C.: United States Department of Housing and Urban Development, 1978.

Citizen Participation and the Development of Local Democracy. Strasbourg: Council of Europe, 1978.

Citizen Participation in Model Cities: A HUD Guide. Washington, D.C.: United States Department of Housing and Urban Development, 1968.

Citizen Participation Today: Proceedings of a Staff Conference. Chicago: United States Department of Housing and Urban Development, Region IV, 1968.

Commonwealth of Massachusetts. *The Acts and Resolves of the Province of the Massachusetts Bay*. Vol. 1. Boston: Wright and Potter, 1869.

_____. *The Acts and Resolves of the Province of the Massachusetts Bay*. Vol. 2. Boston: Wright and Potter, 1874.

_____. *The Acts and Resolves of the Province of the Massachusetts Bay*. Vol. 3. Boston: Wright and Potter, 1878.

_____. *Report of the Commission to Complete the Work of Revising and Codifying the Laws Relating to Towns*. Boston: Senate No. 2, 1920.

_____. *Report Submitted by the Legislative Research Council Relative to Town Meetings in Regional Schools*. Boston: House of Representatives No. 3687, 1961.

Community Planning Districts. New York: City Planning Commission, 1968.

The Community Planning Process in San Diego County: A Preliminary Assessment. San Diego: Institute of Public and Urban Affairs, San Diego State University, 1977.

Community Relations in Superfund: A Handbook. Washington, D.C.: United States Environmental Protection Agency, 1983.

Complaint Handling by New York City Community Boards. New York: New York City Community Assistance Unit, 1982.

Congressional Budget Office. *Proposition 13: Its Impact on the Nation's Economy, Federal Revenues, and Federal Expenditures*. Washington, D.C.: United States Government Printing Office, 1978.

Constitution of the Commonwealth of Massachusetts. Boston: Secretary of the Commonwealth, 1981.

Coterminality for New York City. New York: Community Board Assistance Unit, 1979.

Department of the Environment. *Participation in Road Planning: A Consultation Paper*. London: Her Majesty's Stationery Office, 1973.

Dorchester Town Records: Fourth Report of the Record Commissioners of the City of Boston. 2nd ed. Boston: Rockwell and Churchill, 1883.

Education and Citizenship: A Conference Report. Denver: Office of Education, United States Department of Health, Education, and Welfare, 1976.

Executive Order No. 6: Establishment of a Community Board Assistance Unit and a Community Liaison Unit. New York: Office of the Mayor, 1978.

Final Report of the Billerica Charter Commission. Billerica, Mass.: The Town of Billerica, 1978.

Final Report of the Methuen Charter Commission. Methuen, Mass.: The Town of Methuen, 1977.

Final Report of the Task Force on Tenant Participation in the Management of Low-Income Housing. Washington, D.C.: United States Department of Housing and Urban Development, 1978.

Functional Decentralization at Local and Regional Level. Strasbourg: Council of Europe, 1981.

Galbreath, C. B., comp. *Initiative and Referendum: Published for the Constitutional Convention of 1912*. Columbus, Ohio: The F. J. Heer Printing Company, 1912.

Getting Together: A Community Involvement Workbook. Raleigh, N.C.: The Governor's Office of Citizen Affairs, 1978.

Gray, Justin, et al. *Effective Citizen Participation in Transportation Planning*. Vol. 1.: *Community Involvement Processes*. Washington, D.C.: Federal Highway Administration, 1976.

A Guide to Ballot Questions. Boston: Office of the Secretary of the Commonwealth, 1982.

A Guide to Citizen Participation. Boston: Massachusetts Department of Community Affairs, 1976.

Guidelines for the Development and Implementation of Community Involvement Programs. Olympia, Wash.: Washington State Highway Department, 1975.

Guidelines for Regional and Central Boards of Education. Detroit: Board of Education, 1970.

Hanchey, James R. *Public Involvement in the Corps of Engineers Planning Process*. Fort Belvoir, Va.: United States Army Engineer Institute for Water Resources, 1975.

Handbook for Community Board Members. New York: New York City Community Board Assistance Unit, 1982.

The Impact of Coterminal Service Districts on the Delivery of Municipal Services. New York: State Charter Revision Commission for New York City, 1973.

Impact of School Decentralization in New York City on Municipal Decentralization. New York: State Charter Revision Commission for New York City, 1974.

Initiative and Referendum: An Informational Report. Austin: Texas Advisory Commission on Intergovernmental Relations, 1979.

Initiative and Referendum: Its Status in Wisconsin and Experiences in Selected States. Madison: Wisconsin Legislative Reference Bureau, 1976.

Interim Report. Miami: Dade County Charter Review Commission, 1982.

Johnson, Charles. *Nonvoting Americans*. Washington, D.C.: United States Bureau of the Census, 1980.

Kaiser, John A. *Citizen Feedback*. New York: Office of the Mayor, 1971.

Kittredge, Henry C. *Barnstable 1639–1939*. Barnstable, Mass.: Tercentenary Committee, 1939.

Lawmaking by Initiative. Springfield: Illinois Legislative Council, 1982.

Lawrence Johnson and Associates, Incorporated. *Citizen Participation in Community Development: A Catalog of Local Approaches*. Washington, D.C.: United States Department of Housing and Urban Development, 1978.

Lend a Hand in Your Community Board. New York: New York City Community Assistance Unit, 1980.

Letter Report B–210338/B202116, dated September 19, 1983, to Representative F. James Sensenbrenner of Wisconsin from the Comptroller General of the United States. Washington, D.C.: United States General Accounting Office, 1983.

Local Charter Procedures. Boston: Office of the Secretary of the Commonwealth, 1983.

Massachusetts Information for Voters: 1980. Boston: Office of the Secretary of the Commonwealth, 1980.

May, Judith V. *Citizen Participation: A Review of the Literature*. Davis: Institute of Governmental Affairs, University of California, 1971.

McKinsey and Company, Incorporated. *The Impact of Coterminal Service Districts on the Delivery of Municipal Services*. New York: State Charter Revision Commission for New York City, 1973.

A More Efficient and Responsive Municipal Government. New York: State
    Charter Revision Commission for New York City, 1977.
National Commission on Neighborhoods. *People, Building Neighborhoods.*
    Washington, D.C.: United States Government Printing Office, 1979.
National Commission on Urban Problems. *Building the American City.* Wash-
    ington, D.C.: The United States Government Printing Office, 1968.
*Neighborhood Oriented Programs of the Federal Government: A Compendium
    of Funding and Technical Assistance Resources for Neighborhood Organ-
    izations.* Washington, D.C.: United States Department of Housing and
    Urban Development, 1979.
Neighborhoods: A Self-Help Sampler. Washington, D. C.: United States Depart-
    ment of Housing and Urban Development, 1980.
*1984 Information Manual on Campaign Disclosure Provisions of the Political
    Reform Act.* Sacramento: California Fair Political Practices Commission,
    1984.
The Nova Institute. *Sanitation: A Guide to Community Board Participation
    in Planning the Delivery of City Services.* New York: New York City
    Department of Sanitation, 1979.
Participation of the Poor in Community Decision-Making Process. Washington,
    D.C.: United States Office of Economic Opportunity, 1969.
*The Popular Interest versus the Public Interest . . . A Report on the Popular In-
    itiative.* Albany: New York State Senate Research Service, 1979.
Performance of Urban Functions: Local and Areawide. Washington, D.C.: United
    States Advisory Commission on Intergovernmental Relations, 1963.
Planning and Management Consultants Limited. *Public Involvement Tech-
    niques.* Fort Belvoir, Va.: United States Army Engineer Institute for
    Water Resources, 1980.
*Preliminary Recommendations of the State Charter Revision Commission for
    New York City.* New York: The Commission, 1975.
Priscoli, Jerry D. *Why the Federal and Regional Interest in Public Involvement
    in Water Resources Development.* Fort Belvoir, Va.: United States Army
    Engineer Institute for Water Resources, 1978.
Proposition 2½ and Funding Local Pension Costs. Boston: Massachusetts Sen-
    ate Committee on Ways and Means, 1983.
Public Participation in Revenue Sharing. Washington, D.C.: Office of Revenue
    Sharing, United States Department of the Treasury, n.d.
Reapportionment: Initiative Constitutional Amendment and Statute. Sacramen-
    to: California Secretary of State, 1984.
Recall: At Issue in Utah. Salt Lake City: Utah Office of Legislative Research,
    1976.
Reconnection for Learning: A Community School System for New York City.
    New York: Mayor's Advisory Panel on Decentralization of the New York
    City Schools, 1967.
*The Records of the Town of Cambridge (Formerly Newtowne) Massachusetts:
    1630–1703.* Cambridge: Printed by order to the City Council under direc-
    tion of the City Clerk, 1901.
The Removal of State Public Officials from Office. Madison: Wisconsin Legis-
    lative Reference Bureau, 1980.

Report of the Committee to Consider the Subject of a Representative Form of Town Government. Athol, Mass.: May 15, 1963.

Report of the Committee to Study the Representative Form of Town Meeting for Holden. Holden, Mass.: n.d.

Report of the Committee Studying Changes in the Town Government. Framingham, Mass.: March 1965.

Report of the Joint Subcommittee Studying the Initiative and Referendum to the Governor and the General Assembly of Virginia. Richmond: The Senate, 1980. (Published as Senate Document No. 30.)

Report of the Joint Subcommittee Studying the Initiative and Referendum to the Governor and the General Assembly of Virginia. Richmond: The Senate, 1981. (Published as Senate Document No. 4.)

Report of the Legislative Interim Committee on Intergovernmental Affairs. Salem, Ore.: The Committee, December 1976.

A Report of the Record Commissioners of the City of Boston, Containing the Boston Records from 1700 to 1728. Boston: Rockwell and Churchill, 1883.

Report Relative to Recall of Public Officers. Boston: Massachusetts Legislative Research Council, 1979.

Report Relative to Revising Statewide Initiative and Referendum Provisions of the Massachusetts Constitution. Boston: Massachusetts Legislative Research Council, 1975.

Report of the Representative Town Meeting Review Committee. Auburn, Mass.: January 14, 1963.

Report of the Seminar on Citizen Participation in the Planning, Implementation, Management of Human Settlements. Geneva: Economic Commission for Europe, 1980.

Report of the Subcommittee on Initiative and Referendum to the Majority Leader of the New York State Senate. Albany: New York State Senate, 1980.

Report of the Town Convention. Boston: 1804.

San Francisco Voter Information Pamphlet: Special Recall Election April 26, 1983. San Francisco: Registrar of Voters, 1983.

Second Report of the Record Commissioners of the City of Boston. Boston: Rockwell and Churchill, 1877.

Several Rules, Orders, and By-Laws Made and Agreed Upon by the Freeholders and Inhabitants of Boston of the Massachusetts, at their Meeting May 12, and September 22, 1701. Boston: Bartholomew Green, 1702.

Shurtleff, Nathaniel B., ed. *Records of the Governor and Company of the Massachusetts Bay in New England.* Vols. 1 and 2. Boston: From the Press of William White, Printer to the Commonwealth, 1853.

_____. *Records of the Colony of New Plymouth in New England.* Boston: From the Press of William White, Printer to the Commonwealth, 1855.

Spiegel, Hans B. C., et al. *Neighborhood Power and Control Implication for Urban Planning.* Springfield, Va.: Federal Scientific and Technical Clearinghouse, 1968.

Stenberg, Carl W. *The New Grass Roots Government?* Washington, D.C.: United States Advisory Commission on Intergovernmental Relations, 1972.

A Study of Ballot Measures: 1884–1980. Sacramento: Office of the Secretary of
State, 1981.

A Study of Voters & Non-Voters in Travis County. Austin, Texas: Travis County
Voter Registration Division, 1983.

Task Force on Jurisdiction and Structure. *Re-Structuring the Government of
New York City.* New York State Study Commission for New York City,
1972.

Toward Action and Change: Decentralization. New York: Council of Supervisors
and Administrators, 1975.

Violence in the City—An End or a Beginning? Los Angeles: The Governor's
Commission on the Los Angeles Riots, 1965.

*A Volume of Records Relating to the Early History of Boston Containing Boston
Town Records, 1784–1813.* Boston: Municipal Printing Office, 1903.

*A Volume of Records Relating to the Early History of Boston Containing Boston
Town Records, 1796–1813.* Boston: Municipal Printing Office, 1905.

*A Volume of Records Relating to the Early History of Boston Containing Boston
Town Records, 1814–1822.* Boston: Municipal Printing Office, 1906.

Water and Power Resources Service. *Public Involvement Manual.* Washington,
D.C.: United States Department of the Interior, 1980.

Working Together: A Handbook for Citizen Advisory Groups. Salem: Ore.:
Salem Public Schools, 1981.

Zimmerman, Joseph F. *Community Relations and Citizen Involvement in Urban Transportation Planning and Development.* Geneva: Economic Commission for Europe, 1976.

_____. *Measuring Local Discretionary Authority.* Washington, D.C.: United
States Advisory Commission on Intergovernmental Relations, 1981.

_____. *Pragmatic Federalism: The Reassignment of Functional Responsibility.*
Washington, D. C.: United States Advisory Commission on Intergovernmental Relations, 1976.

_____. *State Mandating of Local Expenditures.* United States Advisory Commission on Intergovernmental Relations, 1978.

Articles

Aberbach, Joel D. "Alienation and Political Behavior." *The American Political
Science Review* 63 (March 1969): 86–99.

Aberbach, Joel D., and Jack L. Walker. "The Meaning of Black Power: A Comparison of White and Black Interpretations of a Political Slogan." *The
American Political Science Review* 64 (June 1970): 367–88.

"Abuse of Recall Power Substitutes Popularity for Leadership." *Georgia County
Government Magazine* 31 (May 1979): 50.

Adams, Charles Francis. "The Genesis of the Massachusetts Town, and Development of Town Meeting Government." *Proceedings of the Massachusetts
Historical Society* 7 (January 1892): 172–211.

Adler, Madeleine, and Jewel Bellush. "A Look at District Managers." *New York
Affairs* 6 (1980): 49–53.

Adlow, Elijah. "Lemuel Shaw and Municipal Corporations." *Massachusetts Law Quarterly* 44 (July 1959): 53–98.

Aleshire, Robert A. "Organizing for Neighborhood Management: Drawing on the Federal Experience." *Public Management* 53 (January 1971): 7–9.

———. "Planning and Citizen Participation: Costs, Benefits, and Approaches." *Urban Affairs Quarterly* 5 (June 1970): 369–93.

Alexander, John W., and Morroe Berger. "Is the Town Meeting Finished?" *The American Mercury* (August 1959): 144–51.

Arnaudo, Patricia, and Terry Pell. "Citizen Participation in the Executive Budget Process." *Urban Data Service Reports* 6 (June 1974): 1–13.

Arnstein, Sherry R. "A Ladder of Citizen Participation." *Journal of the American Institute of Planners* 35 (July 1969): 216–24.

Aron, Joan B. "Citizen Participation at Government Expense." *Public Administration Review* 39 (September/October 1979): 477–85.

Aronowitz, Stanley. "The Dialectics of Community Control." *Social Policy* 1 (May/June): 47–51.

"Austin Vote Backs a Nuclear Freeze." *The New York Times*, September 13, 1982, p. A16.

Baer, Jon A. "Municipal Debt and Tax Limits: Constraints on Home Rule." *National Civic Review* 70 (April 1981): 204–10.

Bailey, R. Lance, and Cortus T. Koehler. "Citizens in the Planning Process: How Sacramento County Does It." *National Civic Review* 71 (September 1982): 415–24.

Barrett, Gil. "Recall Act is Being Used to Punish Local Leaders for Differences of Opinion." *Georgia County Government Magazine* 33 (October 1981): 2.

Bartley, Bruce, "Recall Elections Hit High Mark in State." *Eugene Register-Guard* (Oregon), December 9, 1979, p. 25A.

Batie, Sandra S., and Samuel M. Johnson. "Public Participation in Land Use Planning: A Case Study." *Land: Issues and Problems* (Virginia Polytechnic Institute and State University) (June 1977): 1–4.

Bavas, Andrew L. "Citizen's Watchdog Organizations: The Links to Local Government." *National Civic Review* 66 (July 1977): 333–38 and 345.

Bell, Charles. "California's Continuing Budget Conflict." *Comparative State Politics Newsletter* 4 (October 1983): 9–11.

Bennetts, Leslie. "Local Boards Air the Voice of the People." *The New York Times*, May 16, 1981, p. 27.

Bentley, Philip. "'It's Your Money'—A Defense of Proposition Campaigns." In *The Challenge of California: Text and Readings*, edited by Eugene C. Lee, and Larry L. Berg, 2nd ed., pp. 101–4. Boston: Little, Brown, 1976.

"Berkeley Votes to Bar Its Funds from South Africa and Curb Marijuana Enforcement." *The New York Times*, April 19, 1979, p. A17.

Bickford, Jewelle W. "The Road to Coterminality." *New York Affairs* 6 (1981): 36–44.

Bjur, Wesley E., and Gilbert B. Siegel. "Voluntary Citizen Participation in Local Government: Quality, Cost and Commitment." *Midwest Review of Public Administration* 11 (June 1977): 135–49.

Blair, William G. "3 School Boards Seeking an End to Suspensions." *The New York Times*, February 17, 1983, p. B5.

Bone, Hugh A. "The Initiative in Washington: 1914–1974." *Washington Public Policy Notes* 2 (October 1974): 1–6.

Boynton, Nat. "School Budget Revolt: The Niskayuna Story." *The Spotlight* (Delmar, N.Y.), April 21, 1982, pp. 1, 3.

Bradbury, Katharine L., and Helen F. Ladd. "Proposition 2½: Initiative Impacts, Part I." *New England Economic Review* (January/February 1982): 13–24.

———. "Proposition 2½: Initial Impacts, Part II." *New England Economic Review* (March/April 1982): 48–62.

Brady, Patrick J. "Citizens Become Involved in North Tonawanda." *New York State Municipal Bulletin* (July/August 1982): 6–7.

Breckenridge, Adam C. "Nebraska as a Pioneer in the Initiative and Referendum." *Nebraska History* 34 (September 1953): 215–23.

Browne, William P. "Municipal Interest Groups: What Role for Smaller Cities?" *State and Local Government Review* 10 (May 1978): 51–55.

Brudney, Jeffrey L. "Local Coproduction of Services and the Analysis of Municipal Productivity." *Urban Affairs Quarterly* 19 (June 1984): 465–84.

Bryan, Frank M. "Town Meetings – A Relic." *The New York Times*, April 3, 1982, p. 25.

Burke, Edmund M. "Citizen Participation Strategies." *Journal of the American Institute of Planners* 34 (September 1968): 287–94.

"California Court Upsets Legislative Initiative." *Public Administration Times* 8 (January 1, 1985): 6.

Callahan, John, and Donna E. Shalala. "Some Fiscal Dimensions of Three Hypothetical Decentralization Plans." *Education and Urban Society* 2 (November 1969): 40–53.

Calvert, Jerry W. "Linking Citizen Preferences to Legislative Choices: The Role of Political Parties." *State and Local Government Review* 14 (May 1982): 68–74.

Carroll, Maurice. "Community Boards Learn How to Flex More Muscle." *The New York Times*, December 19, 1982, sec. 4, p. E6.

———. "Neighborhoods Gain New Power in Political Shift." *The New York Times*, February 19, 1979, p. B1.

Casstevens, Thomas W. "Reflection on the Initiative Process." In *The California Governmental Process: Problems and Issues*, edited by Eugene C. Lee, pp. 88–91. Boston: Little, Brown, 1966.

Chambers, Marcia. "Political Sway of Teachers Union Now Pervasive in Most Districts." *The New York Times*, June 26, 1980, pp. 1, B6.

Chandler, Alfred D. "Remarks of Alfred D. Chandler." *Massachusetts Law Quarterly* 4 (February 1919): 77–91.

Church, Foster. "Politicians Live Under Recall Threat." *The Oregonian*, September 9, 1979, p. B-1.

"Citizens Units Found Outspent on Issues." *The New York Times*, August 20, 1979, p. A17.

Clark, Terry N. "Modes of Collective Decision-Making: Eight Criteria for Evaluation of Representative, Referenda, Participation and Surveys." In *Citizen Preferences and Urban Public Policy: Models, Measures, Uses*, edited by Terry N. Clark, pp. 13–22. Beverly Hills, Calif.: Sage Publications, 1976.

Clendinen, Dudley. "How Peterborough, N.H., Voted for Nuclear Freeze." *The New York Times*, March 26, 1982, p. B5.

Cleveland, Willis W., and Charles L. Usher. "The Ecology of Referenda Outcomes in Georgia." *State and Local Government Review* 14 (January 1982): 37–42.

Cline, Robert J., and John Shannon. "Municipal Revenue Behavior after Proposition 13." *Intergovernmental Perspective* 8 (Summer 1982): 22–28.

Coduri, Joseph E. "The Recall Election in Rhode Island Local Government." *BRG Newsletter* (University of Rhode Island) 22 (Winter 1981): 1, 4.

Cohen, David K. "The Price of Community Control." *Commentary* 48 (July 1969): 23–32.

Cole, Richard L., and David A. Caputo. "The Public Hearing as an Effective Citizen Participation Mechanism: A Case Study of the General Revenue Sharing Program." *The American Political Science Review* 78 (June 1984): 404–16.

"Courts Intervene in the Initiative Process." *Public Administration Times* 8 (March 1, 1985): 3.

Couturier, Jean J. "Public Involvement in Government Labor Relations." *National Civic Review* 67 (July 1978): 312–16, 348.

Coxson, Harold P. "Impact of Proposition 13 on Labor Relations in the Public Sector: A Private Sector View." *State and Local Government Review* 11 (September 1979): 89–92.

Crouch, Winston W. "Direct Democracy: A Balance Wheel." In *The California Governmental Process: Problems and Issues*, edited by Eugene C. Lee, pp. 80–84. Boston: Little, Brown, 1966.

Cummings, Judith. "Ruling on Transit Stirs Coast Hopes." *The New York Times*, May 8, 1982, p. 8.

_____. "San Francisco Absentees Decide Smoking and Building Measures." *The New York Times*, November 10, 1983, p. D26.

Cunningham, James V. "Citizen Participation in Public Affairs." *Public Administration Review* 32 (October 1972): 589–602.

Cunningham, Richard H. "Every Citizen a Legislator; But It Takes Good Citizens." *Worcester Telegram* (Massachusetts), March 5, 1964, p. 6.

_____. "Forty Massachusetts Communities Now Use the Representative Town Meeting Idea." *Worcester Telegram* (Massachusetts), March 4, 1964, p. 6.

_____. "Representative Town Meetings: The Shrewsbury Experience." *Worcester Telegram* (Massachusetts), March 6, 1959, p. 6.

_____. "What's Gone Wrong with the Old Town Meeting?" *Worcester Telegram* (Massachusetts), March 3, 1959, p. 6.

Cupps, D. Stephen. "Emerging Problems of Citizen Participation." *Public Administration Review* 37 (September/October 1977): 478–87.

Dahl, Robert A. "The City in the Future of Democracy." *The American Political Science Review* 61 (December 1967): 953–70.

Dauer, Manning J., and Mark Sievers. "The Constitutional Initiative: Problems in Florida Politics." *National Civic Review* 74 (July–August 1985): 316–19.

Davies, Lawrence E. "California Faces Ballot Problem." *The New York Times*, July 8, 1962, p. 47.

"Decentralized Schools' Next Decade." *The New York Times*, July 1, 1980, p. A18.

Dixon, Robert G. "Rebuilding the Urban Political System: Some Heresies Concerning Citizen Participation, Community Action, Metros, and One Man-One Vote." *The Georgetown Law Journal* 58 (March-May 1970): 955–86.

Dodge, William R., Jr. "Public Involvement in Local Government in the 1970's." *Management Information Service Report* 6 (January 1974): 1–14.

Dolan, Paul. "Pseudo-Ombudsmen." *National Civic Review* 58 (July 1969): 297–301, 306.

Douglas, Walter E. "A Coalition Approach Works for a New Detroit." *National Civic Review* 73 (March 1984): 118–24, 145.

Eisenberg, Pablo. "Citizen Monitoring: The Community Block Grant Experience." *Journal of Community Action* 1 (September/October 1981): 4–11.

Ellis, Mimi. "An Agency Perspective." *New York Affairs* 6 (1980): 31–32.

Endicott, William. "The Ballot Initiative: Whom Does It Serve?" In *The Challenge of California: Text and Readings*, edited by Eugene C. Lee and Larry L. Berg, 2nd ed., pp. 105–8. Boston: Little, Brown, 1976.

Esser, George H., Jr. "Involving the Citizen in Decision-Making." *Nation's Cities* 6 (May 1968): 11–13.

Everson, David H. "Ballot Initiatives: How Popular are Popular Referendums?" *Legislative Policy* (March/April 1984): 42–46.

———. "The Effects of Initiatives on Voter Turnout: A Comparative State Analysis." *The Western Political Quarterly* 34 (September 1981): 415–25.

"The Fading Town Meeting." *National Civil Review* 54 (October 1965): 464–65, 522.

Fainstein, Susan S., and Norman I. Fainstein. "Local Control as Social Reform: Planning for Big Cities in the Seventies." *Journal of the American Institute of Planners* 42 (July 1976): 275–85.

Ferman, Louis A., ed. "Evaluating the War on Poverty." *The Annals* 385 (September 1969): entire issue.

Fesler, James W. "Approaches to the Understanding of Decentralization." *The Journal of Politics* 27 (August 1965): 536–66.

Finer, Herman. "The Case for Local Self-Government." *Public Administration Review* 3 (Winter 1943): 51–58.

Finifter, Ada W. "Dimensions of Political Alienation." *The American Political Science Review* 64 (June 1970): 389–410.

Fitzgerald, Michael R., and Robert F. Durant. "Citizen Evaluations and Urban Management: Service Delivery in an Era of Protest." *Public Administration Review* 40 (November/December 1980): 585–94.

Fordham, Jefferson B. "Judicial Nullification of a Democratic Political Process – The Rizzo Recall Case." *University of Pennsylvania Law Review* 126 (November 1977): 1–18.

———. "The Utah Recall Proposal." *Utah Law Review* (1976): 29–37.

Fossel, Peter V. "How Best to Run a Small Town." *Yankee* (December 1977): 108–11 and 114–18.

Fowler, Glenn. "Community Board Wrap-Up." *New York Affairs* 6 (1980): 7–9.

———. "Facing Charges, District 3 Chief Quits School Job." *The New York Times*, March 13, 1982, p. 27.

Franklin, Ben A. "Petitions Block a Maryland Law to Combat Bias." *The New York Times*, June 2, 1963, pp. 1, 70.

Frederickson, H. George, and Ralph C. Chandler, eds. "Citizenship and Public Administration." *Public Administration Review* 44 (March 1984): 99–206.

Gable, Richard W. "The Sebastiani Initiative: A California Wine Gone Sour." *National Civic Review* 73 (January 1984): 16–23.

"Generals of the California Taxpayers' Revolt." *The New York Times*, June 8, 1978, p. 25.

Gittell, Marilyn. "Community Control of Education." In *Urban Riots: Violence and Social Change*, edited by Robert H. Connery, pp. 60–71. New York: The Academy of Political Science, 1968.

_____. "Decentralization and Citizen Participation in Education." *Public Administration Review* 32 (October 1972): 670–86.

Glass, James J. "Citizen Participation in Planning: The Relationship Between Objectives and Techniques." *Journal of the American Planning Association* 45 (April 1979): 180–89.

Gold, Steven. "Is the Tax Revolt Dead?" *State Legislatures* 10 (March 1984): 25–27.

Goldman, Ari L. "Anker Reinstates the Queens Board He Suspended in the Dispute Over Collection of School Racial Data." *The New York Times*, April 6, 1978, p. 35.

_____. "Poll Finds 70% of Residents Back Ousted Queens Board." *The New York Times*, March 20, 1978, pp. 1, D8.

Gottehrer, Barry, and Tim Hutchens. "New York City in Crisis: Mayor's Multitudinous Committees." *The New York Herald Tribune*, February 22, 1965, p. 7.

Greenblatt, Robert, and Edward T. Rogowsky. "A Case Study: The Brooklyn Board." *New York Affairs* 6 (1980): 19–24.

Greene, Kenneth R. "Municipal Administrators' Receptivity to Citizens' and Elected Officials' Contacts." *Public Administration Review* 42 (July/August 1982): 346–53.

Greenhouse, Linda. "Voters Can Be For and Against a Proposition One in Yonkers." *The New York Times*, November 4, 1972, p. 19.

Grollman, Judith E. "Decentralization of Municipal Services." *Urban Data Service Reports* 3 (February 1971): entire issue.

Grumet, Barbara R. "Who is 'Due' Process?" *Public Administration Review* 42 (July/August 1982): 321–26.

"Guidelines for Organization and Operation of Community Action Programs." *Management Information Service* (International City Managers' Association) (May 1967): 1–32.

Gunn, Priscilla F. "Initiatives and Referendums: Direct Democracy and Minority Interests." *Urban Law Annual* 22 (1981): 135–59.

Hager, Philip. "Remapping Vote Voided by High Court." *Los Angeles Times*, September 15, 1983, pp. 1, 20.

Hagman, Donald G. "Proposition 13: A Proposition of Conservative Principles." *Tax Foundation's Tax Review* 39 (September 1978): 39–42.

Hallman, Howard W. "Citizens and Budget: Some Local Innovations." *National Civic Review* 69 (April 1980): 191–96.

_____. "Guidelines for Neighborhood Management." *Public Management* 53 (January 1971): 3–5.

"Harrison Moves Toward Village Status." *The New York Times*, June 22, 1974, p. 41.

Hart, David K. "Theories of Government Related to Decentralization and Citizen Participation." *Public Administration Review* 32 (October 1972): 603–21.

Hatfield, Mark O. "Voter Initiative Amendment." *Congressional Record* 125 (February 5, 1979): S1061–65.

Hatry, Harry P., and Louis H. Blair. "Citizens Surveys for Local Governments: A Copout, Manipulative Tool, or a Policy Guidance and Analysis Aid?" In *Citizen Preferences and Urban Public Policy: Models, Measures, Uses*, edited by Terry N. Clark, pp. 129–40. Beverly Hills, Calif.: Sage Publications, 1976.

"Hawaii Court Says Work on Resort Must End." *The New York Times*, October 25, 1982, p. B12.

Healan, Hill. "The Recall Act – Good Intent and Faulty Application." *Georgia County Government Magazine* 33 (February 1982): 103.

Henson, Gerald M. "Education Levels, Participation Rates, and Policy Output Efforts in the Fifty States." *State and Local Government Review* 14 (May 1982): 75–79.

Herbers, John. "Citizens Turn to Private Groups to Administer Local Services." *The New York Times*, May 23, 1983, pp. 1, A15.

_____. "Grass-Roots Groups Go National." *The New York Times*, September 4, 1983, sec 4, pp. 22–23, 42, 46, 48.

Herbert, Adam W. "Management Under Conditions of Decentralization and Citizen Participation." *Public Administration Review* 32 (October 1972): 622–37.

"Hinsdale Won't Vote on Liquor Sales." *Chicago Tribune*, September 2, 1983, sec. 2, p. 2.

Hoff, Ross H. "Mayor, Council, and Electoral Characteristics in Cities under 25,000 Population." *Urban Data Service Report* 13 (December 1981): 1–25.

Holland, James R. "President's Message." *Georgia County Government Magazine* 35 (December 1983): inside front cover.

Howard, Lawrence C. "Decentralization and Citizen Participation in Health Services." *Public Administration Review* 32 (October 1972): 701–17.

Howell, George W., Jr. "Legislation by Direct Democracy: The Mississippi Experience." *Public Administration Survey* 22 (January 1975): 1–8.

Howes, Robert G. "Letter to the Editor." *The Massachusetts Selectman* 19 (October 1960): 34–35.

Hudson, Edward. "Westchester Drums Beat Over Vote on Con Edison." *The New York Times*, October 9, 1979, p. B2.

"Illinois Supreme Court Gives Written Opinion for Placing Legislative Initiative on Ballot." *Election Administration Reports* 2 (January 22, 1981): 5–6.

"The Indirect Initiative." *National Civic Review* 68 (May 1979): 232–34, 243.

Inkeles, Alex. "Participant Citizenship in Six Developing Countries." *The American Political Science Review* 63 (December 1969): 1,120–41.

"INR Campaign Spending Study: Negativism Effective." *The Initiative News Report* 4 (December 2, 1983): 1–5.

"Irate Citizens Exercise Their New Option to Rule by Recall." *Georgia County Government Magazine* 31 (August 1979): 16.

"Jersey High Court Upholds Ballot Bias Ruling." *The New York Times*, October 7, 1981, p. B5.

Johnson, Hiram. "Inaugural Address: 'Power to the People.'" In *The Challenge of California: Text and Readings*, edited by Eugene C. Lee and Larry L. Berg, 2nd ed., pp. 97–98. Boston: Little, Brown, 1976.

Johnson, Thomas A. "Black-Run Private Schools Lure Growing Numbers in New York." *The New York Times*, April 5, 1980, pp. 1, 23.

Johnston, Laurie. "Retirees Volunteer Wealth of Expertise." *The New York Times*, July 7, 1984, pp. 25–26.

Joyce, Michael S. "Voluntarism and Partnership." In *American Federalism: A New Partnership for the Republic*. edited by Robert B. Hawkins, Jr., pp. 193–211. San Francisco: Institute for Contemporary Studies, 1982.

Kaplan, Fred. "Mixed Results for the Freeze." *Boston Sunday Globe*, November 7, 1982, p. A69.

Kato, Kazuaki. "Systems of Citizens' Participation in Japan." *Local Government Review in Japan* 9 (1979): 5–21.

Kaufman, Herbert. "Administrative Decentralization and Political Power." *Public Administration Review* 29 (January/February 1969): 3–15.

Kearney, Tom. "Town Meetings: They Still Work." *Monadnock Observer* (Keene, New Hampshire), March 6, 1982, pp. 2A, 8A–9A.

Kemp, Roger L. "California's Proposition 13: A One-Year Assessment." *State and Local Government Review* 14 (January 1982): 44–47.

Kiser, Larry L. "Toward an Institutional Theory of Citizen Coproduction." *Urban Affairs Quarterly* 19 (June 1984): 485–510.

Kotler, Milton. "Two Essays on the Neighborhood Corporation." In Joint Economic Committee, *Urban America: Goals and Problems*, pp. 170–91. Washington, D.C.: United States Government Printing Office, August 1967.

Krasner, Michael A. "Two Districts: Another Look at School Decentralization." *New York Affairs* 6 (1980): 58–68.

Kristol, Irving. "Decentralization for What?" *The Public Interest* 11 (Spring 1968): 17–25.

Krouse, Richard W. "Polyarchy & Participation: The Changing Democratic Theory of Robert Dahl." *Polity* 14 (Spring 1982): 441–63.

Ladd, Helen F., and Julie B. Wilson. "Who Supports Tax Limitations: Evidence from Massachusetts' Proposition 2½." *Journal of Policy Analysis and Management* 2 (Winter 1983): 256–79.

Langton, Stuart. "Consensus Building/New Roles for Citizens." *National Civic Review* 73 (March 1984): 132–35.

_____. "Training and Education: A New Deal for Citizenship." *National Civic Review* 69 (April 1980): 197–203.

Lawer, Neil. "Boston's Little City Hall Program." *Public Administration Review* 31 (July/August 1971): 456–57.

Lebenstein, David. "A Report Card." *New York Affairs* 6 (1980): 10–18.

Lee, Eugene C. "The American Experience, 1778–1978." In *The Referendum*

Device, edited by Austin Ranney, pp. 46–59. Washington, D.C.: American Enterprise Institute for Public Policy Research, 1981.

_____. "California." In *Referendums: A Comparative Study of Practice and Theory*, edited by David Butler and Austin Ranney, pp. 87–122. Washington, D.C.: American Institute for Public Policy Research, 1978.

_____. "The Initiative and Referendum: How California Has Fared." *National Civic Review* 68 (February 1979): 69–76.

Levine, Marvin J. "The Status of State 'Sunshine Bargaining' Laws." *Labor Law Journal* 31 (November 1980): 709–13.

Levenson, Rosaline. "California Supreme Court Upholds Crime Initiative." *National Civic Review* 72 (February 1983): 105.

_____. "Zoning Initiative Overturned in Cal." *National Civic Review* 72 (September 1983): 442.

Lewis, Anthony. "Tyranny of a Majority." *The New York Times*, June 13, 1977, p. 29.

Lindsey, Robert. "Budget Cuts Begun After Californians Vote to Curb Taxes." *The New York Times*, June 8, 1978, pp. 1, 25.

Lineberry, Robert L., and Edmund P. Fowler. "Reformism and Public Policies in American Cities." *The American Political Science Review* 61 (September 1967): 701–16.

Logalbo, Anthony T. "Responding to Tax Limitations: Finding Alternative Revenues." *Government Finance* 11 (March 1982): 13–19.

Lopach, James J., and Lauren S. McKinsey. "Local Government Reform by Referendum: Lessons from Montana's Voter Review Experience." *State and Local Government Review* 11 (January 1979): 35–39.

_____. "Montana Local Government Review: Reflections on Product and Process." *National Civic Review* 66 (July 1977): 339–45.

Lord, Arthur. "The Representative Town Meeting in Massachusetts." *Massachusetts Law Quarterly* 4 (February 1919): 49–74.

Lynn, Frank. "Political Charges Traded in School Election Fight." *The New York Times*, April 27, 1983, p. B4.

Madison, James. "The Federalist No. 10." In *The Federalist Papers*, pp. 77–84. New York: New American Library, 1961.

Maeroff, Gene I. "Achievement Lagging in Community-Run Schools." *The New York Times*, June 25, 1980, pp. 1, B4.

Magleby, David B. "The Initiative and Referendum in American States." *The University of Virginia News Letter* 56 (February, 1980): 1–4.

"Making Democracy More Interesting." *The New York Times*, November 27, 1978, p. A18.

Mathewson, William C. "Michigan, Five Other States Reject Rollback Proposals," *Michigan Municipal Review* (March 1985): 35.

Mayer, Barton L. "Planning Your Way Through Zoning Amendments." *New Hampshire Town & City* 25 (October 1982): 17–18.

McCaffrey, Jerry, and John H. Bowman. "Participatory Democracy and Budgeting: The Effects of Proposition 13." *Public Administration Review* 38 (November/December 1978): 530–38.

McDonagh, Eileen L., and H. Douglas Price. "Women Suffrage in the Progressive Era: Patterns of Opposition and Support in Referenda Voting, 1910–1918." *The American Political Science Review* 79 (June 1985): 415–35.

McDougall, Gerald S., and Harold Bunce. "Urban Service Distribution: Some Answers to Neglected Issues." *Urban Affairs Quarterly* 19 (March 1984): 355–71.

McGrail, Kenneth R. "New York City School Decentralization: The Respective Powers of the City Board of Education and the Community School Boards." *Fordham Urban Law Journal* 5 (Winter 1977): 239–78.

Merelman, Richard M. "On the Neo-Elitist Critique of Community Power." *The American Political Science Review* 62 (June 1968): 451–60.

"Metropolis Speaks." *Regional Plan News* (August 1974): entire issue.

Milbrath, Lester W. "Evaluating C.P.: Is Participation Worth It All?" *Citizen Participation* 5 (Fall 1983): 3–5, 18.

Miller, S. M., and Martin Rein. "Participation, Poverty, and Administration." *Public Administration Review* 39 (January/February 1969): 15–25.

Miller, Susan. "'Phony' Initiative Propaganda Hit." In *The Challenge of California: Text and Readings*, edited by Eugene C. Lee and Larry L. Berg, 2nd ed., pp. 99–101. Boston: Little, Brown, 1976.

"A Model Voter Registration System." *National Civic Review* 73 (March 1984): 104–17.

Moore, Charles H., and Ray E. Johnston. "School Decentralization and the Politics of Public Education." *Urban Affairs Quarterly* 6 (June 1971): 421–46.

Morales, Diane M. "A Scapegoat Called School Decentralization." *The New York Times*, July 14, 1980, p. A18.

Moynihan, Daniel P. "The New Racialism." *The Atlantic Monthly*, August 1968, pp. 35–40.

Mueller, John E. "Voting on the Propositions: Ballot Patterns and Historical Trends in California." *The American Political Science Review* 63 (December 1969): 1,197–212.

Munro, William B. "Pasadena Uses the Recall." *National Municipal Review* 21 (March 1932): 161–67.

Murphy, Serre, and Ira Wechter. "The Boards and the Budget Process." *New York Affairs* 6 (1980): 45–48.

Myren, Richard A. "Decentralization and Citizen Participation in Criminal Justice Systems." *Public Administration Review* 32 (October 1972): 718–38.

Neal, Arthur G., and Salomon Rettig. "On the Multidimensionality of Alienation." *The American Sociological Review* 32 (February 1967): 54–64.

Netzer, Dick. "The Wrong End of the Stick." *New York Affairs* 6 (1980): 25–28.

Neuberger, Richard L. "The People or Their Representatives?" In *The California Governmental Process: Problems and Issues*, edited by Eugene C. Lee, pp. 85–87. Boston: Little, Brown, 1966.

Newcomer, Kathryn E., Deborah L. Trent, and Natalie Flores-Kelly. "Municipal Debt and the Impact of Sound Fiscal Decision Making." In *The Municipal Year Book: 1983*, pp. 218–28. Washington, D.C.: International City Management Association, 1983.

"North Carolina State Board Voids Referendum Due to FBI Involvement with Electoral Process." *Election Administration Reports* 14 (February 6, 1984): 3-4.

Oakland, William H. "Proposition 13: Genesis and Consequences." *Economic Review* (Federal Reserve Bank of San Francisco) (Winter 1979): 1-19.

"Ohio Rejects Tax Repeal." *The New York Times*, November 10, 1983, p. D26.

Oser, Alan S. "Zoning Appeals Raise Issue of Jursidiction of 2 Boards." *The New York Times*, December 22, 1978, p. A30.

Paine, Robert T., Jr. "The Initiative, the Referendum, and the Recall in American Cities." In *Proceedings of the National Municipal League, 1908*, pp. 223-46. New York: National Municipal League, 1908.

Parker, Joel. "The Origin, Organization, and Influence of the Towns of New England." *Proceedings of the Massachusetts Historical Society* 9 (1866-1867): 14-65.

"Pastor Requires Voter Registration as Condition of School Enrollment." *Election Administration Reports* 12 (September 27, 1982): 6.

Peairs, C. A. "Introduction." *Boston University Law Review* 38 (Summer 1958): 339-46.

Percy, Stephen L. "Citizen Participation in the Coproduction of Urban Services." *Urban Affairs Quarterly* 19 (June 1984): 431-46.

Peterson, Paul E. "Forms of Representation: Participation of the Poor in the Community Action Program." *The American Political Science Review* 64 (June 1970): 491-507.

"Petitions Filed for Referendum to Repeal Bay State Bottle Bill." *The Keene Sentinel* (New Hampshire), February 17, 1982, p. 15.

Pitkin, Hanna F., and Sara M. Shumer. "On Participation." *Democracy* 2 (Fall 1982): 43-54.

Pope, Chris. "Ballot Questions Give Voters Good Chance to Answer Back." *Worcester Telegram* (Massachusetts), November 3, 1982, p. 17A.

Porter, Bruce. "Special Report: LISC – A New Approach to Community Development." *Ford Foundation Letter* 14 (April 1, 1983): 2-3.

Price, Charles M. "Don't Forget the Recall." *Citizen Participation* 1 (July/August 1980): 14-16.

_____. "The Initiative: A Comparative State Analysis and Reassessment of a Western Phenomenon." *Western Political Quarterly* 28 (June 1975): 243-62.

_____. "Recalls at the Local Level: Dimensions and Implications." *National Civic Review* 72 (April 1983): 199-206.

_____. "Seizing the Initiative: California's New Politics." *Citizen Participation* 3 (September/October 1981): 5, 19-20.

"Private Financing of Public Election Issue in Kauai, Hawaii Initiative Vote." *Election Administration Reports* 14 (February 20, 1984): 3-4.

"Proposition 2½ Brings Shift in Massachusetts Tax Burden." *The Keene Sentinel* (New Hampshire), July 28, 1984, p. 5.

"Proposition 13 Five Years Later." *Cal-Tax Research Bulletin* (September 1983): entire issue.

"Proposition 13: A Revolting Development." *Texas Town & City* 65 (July 1978): 5, 7, 9, 28-30.

Purnick, Joyce. "Math Scores Rise in City's Schools." *The New York Times*, June 4, 1984, p. D18.

———. "Reading Scores Fall in City for the First Time in 5 Years." *The New York Times*, May 3, 1984, p. B1.

Ranney, Austin. "The United States of America." In *Referendums: A Comparative Study of Practice and Theory*, edited by David Butler and Austin Ranney, pp. 67–86. Washington, D.C.: American Enterprise Institute for Public Policy Research, 1978.

Ravitch, Diane. "School Decentralization and What it has Come To." *The New York Times*, June 30, 1974, sec. 4, p. E5.

Recall: *Report of the Legislative Interim Committee on Intergovernmental Affairs*. Salem, Oregon: The Committee, 1976, 103–7.

"The Recall Act – Good Intent and Faulty Application." *Georgia County Government Magazine* 33 (February 1982): 103.

"Recall Bid Faces Delay in Arizona." *The New York Times*, January 21, 1973, p. 30.

"Recall Can be Abused." *Georgia County Government Magazine* 31 (September 1979): 58.

"Recall Eliminates Three in Barrow County." *Georgia County Government Magazine* 32 (May 1980): 44.

"Recall Fails Against Barrett of Dougherty." *Georgia County Government Magazine* 33 (February 1982): 67.

"Recall Fever Infects Oregon." *The Sunday Oregonian*, August 12, 1979, p. C2.

"Recall Sought in Four Counties." *Georgia County Government Magazine* 33 (February 1982): 67.

"Recall Successful in Jones and Greene." *Georgia County Government Magazine* 33 (April 1982): 13.

Rehfuss, John. "Citizen Participation in Urban Fiscal Decisions." *Urban Data Service Reports* 10 (August 1978): 1–13.

Rein, Martin. "Decentralization and Citizen Participation in Social Services." *Public Administration Review* 32 (October 1972): 687–700.

Relihan, John P. "Citizen Participation in Peer Review of Residential Group Care Agencies." *Sharing* 3 (Fall 1979): 2.

Riessman, Frank, and Alan Gartner. "Community Control and Radical Social Change." *Social Policy* 1 (May–June 1970): 52–55.

Robbins, L. H. "Democracy, Town Meeting Style." *The New York Times Magazine*, March 23, 1947, pp. 24, 35, 38.

Robbins, William. "Anticrime Patrols Grow in Number and Effect." *The New York Times*, August 30, 1982, pp. 1, A15.

Rohter, Larry. "Reading Scores in City's Schools Hit Their Highest Levels in Years." *The New York Times*, May 14, 1985, pp. 1 and B4.

Romig, Candace. "Political Activists: Four Roads to Power." *State Legislatures* 10 (August 1984): 15–19.

———. "Two Michigan Legislators Recalled." *State Legislatures* 10 (January 1984): 5.

Rosener, Judy B. "Citizen Participation: Can We Measure Its Effectiveness?" *Public Administration Review* 38 (September/October 1978): 457–63.

_____. "Making Bureaucrats Responsive: A Study of the Impact of Citizen Participation and Staff Recommendations on Regulatory Decision Making." *Public Administration Review* 42 (July/August 1982): 339–45.

_____. "Public Hearings: Some Questionable Assumptions." *Citizen Participation* 4 (January/February 1982): 8–9, 18.

Rosenthal, Alan. "Adapting to Popular Democracy." *State Legislatures* 10 (August 1984): 20–21.

Rosin, Alan G. "California Reapportionment Initiative Fails in Court." *Comparative State Politics Newsletter* 4 (October 1983): 11–13.

Routh, Frederick R. "Goals for Dallas: More Participation than Powersharing." *City* 5 (March/April 1971): 49–53.

Rule, Sheila. "Koch 'Disappointed' by Response of City Panels on Homeless." *The New York Times*, January 27, 1983, p. B3.

Sakata, Tokio, "Citizen Movements and the Role of Local Assemblies." *Local Government Review* (Tokyo) (1978): 48–57.

Salisbury, Robert H. "Interest Representation: The Dominance of Institutions." *The American Political Science Review* 78 (March 1984): 64–76.

"San Diego, in a Mail Referendum, Rejects Convention Complex Plan." *The New York Times*, May 7, 1981, p. A20.

Scher, Richard K. "Decentralization and the New York State Legislature." *The Urban Review* 4 (September 1969): 13–19.

Schreiber, Arthur C. "A New Plan for the Recall of Judges." *Journal of the American Judicature Society* 34 (June 1950): 20–22.

Scott, Douglas. "Measures of Citizen Evaluation of Local Government Services." In *Citizen Preferences and Urban Public Policy: Models, Measures, Uses*, edited by Terry N. Clark, pp. 111–28. Beverly Hills, Calif.: Sage Publications, 1976.

Scott, Stanley, and Harriet Nathan. "Public Referenda: A Critical Reappraisal." *Urban Affairs Quarterly* 5 (March 1970): 313–28.

Scott, William G. "Organizational Government: The Prospects for a Truly Participative System." *Public Administration Review* 29 (January/February 1969): 43–53.

"Secretary of State: Foes of Bottle Bill Misleading Voters." *The Evening Gazette* (Worcester, Massachusetts), November 1, 1982, p. 18.

Sengaila, Helen. "Obtaining Public Participation in Educational Decisionmaking: A Case Study of an Australian Initiative." *Planning and Administration* 9 (Autumn 1982): 88–95.

Sentell, R. Perry, Jr. "Remembering Recall in Local Government Laws." *Georgia Law Review* 10 (1976): 883–915.

Shiobara, Tsunefumi. "Community Center with Residents' Participation – The Case of Musashino-Shi, Tokyo." *Local Government Review in Japan* 9 (1979): 55–66.

Shore, William B. "What Do the People Want?" In *The Good Earth of America: Planning Our Land Use*. edited by C. Lowell Harriss, pp. 88–109. Englewood Cliffs, N.J.: Prentice-Hall, 1974.

Shriver, Donald W. "Should the Civilian Complaint Review Board be Reformed: The Case for Change." *Citizens Budget Commission Quarterly* (New York City) (Fall 1983): 1–8.

Simon, Lucinda. "Representative Democracy Challenged." *State Legislatures* 10 (August 1984): 11–15.

"Size Can Make a Difference – A Closer Look." *ACIR Information Bulletin* (September 15, 1970): entire issue.

Skjei, Stephen S. "Urban Systems Advocacy." *Journal of the American Institute of Planners* 38 (January 1972): 11–24.

Sloan, R. D., Jr., and William O. Winter. "State Institutional Reform: Colorado Success Story." *National Civic Review* 72 (April 1983): 207–12.

Smith, Louis H. "Letter to the Editor." *The Massachusetts Selectman* 20 (January 1961): 18.

"State Governments Stall Balanced Budget Drive." *Public Administration Times* 7 (October 15, 1984): 3.

Steger, Mary A. "Group Influence Versus Decision-Making Rules: An Analysis of CDBG Allocational Decisions." *Urban Affairs Quarterly* 19 (March 1984): 373–94.

Stenberg, Carl W. "Citizens and the Administrative State: From Participation to Power." *Public Administration Review* 32 (May/June 1972): 190–97.

———. "Decentralization and the City." In *The Municipal Year Book 1972*, pp. 88–96. Washington, D.C.: International City Management Association, 1972.

Sterzer, Earl E. "Neighborhood Grant Program Lets Citizens Decide." *Public Management* 53 (January 1971): 10–11.

Stewart, Robert G. "The Law of Initiative Referendum in Massachusetts." *New England Law Review* 12 (1977): 455–523.

Stewart, Thomas R., and Linda Gelberd. "Analysis of Judgment Policy: A New Approach for Citizen Participation in Planning." *AIP Journal* 42 (January 1976): 33–41.

Stewart, Tony, and Sydney Duncombe. "Coeur D'Alene Tomorrow: A Look at Citizen Input." *National Civic Review* 70 (September 1981): 410–14, 422.

Story, George. "Living with Open Government." *Public Management* 60 (June 1978): 5–7.

Strange, John H. "Citizen Participation in Community Action and Model Cities Programs." *Public Administration Review* 32 (October 1972): 655–69.

Sturm, Albert L. "State Constitutional Developments During 1982." *National Civic Review* 72 (January 1983): 35–50.

———. "State Constitutional Developments During 1983." *National Civic Review* 73 (January 1984): 24–30, 37.

Sullivan, John H. "What is Proposition 13 Doing Today?" *GRA Reporter* (Governmental Research Association) (Third Quarter 1982): 6–7.

Susskind, Lawrence. "Do We Still Need 2½?" *Impact 2½*, March 15, 1983, pp. 1–2, 7.

Susskind, Lawrence, and Michael Elliot. "Learning from Public Participation in Western Europe." *Urban Innovation Abroad* (Special Supplement) 4 (September 1980): 1–8.

Taguchi, Takashi. "Budget Compilation with Citizen Participation." *Local Government Review in Japan* 9 (1979): 30–43.

Takayose, Shozo. "Management of Community Facilities by the People." *Local Government Review in Japan* 9 (1979): 44–54.

Taylor, Frederick W. "Governmental Efficiency." *Bulletin of the Taylor Socie-ty* (December 1916): 7–13.

"Tax Revolt Measures Defeated by Ohio Voters." *State Legislatures* 10 (January 1984): 5–6.

Teasley, C. E., III, and Luther F. Carter. "Voter Preferences for Governmental Form and Reform." *State and Local Government Review* 14 (May 1982): 86–90.

Terchek, Ronald. "Incentives and Voter Participation: A Research Note." *Political Science Quarterly* 94 (Spring 1979): 135–39.

Tesh, Sylvia. "In Support of 'Single-Issue' Politics." *Political Science Quarterly* 9 (Spring 1984): 27–44.

Tiebout, Charles M. "A Pure Theory of Local Expenditures." *Journal of Political Economy* 64 (October 1956): 412–24.

Tilden, Robert J. "Separation of Powers and the Representative Town Meeting." *Massachusetts Law Quarterly* 42 (March 1957): 24–28.

_____. "Some Fundamentals of Town Meetings." *Massachusetts Law Quarterly* 47 (June 1962): 165–74.

_____. "Town Government." *Boston University Law Review* 38 (Summer 1958): 347–89.

Titus, A. Costandina. "Shaping Attitudes Towards Local Government: Factors that Influence Political Trust and Efficacy." *The Urban Interest* 3 (Fall 1981): 37–45.

"A Tool of Democracy?" *National Civic Review* 67 (September 1978): 352–53.

Tourigney, Ann. "Thoughts and Questions on Citizen Participation." *Sharing* 3 (Summer 1978): 4, 6.

"Tucson Initiative Fails to Make Ballot." *Public Administration Times* 6 (December 15, 1983): 1.

Turner, Wallace. "Developer Pays Expenses for Voting on Zoning on Little Hawaiian Island." *The New York Times*, January 12, 1984, p. A22.

_____. "Effects of Proposition 13 to Strike California Cities." *The New York Times*, January 24, 1983, p. A15.

Tvedt, Sherry. "Enough is Enough: Propositions 2½ in Massachusetts." *National Civic Review* 70 (November 1981): 527–33.

"Ulurp Offers a Voice, Not a Veto." *The New York Times*, June 5, 1984, p. A26.

"U.S. Balanced Budget Measures Taken Off Ballot." *The New York Times*, August 28, 1984, p. B20.

United States Department of Transportation. "Final Policy and Proposed Guidelines on Citizen Participation in Local Transportation Planning." *Federal Register* 45 (October 30, 1980): 71,938–57.

United States Environmental Protection Agency. "Public Participation in Programs Under the Resource Conservation and Recovery Act, the Safe Drinking Water Act, and the Clean Water Act." *Federal Register* 44 (February 16, 1979): 10,285–97.

_____. "Public Participation in the State Implementation Plan – Transportation Revision Process: Expanded Guidelines." *Federal Register* 45 (June 23, 1980): 42,023–29.

"Volunteers: Our Greatest Natural Resource." *Community News* (New York City Community Assistance Unit) 3 (April 1983): 1, 3.

Walker, Alexander J. "Taxpayers' Associations: The 'Opposition' in Government Finance." *The University of Virginia News Letter* 54 (July 1978): 1–4.

Wandersman, Abraham. "A Framework of Participation in Community Organizations." *The Journal of Applied Behavioral Science* 17 (1981): 27–58.

Warren, Robert, Mark S. Rosentraub, and Karen S. Harlow. "Coproduction, Equity, and the Distribution of Safety." *Urban Affairs Quarterly* 19 (June 1984): 447–64.

Watanabe, Yasuo. "Views of the Chief Executive Officer on 'Citizen Participation.'" *Local Government Review* (Tokyo) (1978): 58–76.

Whitehouse, Franklin. "Yonkers Faces Decision on Fiscal Control Board." *The New York Times*, April 11, 1984, p. B3.

Wicker, Tom. "Tale of Two Initiatives." *The New York Times*, October 29, 1982, p. A27.

Wilcox, Herbert G. "Hierarchy, Human Nature, and the Participative Panacea." *Public Administration Review* 29 (January/February 1969): 53–64.

Willis, Benny. "State Officer Says Recalls are Misused." *Eugene Register-Guard* (Oregon), December 14, 1979, pp. 1B–2B.

Wilson, Kenneth D. "Neighborhood Proposal Aimed at Citizen Participation." *Public Management* 53 (January 1971): 12–13.

Winkleman, Michael. "The View from Within." *New York Affairs* 6 (1980): 33–34.

Zabarkes, Arthur. "Different Decision, Different Processes." *New York Affairs* 6 (1980): 29–30.

Zimmerman, Joseph F. "Are Neighborhood Governments a Desirable Institutional Change?" *Planning* 38 (October 1972): 224–30.

———. "Citizen Budgeting in Massachusetts Towns." *The Massachusetts Selectman* 27 (January 1968): 7–10.

———. "Citizen Involvement in Transportation Planning and Development. *Planning and Administration* 3 (Autumn 1976): 65–70.

———. "Citizen Participation in Urban Renewal." *Planning and Civic Comment* 29 (December 1963): 13–14.

———. "Community Building in Large Cities." *Administration* 20 (Summer 1972): 71–87.

———. "Complaint Systems – Links to Government Functions." In *Citizen Participation Certification for Community Development*, edited by Patricia Marshall, pp. 135–37. Washington, D.C.: National Association of Housing and Redevelopment Officials, 1977.

———. "The Development of Local Discretionary Authority in New York." *Publius* 13 (Winter 1983): 89–103.

———. "Electoral Reform Needed to End Political Alienation." *National Civic Review* 60 (January 1971): 6–12.

———. "Ethics in Local Government." *Planning and Administration* 9 (Spring 1982): 33–45.

———. "Ethics in the Public Service." *State and Local Government Review* 14 (September 1982): 98–106.

———. "Evolving Decentralization in New York City." *State and Local Government Review* 14 (January 1982): 16–19.

———. "The Federal Voting Rights Act and Alternative Election Systems." *William & Mary Law Review* 19 (Summer 1978): 621–60.

_____. "Genesis of the Massachusetts Town." *Social Science* 41 (April 1966): 76–83.

_____. "Heading Off City Hall–Neighborhood Wars." *Nation's Cities* 8 (November 1970): 18–21, 39.

_____. "The Heart of Grass Roots Democracy." *Worcester Sunday Telegram Feature Parade* (Worcester, Massachusetts), March 28, 1965, pp. 30–32.

_____. "How Can Local Government Be Made More Responsive?" *The American County* 35 (April 1970): 35–36.

_____. "Lease-Purchase Fails." *National Civic Review* 48 (May 1959): 1–6.

_____. "Neighborhood Control of Schools." In *Revitalizing Cities*, edited by Herrington J. Bryce, pp. 243–56. Lexington, Mass.: Lexington Books, 1979.

_____. "Neighborhood Governments: Goal of New Municipal Reformers." *Connecticut Government* 24 (Summer 1971): 1–4.

_____. "Neighborhoods and Citizen Involvement." *Public Administration Review* 32 (May/June 1972): 201–10.

_____. "The New England Town Meeting: Pure Democracy in Action?" In *The Municipal Year Book 1984*, pp. 102–6. Washington, D.C.: International City Management Association, 1984.

_____. "On the Other Hand." *National Civic Review* 55 (January 1966): 14–20.

_____. "The Open Town Meeting: A Tenacious Institution." *Civic Affairs* 13 (October 1965): 16–19.

_____. "The Politics of Neighborhood Government." *Studies in Comparative Local Government* 5 (Summer 1971): 28–39.

_____. "A Proportional Representation System and New York City School Boards." *National Civic Review* 63 (October 1974): 472–74, 493.

_____. "Regional Governance Models: Greater Dublin and Greater London." *National Civic Review* 71 (February 1982): 86–90.

_____. "Representative Town Meeting." *The Massachusetts Selectman* 25 (April 1966): 7–8, 10, 30.

_____. "Representative Town Meeting: An Evaluation." *The Massachusetts Selectman* 25 (July 1966): 17–18.

_____. "Whither Town Government?" *The Municipal Voice* 4 (December 1966): 6–13.

Zwiebach, Burton. "Democratic Theory and Community Control." *Community Issues* (March 1969): entire issue.

Unpublished Materials

Baker, Gordon E. "American Federalism and the Impulse for Direct Democracy: A Bicentennial Perspective." A paper presented at the National Conference on Government, Williamsburg, Va., November 8, 1976.

Carroll, John J., William E. Hudson, and Mark S. Hyde. "Public Attitudes Towards State Economic Development Policy: Rhode Island's Greenhouse Compact Referendum." A paper presented at the annual meeting of the American Political Science Association, New Orleans, La., August 30, 1985.

Franklin, Robert H. "Referendum and Initiative: Public Policy by Bumper-

Sticker." Hartford: Connecticut Public Expenditure Council, Incorporated, March 10, 1983.

Guy, Joseph L. "Citizen Participation in Model Cities: The Role of Federal Administrators." Albany: Unpublished Ph.D. diss., Graduate School of Public Affairs, State University of New York at Albany, 1973.

"Paul Guzzi Secretary of the Commonwealth Analysis of Election Day Poll." Boston: Secretary of the Commonwealth, 1976.

Hallman, Howard W. "Citizen Priorities and the Local Budget Process." A paper presented at the National Conference on Government, Detroit, Mich., November 12, 1979.

———. "The Neighborhood Movement in the 1980s." A paper presented at the Fifth Annual National Conference on Neighborhood Councils, Pittsburgh, Pa., May 22, 1980.

Heyman, Mark. "The Neighborhood Movement and City Planning: New Directions." A paper presented at the 1979 Annual Meeting of the American Political Science Association, Washington, D.C.

Lee, Eugene C. "The Initiative Process in California." A paper presented at the Eighty-fourth National Conference on Government, Louisville, Ken., November 12–15, 1978.

Magleby, David B. "Direct Legislation: Voting on Ballot Propositions in the United States." Berkeley: Unpublished Ph D. diss., University of California, 1980.

———. "Voter Pamphlets: Understanding Why Voters Don't Read Them." A paper presented at the 1981 Annual Meeting of the American Political Science Association, New York, N.Y.

Magleby, David B., Walt Klein, and Sue Thomas. "The Initiative in the 1980s: Popular Support, Issue Agendas, and Legislative Reform of the Process." A paper presented at the 1982 Annual Meeting of the American Political Science Association, Denver, Colo.

Marini, John. "Administrative Centralization and the 'New Despotism.'" A paper presented at the 1983 Annual Meeting of the American Political Science Association, Chicago, Ill.

Melick, Richard P. "Memo to Town Meeting Members." Natick, Mass.: March 8, 1953.

"Model By-Laws for Massachusetts Towns." Boston: Massachusetts Federation of Taxpayers Associations, Incorporated, 1940.

"Recommendation of the Initiative Committee of the National Municipal League." New York: National Municipal League, 1979.

"Representative Town Meeting in Massachusetts." Boston: Massachusetts Federation of Taxpayers Associations, Incorporated, June 1945.

Rivers, David. "Role of Neighborhoods in Atlanta's Comprehensive Planning Process." A paper presented at the National Conference on Government, Louisville, Ken., November 14, 1978.

Rosener, Judy B. "Democracy and the Administrative State: Can Citizen Oversight Make Bureaucrats Responsive?" A paper presented at the Annual Meeting of the American Society for Public Administration, Baltimore, Md., April 1–4, 1979.

"The Status of Volunteerism." Boulder, Colo.: Volunteer, 1982.

Stenberg, Carl W. "The History and Future of Citizen Participation: An Overview." An address presented at the 1971 National Conference on Public Administration, Denver, Colo., April 19, 1971.

"Testimony of Marcia Molay, Massachusetts Director of Elections, before the New York State Senate Subcommittee on Initiative and Referendum," September 17, 1979.

Zimmerman, Joseph F. "Reforming the Model City Charter." A paper presented at the Eighty-ninth National Conference on Government, Baltimore, Md., November 15, 1983.

Zvesper, John. "Liberal Democracy and Bureaucracy." A paper presented at the 1983 Annual Meeting of the American Political Science Association, Chicago, Ill., September 3, 1983.

INDEX

Absentee voting, 117
Administrative decentralization, 145–49, 175–76
Advisory initiative, 78
Advisory referendum, 40–41, 59
Albergo, Joseph, 142
Alderwood Associates v. Washington Environmental Council, 100n
Alexander, John W., 17–18, 33n
Alshire, Bill, 15n
Alternative proposition, 71, 76–78
Amador Valley Joint Union High School District v. State Board of Equalization, 101n
American Bar Association, 126, 134n
American Municipal Association, 180, 184n
Annexation, 44–45
Application of Cohalan, 66n
Area Citizens Together in Volunteer Endeavors, (ACTIVE), 13
Aristotle, 1, 15n, 17, 53n, 176, 184n
Articles of Confederation and Perpetual Union, 105
Assembly of the State of California v. Deukmejian, 101n
Assessment, 44; "full and fair cash" value, 44
Association of Town Finance Committees, 28
"Austerity" budget, 44

Baer, Jon A., 183n
Balanced federal budget, 84–85
Ballot title, 72
Banfield, Edward C., 155n
Barber, Benjamin R., 160, 162, 174, 183n
Barrett, Gil, 125, 134n
Barto v. Himrod, 62n
Baylies, Francis, 33n

Beard, Charles A., 103n, 123, 127, 133n, 134n
Bell, Charles, 102n
Bennetts, Leslie, 158n
Berger, Morroe, 17–18, 33n
Billett, Allan R., 122
Bird, Frederick L., 119, 123, 127, 128n, 132n, 133n, 134n
Bish, Robert L., 155n, 156n
Blair, William G., 156n
Bone, Hugh A., 95–96, 104n
The Book of the States, 131n
Booth, David A., 64n
Brady, Patrick J., 16n
Bramlette, Laurie, 113, 131n
Brosnahan v. Brown, 100n
Bryce, James, 17, 33n
Buckley v. Secretary of the Commonwealth, 100n
Buckley v. Valeo, 50, 65n
Burchell v. State Board of Election Commissioners, 130n
Butler, David, 165, 183n

California Achievement Test, 143
Carroll, Maurice, 158n
Chambers, Marcia, 157n
Chandler, Alfred D., 28
Charters, 11; drafting and amendment, 11
Childs, Richard S., 55–56, 67n, 164–65
Cipriano v. City of Houma, 66n
Citizen advisory committees, 9, 24, 26
Citizen participation, 1–4, 6–14; benefits, 3–4; costs, 3–4; types, 6–14
Citizens Against Rent Control v. City of Berkeley, 66n
Citizens Committee for New York City, Incorporated, 149–50, 157n

223

ABOUT THE AUTHOR

Joseph F. Zimmerman is a Professor of Political Science at the Graduate School of Public Affairs of the State University of New York at Albany and also serves as Research Director of the New York State Legislative Commission on Critical Transportation Choices and chairman of the section on Representation and Electoral Systems of the American Political Science Association. He previously taught at Worcester Polytechnic Institute and Clark University.

Dr. Zimmerman is the author of *State and Local Government, The Massachusetts Town Meeting: A Tenacious Institution, Pragmatic Federalism, State Mandating of Local Expenditures, Measuring Local Discretionary Authority, The Government and Politics of New York State*, and *State-Local Relations: A Partnership Approach.* He is coauthor of *The Politics of the Veto of Legislation in New York* and editor of several books, including *Government of the Metropolis* and *Subnational Politics.*

Professor Zimmerman received a B.A. at the University of New Hampshire and an M.A. and Ph.D. at Syracuse University.